Adobe® InDesign® CS2 @work

PROJECTS YOU CAN USE ON THE JOB

Cate Brosseau Indiano

SAMS 800 East 96th Street, Indianapolis, Indiana 46240, USA

Adobe® InDesign® CS2 @work: Projects You Can Use on the Job

International Standard Book Number: 0-672-32802-X

Library of Congress Catalog Card Number: 2005901042

Printed in the United States of America

First Printing: August 2005

08   07   06   05   4   3   2   1

Trademarks

All terms mentioned in this book that are known to be trademarks or service marks have been appropriately capitalized. Sams Publishing cannot attest to the accuracy of this information. Use of a term in this book should not be regarded as affecting the validity of any trademark or service mark.

Warning and Disclaimer

Every effort has been made to make this book as complete and as accurate as possible, but no warranty or fitness is implied. The information provided is on an "as is" basis. The author and the publisher shall have neither liability nor responsibility to any person or entity with respect to any loss or damages arising from the information contained in this book.

Bulk Sales

Sams Publishing offers excellent discounts on this book when ordered in quantity for bulk purchases or special sales. For more information, please contact

U.S. Corporate and Government Sales
1-800-382-3419
corpsales@pearsontechgroup.com

For sales outside of the United States, please contact

International Sales
international@pearsoned.com

Acquisitions Editor
Linda Bump Harrison

Development Editor
Songlin Qiu

Managing Editor
Charlotte Clapp

Project Editor
Dan Knott

Indexer
Ken Johnson

Proofreader
Jessica McCarty

Technical Editor
Claudia McCue

Publishing Coordinator
Vanessa Evans

Multimedia Developer
Dan Scherf

Book Designer
Gary Adair

Page Layout
Bronkella Publishing

Contents at a Glance

Table of Contents

About the Author

Cate Indiano, owner and president of DesktopMedia, has been working in the graphic arts industry for the last 17 years training and consulting with graphic arts professionals throughout the Midwest. Cate has a degree in public and corporate communications from Butler University, is a certified technical trainer, and an Adobe certified instructor. She and her staff technically support, train, and consult to the creative and production community of graphic arts.

Not only does Cate relish her work with her clients, but she also is active in curriculum development for DesktopMedia's application-based and skills-based training programs. On the consulting side, workflow is her passion and her clients invite her to examine their hand-offs, expose their inefficiencies, and improve their bottom lines.

Having worked with clients just like you for more than 16 years, this is her first book. She has worked with many graphic arts professionals over the years, and this book is filled with real-world examples of projects she has encountered repeatedly throughout her professional journey.

Acknowledgments

This was the classic example of "I don't know what I don't know," and as I look back over the experience, it's truly miraculous that it has all come together so well. First, you have an inexperienced author, working on a beta version of software, with an unknown editorial staff and learning a new publishing process. Which brings me to my first big THANK YOU, to Linda Harrison, senior acquisitions editor for Sams Publishing, who championed the series, the title, and this unknown author. I thank you for the hand holding, for being easy to work with, and for guiding me through this unique process.

The second round of thank yous goes to the staff that took my work and transformed it into a real book: Songlin Qiu, development editor, who assisted me with the overall game plan; Megan Wade, production editor, who helped me clarify my vision; Claudia McCue, technical editor, who kept me on my toes for absolute technical clarity and accuracy; Dan Knott, project editor, who kept the project on track; and Dan Scherf, media developer, who has made the projects come to life on the publisher's website.

Now on to the personal personnel—as it turns out, I am also the mother of two beautiful teenage girls who, in addition to my company, keep me quite busy. When I told them their mother was writing a book, they were like, "Cooool, will you be on *Oprah?*" I told them it was not that kind of a book, and while I did my best to explain this book and the series, their eyes glazed over. Having said that, they've been terribly supportive and are both anxious for a copy to show off to their friends.

I want to thank my parents, who have been instrumental throughout this entire period of exploration and adventure. They have helped me enormously with my children and I am deeply grateful. I do believe that they are proud parents of their author daughter, even if she's 43 years old. I am the consummate late bloomer, but they have always been supportive of everything I do.

To my brother, Edward, who steers the ship for me at DesktopMedia and who tirelessly champions our services despite the ups and downs of a fickle industry and demanding economy, I thank you for everything you have done for me and for DesktopMedia.

I want to thank my father, Pete Brosseau, for contributing some of his photography to this book. He's been taking pictures both professionally and personally for so long, I had a nice selection to choose from. So a big thank you to him for sharing his work for the book.

Finally, to my husband Michael, who has encouraged my career goals for these last 20 years, I thank you for allowing me to pursue this assignment in the midst of much family transition. It meant having to shoulder more family responsibilities, and I appreciate your efforts and thank you for allowing me this great adventure.

I don't believe in accidents or coincidences. I believe there was something greater at work here than serendipity when Linda's email popped into my inbox. I do believe we are presented with opportunities every day but often we're so busy we don't recognize them in time, or not even at all. I really wanted to take this opportunity and see what was out there. I would love to hear from all of you. I know what it's like to be presented with a tool but not have the skills or the understanding to execute an assignment. It was with you in mind that I wrote this book. I hope it helps you enjoy your InDesign CS2 experience as well as execute, with confidence, your own publishing assignments.

We Want to Hear from You!

As the reader of this book, *you* are our most important critic and commentator. We value your opinion and want to know what we're doing right, what we could do better, what areas you'd like to see us publish in, and any other words of wisdom you're willing to pass our way.

You can email or write me directly to let me know what you did or didn't like about this book—as well as what we can do to make our books stronger.

Please note that I cannot help you with technical problems related to the topic of this book, and that due to the high volume of mail I receive, I might not be able to reply to every message.

When you write, please be sure to include this book's title and author as well as your name and phone or email address. I will carefully review your comments and share them with the author and editors who worked on the book.

Email: graphics@samspublishing.com

Mail: Mark Taber
         Associate Publisher
         Sams Publishing
         800 East 96th Street
         Indianapolis, IN 46240 USA

Reader Services

For more information about this book or another Sams Publishing title, visit our website at www.samspublishing.com. Type the ISBN (excluding hyphens) or the title of a book in the Search field to find the page you're looking for.

Introduction

When we first started discussing this series, I kept thinking of it as curriculum and then I adjusted my thinking to "self-taught" curriculum. Remember, I'm a trainer—hands-on, onsite, instructor-led is our mantra. Throughout the years, I can't remember finding a published work I felt contained exercises geared to our customer base. They either were too basic or taught features that would be infrequently used.

So, in developing the outline for the book, it was important that I kept in mind you, the reader. Who are you? I imagine you are in some form of marketing, communications, publishing, or graphic arts. Your educational background might be in design, but odds are it's not. You might have hired into this job or your job might have evolved into this position. You might have some minimal page layout experience; you might not.

But one thing's for sure: You need a practical guide to step you through common layouts and publications using the features of an application you barely know, if at all. In addition, you probably have little or no experience with regard to media production and distribution. So, in addition to InDesign skills, you are going to get a healthy dose of practical production advice from me.

Organization of This Book

This book is divided into two parts:

- ▶ Part I, "Getting Started," takes you on a tour of InDesign CS2, the newest version from Adobe. It was important not to make assumptions about what you do and do not know about InDesign, so we've made sure that all the tools, palettes, and basic conventions of InDesign are covered, as well as how it integrates with other Adobe products.

- ▶ Part II, "Projects," contains a variety of projects you'll likely be asked to complete on the job. The projects start from the common, but fairly simple, assignment of developing business collateral and move through progressively more complex projects like preparing advertisements, product sheets, brochures, interactive presentations, newsletters, catalogs, order forms, and even annual reports. This portion of the book will prepare you for almost any marketing requirement you may be asked to fulfill.

  If you have your own resource files, fonts, logos, and images, feel free to use them as you work through each project. But if you don't have those assets readily available, we've provided them for you on the publisher's website.

- ▶ In Part III, "Appendixes," you'll find Appendix A, "Glossary," which lists and defines the key terms used throughout the book. Appendix B, "Resources," provides additional information on popular plug-ins you might want to get, links where you can find user groups and associations, training information, and a list of web and print publications.

Downloading the Book's Project Files

The chapter-by-chapter project and media files are available at the publisher's website via Zip files.

To download the book's project files, go to http://www.samspublishing.com. Enter this book's ISBN (without the hyphens) in the Search box and click Search. When the book's title is displayed, click the title to go to a page where you can download the project Zip files.

> 🚫 **CAUTION**
>
> Be sure you extract all the files from each Zip file with the option (for PC users) Use Folder Names selected so you can get the same folders on your computer as included in each Zip file. Mac users can simply double-click the downloaded Zip file and the folder structure should appear intact, as named.

Conventions Used in This Book

This book uses the following conventions:

- *Italic* is used to denote key terms when they first appear in the book.

 TIP

Tips provide shortcuts to make your job easier or better ways to accomplish certain tasks.

 NOTE

Notes provide additional information related to the surrounding topics.

 CAUTION

Cautions alert you to potential problems and help you steer clear of disaster.

The end result is a book that should sit on your desk as a reference for you to use. It should contain the majority of projects you will ever execute. I hope it's useful to you—I wrote it as if you were my student.

 **@work resources**

- This indicates specific files that are available for download on the Sams website.

PART I: Getting Started

In this chapter we will explore InDesign CS2—the basic interfaces for this product including the Tool palette, primary palettes, secondary palettes, and new features specifically introduced with CS2.

Choosing InDesign

It probably goes without saying that, in purchasing this book, you already own Adobe InDesign CS2. However, if by chance you are researching your purchase, I suggest you investigate the Adobe website, using the following URL: http://www. adobe.com/products/indesign/conversion.html.

Here you will find a number of resources guiding you through productivity and return on investment studies as well as conversion issues to consider. See more about converting in Chapter 3, "Converting to InDesign from Another Application."

If, on the other hand, you have made your purchase and are ready to get started, may I first congratulate you on an excellent decision. You have chosen a superior page layout product that includes robust layout features, tight integration with the most popular Adobe products (collectively known as the Creative Suite), and rich creative and design features that would satisfy the most discriminating designer.

As I've indicated in the introduction, I will not assume you are simply upgrading from a previous version of InDesign. In this chapter, I cover the most commonly used features as well as point out new features to the readers who are upgrading.

Creative Suite Advantages

The advantages of purchasing the Creative Suite are innumerable. To be able to purchase these powerful and creative products for a price comparable to the cost of a single standalone competitor is truly remarkable. Think carefully when choosing between the Standard and Premium editions of Creative Suite. The Standard Edition includes InDesign, Illustrator, Photoshop, Version Cue, Bridge, and Stock Photos. The Premium Edition adds Acrobat 7 Professional and GoLive to this list, thereby extending your content distribution enormously.

Adobe Bridge (New Feature) and Version Cue

These file management applications are available with Adobe's individual application purchases as well as both the Standard and Premium versions of Creative Suite. Bridge and Version Cue allow you to work, collaborate, and manage within an all-Adobe workspace.

Adobe describes Bridge as "the new navigational control center built for Adobe Creative Suite and its components." It enables you to browse and organize your project files while providing centralized access to your project files, applications, and settings. For example, Bridge can manage the PDF review process as well as the color settings. You can organize, browse, locate, and view assets using Bridge instead of your operating system's file navigation (via the Use Adobe Dialog button or Use OS Dialog button).

For those of you familiar with the File Browser in previous versions of Photoshop, think of Bridge as a more robust version of File Browser but now shared by all the Adobe Creative Suite applications. Bridge enables you to store your projects locally on your hard drive. If you are in a workgroup setting and you own Creative Suite Standard or Premium, you can install Bridge and Version Cue and configure them to store your projects on your server. Take a look at Adobe Bridge in Figure 1.1.

Version Cue allows you to file share, manage versions of your projects, track alternative versions and the status of project files, maintain communication with others about the status of the project (in use, synchronized, and so on), and perform utilitarian processes such as backing up Version Cue projects. Managing projects in a universal workspace shared by all users enables easier collaboration across workgroups. Figure 1.2 shows where you access Version Cue in Bridge. Later in this chapter, you will see the indicator in the InDesign window.

FIGURE 1.1   The Adobe Bridge interface.

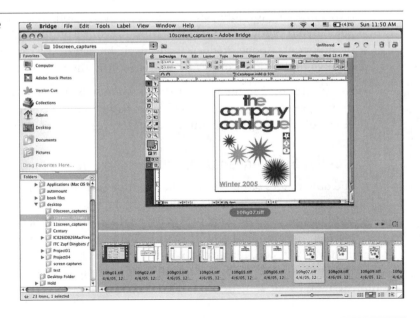

CHAPTER 1: Exploring InDesign

FIGURE 1.2   The Version Cue feature in Bridge.

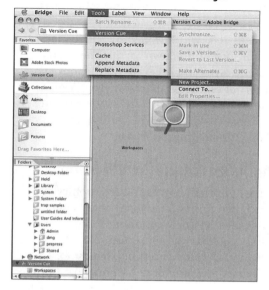

both the palette and a new style I created to demonstrate the feature.

FIGURE 1.3   The Object Styles palette.

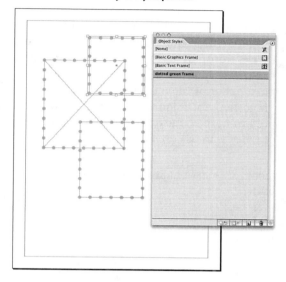

PageMaker Users

While Chapter 3 specifically covers converting PageMaker files, I thought it would be worthwhile to include some thoughts in this chapter about exploring. InDesign CS2 has added specific Pagemaker features for users who are now making the switch. It contains the following: a PageMaker tool palette; PageMaker keyboard shortcut sets; and plug-ins that enable features such as InBooklet, automated bullets and numbering, data merge, and so on.

Object Styles (New Feature)

Just like paragraph styles or character styles, object styles in InDesign CS2 enable you to define graphic, text, and frame attributes as saved styles you can apply repeatedly to achieve consistency in your design and increase your productivity. Featured in Chapter 9, "Developing a Newsletter," you will use this new feature to create consistent text frames. See Figure 1.3 for an example of

Photoshop and PDF Layer Support (New Feature)

InDesign CS2 enables you to import layered Photoshop files, selectively showing and hiding Photoshop layers without altering the image in Photoshop. Additionally, the visibility of Layer Comps in a Photoshop file can be controlled in InDesign, without exiting to Photoshop. Maintaining those layers gives you greater flexibility in experimenting with alternative versions as you create. Layers themselves are covered in Chapter 8, "Putting Together an Interactive Presentation."

Transparency

Continued support exists for transparency, including drop shadows, feathering, and changing the opacity and color blending modes of any object (imported or created directly in InDesign). Transparency is invoked when using any of the features previously mentioned. Flattening can be previewed via the Flattener Preview palette. The act of flattening can be managed via the Pages palette or the Print or Export dialog boxes. Transparency is featured in several chapters throughout this book. The two primary palettes are shown in Figure 1.4, but bear in mind that drop shadows and feathering also invoke transparency. You can quickly identify transparency in use by looking at the Pages palette. Borrowing a convention from Photoshop, InDesign uses a checkerboard pattern in the page icons to indicate transparency is in use on a certain page.

FIGURE 1.4   The Transparency and Flattener Preview palette.

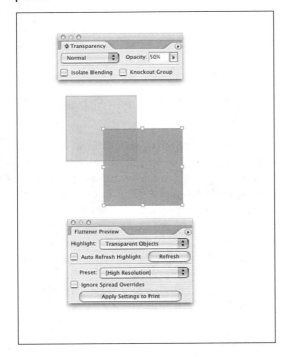

OpenType Font Support

Continued support also exists for Adobe OpenType, a new font standard jointly innovated by Adobe and Microsoft. It combines the best of all font structures—

single file structure, cross-platform compatibility, and extended character set support. Access to all the characters of your OpenType fonts is easy with the Glyphs palette, found on the Type pull-down menu. The Glyphs palette gives you access to all the font characters of all the typefaces in every font family you own. Use of the Glyphs palette is featured in Chapter 5, "Creating an Advertisement and a Poster."

Anchored Objects (New Feature)

In an improvement to inline graphics or anchored frames, anchored objects are controlled via new commands found on the Object pull-down menu. You select Anchored Objects, Options, Inserting, Releasing. The previous implementation of anchored frames restricted the frames to the interior of the text frame in which they were anchored, but anchored objects are tethered to their text anchor; however, they can float outside the text frame itself. You can find more on this feature in Chapter 10, "Designing a Product Catalogue." See Figure 1.5 for an example of anchored object options.

Tables

Tables are one of the most important features of InDesign. Although they are far more robust than other products on the market, they're easy to use. Tables can be created and enhanced using either the Table pull-down menu or the Table palette. You can import tables from Microsoft Word and Excel, as well as copy and paste tables from those applications. Tables can incorporate both text and graphics. You have complete control over the way every table cell looks, including its fills, strokes, and tint fills applied in a pattern, such as every other row. You can format text, tab it, indent it, rotate it, and style it any way you choose. Tables are featured in Chapters 9, 10, and 11.

FIGURE 1.5   The Anchored Object Options window.

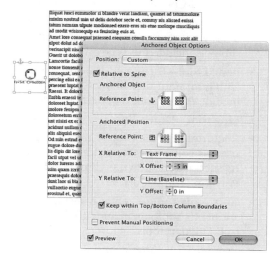

Direct Export to PDF

Expanded support for PDF export includes support for presets, PDF industry standards, and version compatibility. PDF presets can be customized, saved, and shared with others. If you own Creative Suite, PDF presets can be set universally for all CS2 applications from a common repository shared by all applications within the suite. Almost every chapter in this book steps you through the creation of a PDF.

Snippets (New Feature)

You can export InDesign objects as snippets that can be shared by other Adobe applications almost like shared libraries. The steps are simple: To create a snippet, simply select an object or several objects; go to the File pull-down menu; and select Export, InDesign Snippets. Note that the file extension for snippets is .inds. Whatever you have selected is saved as an independent file that you can browse and use via the Place command—you can even drag and drop it from Adobe Bridge! Figure 1.6 shows an example of a snippet.

The InDesign CS 2 Window

Figure 1.7 shows the InDesign CS 2 window. In addition to identifying the various components of the InDesign window, it's important to point out components that are new to this

FIGURE 1.6   Snippets in Bridge.

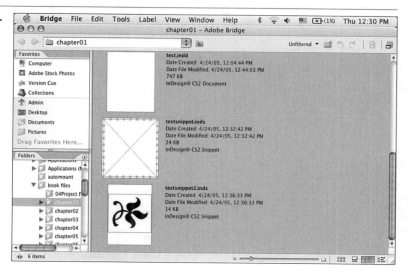

specific version. At the bottom of the window, directly to the right of the page indicator—and new to this version—is the Version Cue status bar. It lets you know the current state of your file, such as never saved, open, version, alternate, and so on.

InDesign CS2 Tools

This section covers the set of tools available in InDesign CS2. The following list details each tool's role as shown in Figure 1.8:

- ▶ **Selection tool**—Selects, moves, and reshapes objects.
- ▶ **Direct Selection tool**—Selects, moves, and reshapes anchor points and handles. Selects and repositions graphics inside frames (it becomes a hand tool in this state).
- ▶ **Pen tool**—Bézier drawing tool that enables you to create anchor points and paths. Its subtools include the Add

Anchor point tool, Delete Anchor point tool, and Convert Direction point tool.

- ▶ **Type tool**—Creates text frames and enables you to insert and highlight text. Its subtools include the Type on a Path tool.
- ▶ **Pencil tool**—Facilitates drawing a vector with a familiar utensil. Its subtools include the Smooth tool and Erase tool.
- ▶ **Line tool**—Draws lines.
- ▶ **Rectangle Frame tool**—Creates frames used as containers for placed graphics. Its subtools include the Ellipse and Polygon Frame tools.
- ▶ **Rectangle tool**—Creates a rectangular shape. Its subtools include the Ellipse and Polygon tools.
- ▶ **Rotate, Scale, Shear, and Free Transform tools**—These all are transformation tools. Transformation tools rotate, distort, skew, or scale objects in InDesign. They can be executed via the Object pull-down menu, the Control

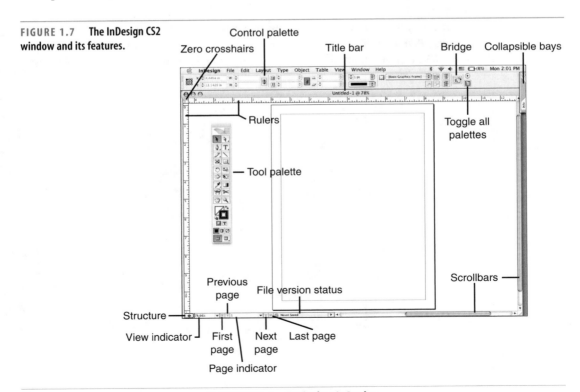

FIGURE 1.7 **The InDesign CS2 window and its features.**

Control palette

Zero crosshairs

Title bar

Bridge   Collapsible bays

Rulers

Toggle all palettes

Tool palette

Previous page

File version status

Scrollbars

Structure

View indicator

First page

Next page

Last page

Page indicator

palette, and the Transform palette (found by going to the Window pull-down menu and selecting Object & Layout).

▶ **Eyedropper tool**—Samples a number of attributes from one element and applies them to another. Its subtool include the Measure tool. Double-click this tool to manage its settings.

▶ **Gradient tool**—Manages the direction and length of a gradient fill.

▶ **Button tool**—Designates elements as buttons to which actions can be attached.

▶ **Scissors tool**—Cuts apart paths.

▶ **Hand tool**—Moves the page around in the window, similar to the scrollbars.

▶ **Zoom tool**—Magnifies the page by zooming in (enlarging the view) and zooming out (shrinking the view) with the Option (Mac) or Alt (PC) key.

The tools in the Tool palette are shown in Figure 1.8.

FIGURE 1.8 **The InDesign CS2 tools.**

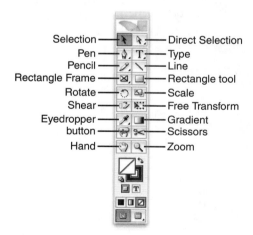

InDesign CS2 Primary Palettes

This section covers the primary palettes, which you will use regularly. Each is described in detail.

Figure 1.9 shows the Character palette. This floating interface enables you to manage character level formatting, including font, size, leading, kerning, tracking, horizontal and vertical scale, baseline shift, skew, language control, type styles, underline and strikethrough options, and OpenType options.

FIGURE 1.9 **The Character palette.**

The Paragraph palette (shown in Figure 1.10) is the floating interface that enables you to manage paragraph level formatting, including alignment, indentation, paragraph spacing, drop caps, hyphenation, lock to baseline grid, justification, keeps, nested styles, paragraph rules, and bullet and numbering options.

FIGURE 1.10 **The Paragraph palette.**

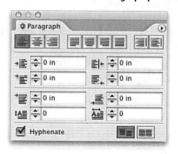

The Stroke palette, shown in Figure 1.11, lets you manage the stroke format of an InDesign element, including weight, cap and join styles, stroke alignment (this new feature has the following options: Align Stroke to Center, Align Stroke to Inside, and Align Stroke to Outside of Object), and stroke styling options.

and columns (and their respective widths and heights); text alignment and rotation; indentation; and the formatting of cells, rows, and columns.

FIGURE 1.11   **The Stroke palette.**

FIGURE 1.12   **The Swatches palette.**

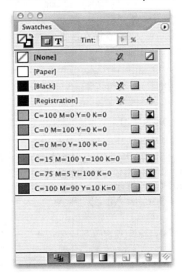

The Swatches palette, shown in Figure 1.12, enables you to manage saved colors, tints, gradients, and inks, including defining, applying, editing, and deleting them. Adding unnamed colors is also a powerful feature of the Swatches palette because it enables you to add previously undefined colors to it, thereby saving the colors like styles. If you update the swatch, the object is also updated wherever the color is assigned.

The Links palette is a floating interface that enables you to manage the links between the InDesign layout and the resource files placed in InDesign (see Figure 1.13).

The Pages palette, shown in Figure 1.14, lets you manage the pages in a layout, including pages, master pages, master page items, numbering, sectioning, and page flattening.

Figure 1.15 shows the Transform palette, a floating interface that enables you to change the location, size, rotation, and shear attributes of a transformation.

The Table palette, shown in Figure 1.16, is a floating interface that enables you to manage and edit tables in InDesign, including rows

FIGURE 1.13   **The Links palette.**

The Layers palette is a floating interface that enables you to create, manage, and delete layers. Placing elements on layers gives you

CHAPTER 1: Exploring InDesign

greater control over managing a complex layout (see Figure 1.17).

FIGURE 1.17   The Layers palette.

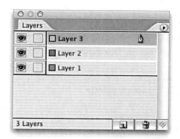

FIGURE 1.17   The Layers palette.

FIGURE 1.14   The Pages palette.

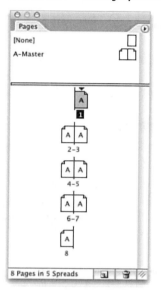

InDesign CS2's Secondary Palettes

This section covers the secondary palettes, which I feel you will use often, but perhaps not regularly. Each is covered in detail here.

The Tabs palette is a floating interface that enables you to create, edit, and manage tab stops and leaders (see Figure 1.18).

FIGURE 1.18   The Tabs palette.

FIGURE 1.15   The Transform palette.

The Align palette is a floating interface that lets you align and distribute objects relative to each other (see Figure 1.19).

FIGURE 1.19   The Align palette.

FIGURE 1.16   The Table palette.

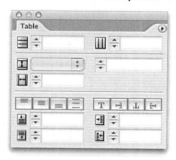

The Transparency palette is a floating interface, shown in Figure 1.20, that enables you to change the opacity of its fills and strokes. This palette also lets you utilize Blending Modes much like those in Photoshop.

FIGURE 1.20   The Transparency palette.

The Paragraph Styles palette, a floating interface, enables you to define, edit, and apply paragraph styles. The palette itself contains saved paragraph formats (see Figure 1.21).

FIGURE 1.21   The Paragraph Styles palette.

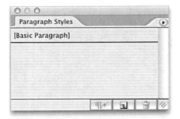

The Character Styles palette is a floating interface that enables you to define, edit, and apply character styles. The palette itself contains saved character formats (see Figure 1.22).

FIGURE 1.22   The Character Styles palette.

Figure 1.23 shows the Gradient palette, a floating interface that enables you to create linear and radial gradients. They can later be saved as swatches in the Swatches palette.

FIGURE 1.23   The Gradient palette.

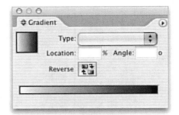

The Color palette is a floating interface that enables you to create colors. They can later be saved as swatches in the Swatches palette (see Figure 1.24).

FIGURE 1.24   The Color palette.

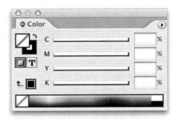

Figure 1.25 shows the Pathfinder palette, a floating interface that enables you to combine and convert shapes. This palette also provides vertical and horizontal distribution of selected objects.

FIGURE 1.25   The Pathfinder palette.

The Object Styles palette is a new palette. This floating interface allows you to define, edit, and apply object styles. The palette itself contains saved object attributes (see Figure 1.26).

FIGURE 1.26   The Object Styles palette.

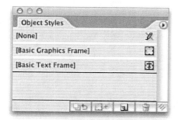

The Text Wrap palette is shown in Figure 1.27. It's a floating interface that enables you to manage the flow of text around an object.

FIGURE 1.27   The Text Wrap palette.

The Separations Preview palette, shown in Figure 1.28, allows you to view a layout in each separate color, as it will be produced by your commercial print provider.

The Flattener Preview palette, shown in Figure 1.29, lets you view different effects that flattening controls have over elements or pages that involve transparency.

FIGURE 1.29   The Flattener Preview palette.

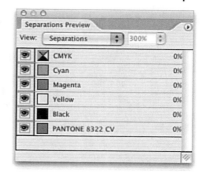

FIGURE 1.28   The Separations Preview palette.

Final Thoughts

For new users, this chapter acquainted you with the features of InDesign CS2—specifically tools and palettes. For users of previous versions of InDesign, this chapter pointed out some of the new and notable features in this upgrade.

As you work your way through the projects in this book, you will likely reference this chapter to clarify the role of a palette or tool as it relates to the exercise you are working with. You might even seek out certain projects that contain a feature you are interested in using as well!

CHAPTER 2: Planning for Production

Why plan? The answer might seem obvious, yet how many of us thoroughly plan our content creation and distribution exercises in this fast turnaround, impossibly deadline-driven industry? You really should preplan. This step solicits feedback from all the resources before the project is created, saving costly time and money and avoiding the mistakes that impact production. When you know your goal, you can plan the finished product or service. In addition, you have all your questions answered, the budget approved, the message approved, the distribution method chosen, so you simply need to plan the manufacturing steps, coordinate your resources, and implement your timeline.

Many tasks are required to publish content and several hand-offs. You will be collaborating internally with sales and marketing professionals, engineers, and operations staff; you'll also communicate externally with photographers, print service providers, graphic artists, and web developers. So, when you tackle the assignment of publishing content, planning is very important.

You shouldn't create something you can't actually produce or manufacture, and you don't want to spend a lot of time and money arriving at a deadline only to find out you are going to cost the company more time and money because you didn't realize the implications your creativity had on budget and manufacturing.

Essentially you are involved in a four-step process:

1. **Plan**—Map your marketing initiative and plan your distribution points.
2. **Create**—You first create the look, feel, and message of the content.
3. **Review/Edit/Approve**—All contributors give feedback, and revisions occur and are approved.
4. **Produce**—You publish your content using your chosen distribution method. Depending on your distribution method(s), you might need to involve external vendors, such as a commercial print service provider.

After your message has been approved and you have planned your distribution, you probably have already begun the manufacturing process. However, unlike most manufacturing processes, the manufacturer—in this case, the print service provider—does not control the beginning of manufacturing process. You do.

FIGURE 2.1 Your creative workflow: plan, create, approve, produce.

FIGURE 2.1 Your creative workflow: plan, create, approve, produce.

Plan   Create   Approve   Produce

 NOTE

Please be aware that publishing is classified as a manufacturing process. After all, manufacturing is the act of producing or processing something.

Let's say you work for an auto manufacturer and are in the advanced product concepts department, tasked with coming up with new ideas for cars. Car designers collaborate with engineers throughout the design process to ensure that the design can be translated into a product with the materials and machinery at hand.

What would happen to any manufacturing process if, say, 70% of the materials were so flawed that they had to be fixed before manufacturing could begin? Could a printer stay in business if her paper vendor kept supplying her with 70% flawed stock? Of course not, yet 70% of all incoming *digital* files supplied by their customers contain serious flaws, which require analysis, intervention, and repair. That's quite a challenge.

So, it's important that the creative people collaborate with the manufacturing people— the print service provider, document manager, web developer, and so forth—to ensure that the manufacturing process can achieve the

requested product and that the process flows smoothly, on time, and on budget.

You know the old adage, "failing to plan is planning to fail." Failure to plan costs time and money no matter what industry you are in, and the bottom line is affected. Affect the bottom line enough, and there will be no content to distribute.

You need to answer the following questions: What is the message? Who will we send it to? and How will we get it there?

Distribution (via Print, PDF, and the Web)

What do I mean when I say *distribution*? The sharing or delivery of content to its intended recipient requires that you know how to best deliver that content. For example, would you send an email to someone who doesn't have a computer? Careful consideration and planning needs to take place by studying the demographics you are trying to market to, which will help you decide how to best reach them—via print, disk, or the Web. Be sure to ask these questions:

▸ Who is your audience?

▸ How will your content, message, brand, product, and service be distributed?

- How quickly does this information need to reach them?
- Which distribution method has proven most effective in the past?
- Which distribution method has proven least effective?

Print

All the answers to these questions should drive you toward a distribution solution for your publication. We have been living in a print-centric world for quite some time now—since Gutenberg. So, the first questions to be answered are Will this be a printed piece? Do I need ink on paper to convey this message—is that what my customer expects or wants? How important is color, clarity, and resolution to the message I'm trying to convey?

Despite the popularity of the Internet and email, print is still a viable distribution method. People still love to curl up with a good book (or magazine or catalog), but can you really curl up with a good computer? Can any other medium convey images of clothing, food, or jewelry as well as print? The answer of course, is "no," and this is why, despite the onslaught of web and email communications, print is still a viable method of distributing content. Printed material is portable and doesn't require the recipient to own a computer or have an Internet connection. Everyone has a mailing address but not necessarily an email address. Remember the demographics you are marketing to.

It's just that now print is not the only method, it's not the quickest method (particularly when you factor in mail or some other delivery option), and it's not the least expensive method (particularly when you include postage rates).

But 9 times out of 10, when you sit down to plan content distribution, the first question you are still likely to ask is, "Is this going to be printed?"

PDF

Perhaps content publishing will take place in more than one form. Will you print your company newsletter *and* make it available on your website? Is it easier to email the content than to physically mail it? For either choice, do you have the necessary data to support either function, and is it accurate? Or perhaps you'll direct everyone to a URL somewhere on your website where they will be instructed to download a document (keeping the overhead of an email message to a minimum).

Portable Document Format (PDF) is an excellent choice for easily repurposing content into a digital form that is readable by the masses. The PDF file format has become a document exchange standard and is an excellent choice for supplementing a printed piece with a digital one. But, can you make a bad PDF? Well, sure you can. You must consider how you will make a PDF; what version of the PDF software you'll use; and the color model, resolution, and file size you'll use. You also must determine who will make this PDF to ensure that everyone can open and read it.

The distribution method you choose might be a passive method, instead of active. You won't push content to specific people or addresses, but drive people to a location. What it this location? Is it a website? Rather than pushing many pieces of information to many locations, with the inherent risks of the pieces not reaching their destinations, the destinations being incorrect, and the process being quite costly, you can drive everyone to the same destination, thereby ensuring that the same content is delivered each time. It also enables you to change the content frequently and cost effectively.

When we talk about publishing content via the Web, we have moved from a two-dimensional, subtractive color model and a manufacturing process known as *print* to a viewing-only, additive color model and development-based service known as *web*. Will you design differently for web than for print? Are the resources that are required for print different from those required for web? The answer is "yes and no." PDF is the bridge between the two media because it can be repurposed for both distribution methods. Web pages are not well suited to be printed, and print files are not well suited to be posted as web pages.

Web

One of your choices for moving your content to the Web might include Adobe's GoLive, which creates standards-based websites. You can create web pages in GoLive and work with Adobe Photoshop, Adobe Illustrator, and Adobe PDF files directly within GoLive. InDesign's Package for GoLive offers you the ability to repurpose your layout and graphics into file formats, colors, and resolutions appropriate for web instead of print.

Does this mean you have to design once, twice, or three times to distribute your content in three different ways?

Many of us have been doing this for a while now. But this isn't an efficient use of time and resources. Especially because our goal should always be to deliver the same, consistent content regardless of the distribution method. This is where *XML* comes in.

If you are going to be tasked with the repurposing of content to a variety of best-fit distribution methods for marketing, what are you going to do? How are you going to accomplish this efficiently? The answer might be XML, depending on your resources and handoffs. What is XML, and how can it be used to repurpose content? XML stands for Extensible Markup Language. It can be used to store any kind of structured document and can include information so that it can pass between different computing systems that might not be able to talk to each other. It describes the *meaning* of information, not how it's displayed. And separating content from presentation is the key to XML's importance.

You might already have experience tagging text with style sheets. Think of style sheets as a tagging mechanism. XML tags, while concerned only with the content of information (and not its presentation), can be used as a method of targeting incoming content in InDesign. Mapping XML tags to paragraph and character styles in InDesign can facilitate automated workflows. And the same tagged XML can be used in GoLive with Cascading Style Sheets (CSS) to allow flexible repurposing of content, changing the presentation of content quickly by modifying the externally referenced CSS file.

> ### ⊗ NOTE
> Although the subject of XML is outside the scope of this book, if you're interested in a primer on the subject, pick up *XML for the World Wide Web: Visual QuickStart Guide* by Elizabeth Castro (PeachPit Press, ISBN: 0201710986).

To recap, what is the message, who will we send it to, and how will we get it there?

Budget

You also must determine how much all this is going to cost. I've never worked with an organization that didn't care about the cost of a marketing project, but I have worked with many that did not have a budgeting process (the projected budget) for publishing or a tracking methodology (the actual cost) to measure these processes.

But, believe it or not, the steps we've discussed leading up to the publishing of content cost something, and I encourage you and your organization to attach values to the marketing and publishing cost centers. To do this, you must have some idea of how many times a year you will publish content, in what ways, and what the previous year's cost was so you can budget for this year's costs.

Having a good working relationship with your print service providers, web developers, or email partners is vital to the budgeting process. Preplanning will help these service providers give you a more accurate estimate or quote for services.

Resources will contribute to the cost of your project, including

- ▶ **Photography**—How you secure the images for your work will contribute greatly to the cost of the project. You can choose to hire a photographer or use a stock photography service. If you use stock photography, be sure to check out Adobe Stock Photography. If you collaborate with a photographer, make sure that you agree upon his services, the color mode and resolution he will supply, and the file format you would like. If the photographer wants to color correct, question this. Will he collaborate with your print service provider or web developer? And just what will he

correct for? If both distribution methods are involved, it probably doesn't make sense to pay for this service.

- ▶ **Graphic design**—Perhaps you've commissioned a graphic artist to develop icons for your newsletter/website. If so, you need to figure out what specifications to give her. Is there a *color palette* she needs to work from, such as one that includes the company spot colors? And which fonts should be used? Will she need to supply the icons for web or print, or both? For more information, see the section "File Standards," later in this chapter.

- ▶ **Fonts**—Do you own the *fonts* you want to use, or will you purchase new ones for the project? (This is more likely for outside ad agencies than in-house, but see the Adobe OpenType font library at http://studio.adobe.com/us/type/main.jsp for more information.)

- ▶ **Web development**—Costs will mostly involve the cost of time but can also involve the cost of hosting or tracking services as well as making updates to the site or page if you want to refresh the content on a regular basis. If you are capturing data from the site, database development, tracking, and maintenance might be involved as well.

- ▶ **Mail**—Your printed content factors in greatly when budgeting for content distribution. It is important that you have a working knowledge of postal regulations and discounts available depending on how much work you want to put into sorting, bar coding, and delivering your mail. If this is not a function you choose to make available in-house, consider a mailing service. Depending on your quantities, it can save you significant dollars. Additionally, many mailing services now offer to warehouse your customer data and maintain this contact information. (For instance, when a piece of mail or email comes back as undeliverable, the service updates the database to maintain its integrity.)

▶ **Editorial considerations**—Some, such as whether the content will come from within, have associated costs. You might hire a writer, technical writer, or translator for your publication. What tool will he use to create copy? Will he spell-check his content? Do you want him to format the text and, if so, will you supply him with styles that will import correctly into InDesign?

Add the cost of your outside resources, internal resources, your time, marketing's time, and the distribution costs to arrive at a number for approval.

You must answer all these questions: What is the message? Who will you send it to? How will you get it there? What's it going to cost? After you know the answers to these, you can decide which production methodology is most effective for both delivery and cost, which leads us to specific production options.

Specific Production Options

Within the context of print, planning for production involves paper (stock and *substrate*), ink or toner, and the printing method (*digital* and *offset* or alternative print technologies such as *flexographic*, *serigraphic* (or screen) printing, and so on). All these elements involve careful planning of the manufacturing process.

Offset and digital are the most common methods of printing marketing publications. Flexography is found in package and label printing. Screen and wide format digital are most often used for signage and printing on unusual surfaces or specialty items. Letterpress is still used for engraved stationery, stamping of forms, and ticketing.

As you will often hear throughout the book, I strongly recommend establishing a good working relationship with your print service provider. When you are in the beginning stages of a project and have determined that some portion of it will be printed, be sure to involve your service provider. Sit down with them and discuss your options, manufacturing processes, and the costs associated with each idea you have.

They can make useful and cost-effective suggestions regarding stock and ink. They will engineer the layout to the stock in the most practical, efficient, and least wasteful process possible. They will also recommend or caution you on your ink choices based on what will happen to the piece after it's distributed. If they can offer a variety of technologies, they will guide you to appropriate choices for offset, digital, letterpress, screen, or flexo printing.

Binding and finishing should also be discussed and planned for because these add to the expense as well as the timeline for delivery of the finished pieces. If you have a multiple-page document, you should choose from a mechanical bind, saddle stitching, perfect binding, or case binding. If you have a job that requires folding (such as folders, stationery, or brochures), discuss the exact fold sequence and, if possible, make up a dummy. This will assist your print service provider when estimating the job. Uncommon folds can require a change in equipment setup, employing handwork, or sending the job out to a specialty shop to accommodate the request. Special finishing requirements such as coatings, die cuts, stamping, or embossing, will likely be sent to a specialty shop, take longer, and cost more.

 TIP

Remember that the more straightforward the resources of paper and stock and the simpler the digital file, the less your service provider will have to do to the electronic file when it reaches them. And that means a faster turnaround and lower price.

Checklist for Print Production

I wanted to put together a guideline to assist you through the print production process. Consider how you organize your digital information, including your filenaming conventions and folder structure. I suggest using a folder with the job name/number and putting your layout(s) within that folder. Then use subfolders for fonts, images, and text files.

It's also useful to identify, in advance, where all your resource files will be coming from—both internally and externally. The remainder of the form answers the following questions:

- ▶ Who will review and approve the critical steps of your project?
- ▶ What production options have been planned for the job?
- ▶ If you are mailing this project, what are the requirements?
- ▶ And finally, what did all this end up costing the company?

Figure 2.1 presents an example of a checklist you can use to guide you through the planning process.

PDF Prep for Press, Print, or View

When creating a standard file exchange for distribution, there's no question that PDF is the way to go. Creating a PDF for distribution via InDesign CS2 couldn't be easier with its newly enhanced PDF presets. Simply choose the appropriate preset (the equivalent of job options), tweak the settings to best fit your production, and export. You will be making several PDFs throughout the book.

If your job is destined for press, consider the PDF/x file structure; it's a PDF with a structure that guarantees minimal intervention by your print service provider. The *PDF/x* file format originated with newspapers and publishers trying to get advertising submissions standardized and minimize the amount of time spent on these ads. The PDF/x format not only creates a PDF, but also ensures that key ingredients necessary for most print service providers are found in the file, including trim and media box information, color specifications (*CMYK* as well as spot color), and trapping information. You can create a bad PDF, so take the time to collaborate with your service provider on these settings.

But not all PDFs are headed to your print service provider. If your job is headed for digital output, externally or internally, you will probably choose the PDF preset for Print, but make sure you ask your provider for specifications. New digital presses such as Xerox's iGen3 and HP's Indigo rival offset quality, and your service provider might ask you to follow PDF for press guidelines.

Print Planning Checklist

Job Name: _____

Job Number: _____

Timeline/Deadline: _____

Description of project: _____

_____

Internal Resources identified:

❏ marketing ❏ shipping   ❏ _____   ❏ _____   ❏ _____   ❏ _____   ❏ _____

External Resources identified:

❏ photography   ❏ graphic artist   ❏ copywriter   ❏ print service   ❏ mailing

❏ _____   ❏ _____   ❏ _____   ❏ _____   ❏ _____   ❏ _____   ❏ _____

File requirements:

❏ Page Layout   _____   _____   _____   _____   _____

❏ Editorial   _____   _____   _____   _____   _____

❏ Images   _____   _____   _____   _____   _____

❏ Graphics   _____   _____   _____   _____   _____

❏ Print Service Provider   _____

❏ Stock/Ink _____

❏ Page Count _____

❏ Print Method _____

❏ Binding _____

❏ Finishing _____

Review and approval methods and proofing requirements:

_____

_____

Mailing Requirements

_____

_____

Internal Costs: _____

External Costs: _____

Mailing Costs: _____

Budget (projected): _____

Actual: _____

PDFs for print slightly lowers the overhead for resolution and compression for your file (meaning the quality expectations are lower for digital output), and the file size should be smaller and somewhat more compact. It is designed for laser output, but you might end up distributing this file via email and have the recipient print it. For example, it might be a form the recipient needs to fill out and sign. Anything you want to distribute electronically but still want to print well should be done via PDF for print.

Finally, PDF distribution can be for read-only purposes. Whether it's for distribution via email or it's to be viewed on the company website, the goal is to make a small PDF with low-resolution images and *RGB* color. You use RGB color because the device the viewer will be using—a monitor—is an RGB device. Choosing the Smallest File Size preset is recommended for this purpose.

Checklist for PDF Production

The following is a guideline to assist you through the PDF production process. Consider how you organize your digital information, including your filenaming conventions and folder structure. I suggest using a folder with the job name/number and placing your layout(s) within that folder. Then use subfolders for fonts, images, and text files.

It's also useful to identify, in advance, where all your resource files will be coming from—both internally and externally. The remainder of the form answers the following questions:

▶ Who will review and approve the critical steps of your project?

▶ What interactivity has been planned for the job?

▶ Will this PDF be distributed electronically via email, be distributed via website, or be burned to CD?

▶ And finally, what did all this end up costing the company?

See Figure 2.2 for an example of a checklist you can use to guide you through the PDF planning process.

For Web

When planning for web distribution, someone else will likely actually be compositing the web page or site in question. Many people still hire out this function because it is still uncommon to find a web and print skill set in the same person. However, it is essential that you understand the basic construction, terminology, language, and file format requirements.

It is also important for you to understand the limitations of web compared to print with regard to typography and graphic presentation. You can provide interactivity and dimension with your web page that you can't on a two-dimensional piece of paper. You can enrich content with animation, sound, images, and movies to engage the user in a different way and provide a different experience.

Collaborate with your service provider to submit the content she needs in the best possible format. You might have to repurpose your graphics, export your images, stories, and a PDF visual guide via Package for GoLive, or supply her with additional resources you wouldn't ordinarily store.

PDF Planning Checklist

Job Name: _____

Job Number: _____

Timeline/Deadline: _____

Description of project: (based on previous job)   _____

_____

Internal Resources identified:

❏ marketing ❏ IT   ❏ _____   ❏ _____   ❏ _____   ❏ _____

External Resources identified:

❏ ISP   ❏ web developer   ❏ _____   ❏ _____   ❏ _____   ❏ _____

File requirements for the PDF:

❏ Page Layout   _____   _____   _____   _____   _____

❏ Editorial   _____   _____   _____   _____   _____

❏ Images   _____   _____   _____   _____   _____

❏ Graphics   _____   _____   _____   _____   _____

❏ A/V, animate   _____   _____   _____   _____   _____

Interactive additions in Acrobat:

❏ Hyperlinks _____

❏ Bookmarks _____

❏ Page transitions _____

❏ Forms _____

❏ Security _____

Review and approval methods and proofing requirements:

_____

_____

Distribution Requirements (e-mail, web)

_____

_____

Internal Costs: _____

External Costs: _____

Distribution Costs   _____

Budget (projected): _____

Actual: _____

You need to collaborate with your service provider on the structure of the website and the kind of elements that might enrich the recipient's experience. Understand that, just like binding and finishing options, asking for Flash animation will cost more. Weigh the benefits versus the cost. If you take a look at my company's website (www.dm-corp.com), you will see that, rather than integrating Flash animation throughout the site, we opted to just open the website with Flash animation. After you enter the site, it is developed in HTML. This was more cost-effective for us, but we were able to add some visual interest.

Getting people to respond to you is easier when you ask them to spend little time and effort figuring out how to do it. Printed surveys are considered successful when you have around a 2% response rate. This, of course, could mean providing a self-addressed stamped envelope and asking recipients to fill out a form and walk the whole thing to a mailbox or mail stop.

A website allows recipients to fill out a form online, which is fast, easy, and free. No wonder people spend time, money, and planning for capturing data actively and even more time, money, and planning capturing data passively (data such as who visited the site, how many times, and whether they left a cookie behind). The possibilities are endless, as are the number of professionals necessary to create, code, and track this data. And that all costs money.

When planning for web production, first decide what type of content needs to reside on the site, how often it will change, who will change it, and how much it will cost to change it. Sound familiar?

Checklist for Web Production

The following is a guideline to assist you through the web production process. Consider how you organize your digital information, including your filenaming conventions and folder structure. I suggest a folder with the job name/number and putting your layout(s) within that folder. Then use subfolders for fonts, images, and text files.

It's also useful to identify, in advance, where all your resource files will be coming from—both internally and externally. The remainder of the form answers the following questions:

- ▶ Who will review and approve the critical steps of your project?
- ▶ What interactive options have been planned for the job?
- ▶ Will you be capturing customer information from the site?
- ▶ Will this content be pushed out to email or mobile devices as well?
- ▶ And finally, what did all this end up costing the company?

Figure 2.3 shows an example of a checklist you can use to guide you through the web planning process.

Technology Considerations—A Primer

Let's turn our attention to another critical component of your planning decisions: What technology are you going to use in the planning and production of your content?

Technology considerations include *color management*, *vector* versus *raster* graphics, and the appropriate use of graphic file formats. These considerations all play a vital role in compositing your message using InDesign CS2.

Web Planning Checklist

Job Name: _____

Job Number: _____

Timeline/Deadline: _____

Description of project: (based on previous job) _____

_____

Internal Resources identified:

❑ marketing ❑ IT   ❑ _____ ❑ _____ ❑ _____ ❑ _____

External Resources identified:

❑ ISP   ❑ web developer   ❑ graphic artist   ❑ _____ ❑ _____ ❑ _____

File requirements for the web:

❑ Web Layout   _____   _____   _____   _____   _____

❑ Editorial   _____   _____   _____   _____   _____

❑ Images   _____   _____   _____   _____   _____

❑ Graphics   _____   _____   _____   _____   _____

❑ A/V, animate   _____   _____   _____   _____   _____

Additions to page/site:

❑ Flash _____

❑ Rollovers _____

❑ Data capture _____

❑ Smart objects _____

❑ _____

Review and approval methods and proofing requirements:

_____

_____

Distribution Requirements (e-mail, web, mobile devices)

_____

_____

Internal Costs: _____

External Costs: _____

Distribution Costs   _____

Budget (projected): _____

Actual: _____

Software

Technical tools are an important consideration in this process. We all know what it's like to be assigned an important project but not have access to the tools necessary to get the job done. Even if you have no other tool than InDesign CS2, you will still be able to accomplish most of your publishing goals. This book is structured in such a way that InDesign is the only tool you will need, but I would be remiss in not recommending additional tools I have found useful over the years.

I recommend Adobe's Creative Suite 2, which offers the full complement of page layout, illustration, photo editing, revision control, and web development all in one box. You can add to this a good font library (Adobe OpenType) and font management utility (Extensis's Suitcase). Beyond these tools and to enhance your arsenal, consider some plug-ins that will extend the functionality of this tool set. I've recommended a few in Appendix B, "Resources," and you can also visit Adobe's website for a more complete listing of plug-in developers.

I could add more recommendations at this point, but I'm going to stop and advocate not for more tools, but for a better understanding and utilization of the tools you already have. How many of us possess software applications but have not had the time to truly learn them or don't have the resources to educate ourselves? How frustrating is it to know we could be doing more with what we already have but for the lack of education?

Companies must do more with less. You might have taken on some of the marketing functions as a result of downsizing. You might have been in charge of the company

newsletter, and now management expects you to take on additional assignments. I encourage you to acquire the proper tools and find good training—the kind that understands the nature of your work and the skills you need to accomplish your publishing tasks.

Now that the question of tools is out of the way, let's turn our attention to file standards. They might already be set in place, but it's worthwhile to review them. If you follow the recommendations regarding tools, we can break down your file standards into two categories: raster and vector.

File Standards

Raster files are digital files that describe graphic content using pixels of color, in a specific amount (*resolution*). The resolution of a raster image is measured in the number of pixels per inch. An image for a website, for example, typically has a resolution of 72ppi. Why? Because computer monitors are very low-resolution devices, so why include more pixels than your monitor can display? An image intended for print should have a higher resolution—typically twice its line screen (usually this is 300ppi). Raster images are both resolution and device dependent, meaning they have a fixed size and that size is determined by what destination it is bound for. If you try to change the size of the image after you've determined its resolution, you run into a problem. If you enlarge the image, detail degrades, and if you shrink the image, detail degrades.

Vector files are digital files that describe graphic content using lines (*paths*) and fills in the form of mathematical descriptions. These lines and fills can have attributes of color, pattern, and weight attached to them.

They are both resolution and device independent and can therefore be scaled and repurposed for different distribution outlets with no effect on quality.

Your raster work, largely produced in Photoshop, or from a digital camera, or provided from a scanning provider, will vary depending on distribution. If you are preparing to publish via print, your raster considerations (including dimensions, resolution, and color mode) will be guided by the following:

▶ The size at which you will produce an image relative to the original size

▶ The line screen at which you will print, based on ink, stock, and press (consult your vendor)

▶ The number of colors you will produce

If you're using print, you'll likely produce an image that will be scanned to size, at a resolution of at least twice your line screen and probably in either grayscale or *CMYK* color mode. These are all appropriate choices for print. After these are determined, you can move on to decisions about the file format. If you already have a standard in place, stick with it. You'll probably use one of the following: *Tagged Image File Format (TIFF)*, *Encapsulated PostScript (EPS)*, *Joint Photographic Experts Group (JPEG)*, and *Photoshop Layered (PSD)*.

All these file formats have pros and cons. TIFF is an all-raster format that is easy to produce and generally error free. It is an open file format that can be tinkered with in other programs. You can apply color to it (see our brochure project) or apply a filter to create an unusual effect.

On the other hand, EPS is a *metafile*. A metafile is a digital file that can be made up of raster and vector elements. This file standard has a history if your rasters contain clipping paths because it was the first file format to allow for the recording of these paths. This format contains PostScript information in addition to the image. It is self-contained, and other programs cannot tinker with its contents. EPSs can be opened by any application that can create an EPS, and they almost always can be safely edited by the originating application, such as Illustrator, FreeHand, or CorelDraw.

If you are working in "RIP and run" publishing (fast turnaround, lower-quality work), you might have adopted a JPEG standard. It is a common file format that most digital cameras work with, and it generally compresses the information within the file. It is a lossy compression scheme, however, meaning it achieves compression by eliminating data during each file save. This can lead to problems processing these jobs using older RIPS and runs counter to the quality issue many strive for with printed pieces, but it might be ideal for other distribution methods. Should you encounter a JPEG, I recommend opening it in Photoshop and resaving the file as a TIFF.

Finally, if you are using an all-Adobe workflow, you might leave your raster images in a PSD file format. InDesign imports a PSD file without having to flatten it or convert it to some other file format. The PSD format offers the most flexibility and editability of all the raster file formats because it allows you to keep your layers intact.

Your vector work will be largely composed of graphic elements, logos, creative work with type, patterns, borders, charts, and illustrations. It is characterized by crisp outlines and interesting fill colors and patterns. Illustrator is the power of PostScript in the hands of the average user, you and me. You can do much with this file format to enhance your content. Illustrator primarily produces vector art, but it allows for the import and export of the raster file format. Placing raster images in Illustrator renders the Illustrator file subject to the stricures on raster art, as previously discussed, meaning it can no longer be scaled without losing detail. Because Illustrator creates files containing PostScript, your RIP is responsible for converting this mathematical language into basic shapes and fills, which your output device then maps out into spots applied to your stock.

Your file standard options for your vector work are Adobe Illustrator (AI), EPS, and PDF. One of the advantages to using an all-Adobe workflow is the fact that these products accept each other's native file formats. InDesign takes an AI file without having to convert it to some other independent graphic file format.

If you are handing off your files to other departments or entities outside your company, or if you do not have an all-Adobe workflow, you must incorporate file format standards that are accepted by a variety of graphic arts products—and file formats such as PSD and AI do not fall into that category.

Now we've just been talking about print, and part of planning for production involves the distribution of content via PDF or web. Can you use the same file formats for these distribution methods? You can for PDF files because PDFs can contain a variety of graphic file formats within them. As long as they are properly linked to the original application file, the graphic files will be embedded and rendered correctly within the resulting exported PDF. But web is a different animal altogether.

Elements for web pages can be created with Photoshop and Illustrator, but they must be saved in file formats that are compatible with the production goals of web development. It doesn't make any sense to place a high-resolution file within a web page when your monitor is only 72dpi, and it doesn't make sense to display a graphic in CMYK when your monitor is RGB. The production requirements for web are the opposite of those for print.

First, always work in RGB color mode. Second, use web-safe colors. Creating small graphic file sizes is important when you are distributing images on the Web.

In general, web graphics, like print graphics, fall into the two categories of raster and vector. The raster file formats are typically the *Graphical Interchange Format (GIF)* and JPEG. JPEG is recommended for continuous tone images, such as photographs. As mentioned earlier, it is a compressed file format (extremely useful for creating small files) but doesn't support transparency. GIF is used for animations, solid-color images, and images with repetitive color (such as line art and logos). Also, GIF does support transparency. These raster files describe an image with colored pixels (*pixels*, not dots or spots, are small, touching squares of color you can see when you zoom in on a raster image).

⊗ NOTE

You can find more on the topic of transparency throughout the book because this is a key feature of InDesign CS2.

The vector file formats are typically *Scalable Vector Graphics (SVG)* and *Shockwave Flash (SWF)*.

SVG graphics, which are XML based, are typically used for scalable, compact vector web graphics. Because they are scalable, they can be viewed onscreen without sacrificing quality and are ideal for text and colors. SWF is a Macromedia Flash file format, and it creates scalable compact web graphics and is well suited for interactive, animated web graphics.

Organizing and Protecting Versions and Assets

As you can see, depending on your distribution choices, your resources, your digital assets, and their file formats are important. You probably have the same image in different formats and resolutions depending on whether you distribute for print and/or redistribute for web. Many of my clients, in an effort to control their exploding libraries of images, store only one version of an image—a large, high-resolution, RGB file—from which all other files and formats can be generated but not archived.

This strategy makes sense because, by storing a high-resolution file, you ensure that you will always have enough pixels to support whatever distribution method you choose. By storing the largest physical dimensions possible, you account for something as large as signage and as small as web. By storing RGB, you store the largest color gamut available—approximately 16 million colors (more on this in the next section).

As you continue to publish your content, explore and grow your skills, and deliver your message in a variety of ways, you will experience continued pressure on your growing number of digital assets. Thinking through your file format requirements, storage requirements, and the organization of these

assets is something you will have to grapple with sooner rather than later.

Securing your work, production, and assets is critical to your workflow. Be sure you understand the difference between backing up and archiving. Backing up your data is an exercise you should perform daily to protect yourself and your work from catastrophic damage. Many utilities are available and, if you work in a networked server environment, you should store all your data on a server and back up the server daily. Consider what would it mean to you and your company if you lost all your digital content and you'll see the importance of daily backups.

Archiving involves storing your digital assets in an organized manner for future reference. Being able to historically reference your work in a timely manner will pay dividends in efficiencies over time. How many times have you received a request for an image or text that was created a couple of years ago to be reused or repurposed for an upcoming event? Could you get your hands on it quickly and easily? If not, why not? Many applications and hardware options are available on the market today that perform a librarian function for your important assets.

In addition to these organization issues, consider the number of versions of a project that might be circulating at any given time. When you purchase Adobe's Creative Suite 2, you will have a new feature called Version Cue that enables you to organize your projects and easily share them between people and applications. It enables you to track and maintain continuity within your workflow of current versions and manage who is working on what by using a checkout system.

Finally, when you are in the middle of creating content, you must have at least one additional pair of eyes review, comment, and approve your work. One of the best products available is Acrobat 7 Professional, which contains amazing commenting, review cycle, and approval tools based on the superior file format of PDF. With this new version of Acrobat, you can share PDFs with others even if they don't own a full version of Acrobat; Reader 7 is all they need to participate in the review circle. This is truly an essential content publishing tool.

Quality Control for Color

When I use the term *color management*, I'm talking about predicting color from a variety of sources. Color management is most effective and most achievable when you, the creative, control the majority of the process or when your production partner is creating both your scans as well as your output.

Color management involves the proper calibration of devices. To *calibrate* means to ensure that your devices are functioning according to manufacturers' specifications. Often manufacturers provide methods for achieving calibration.

Next, color management involves the characterization of each device. To *characterize* a device means to describe the device in terms of the number of colors it is capable of capturing, displaying, or producing. This characterization is stored in the form of a profile, which is a digital color story attached to an image file.

Finally, color management often involves conversion from one color mode to another. For print, that might be converting from RGB to CMYK. For web, it might be the opposite. As you repurpose content for alternative

distribution methods, converting from one color model to another becomes commonplace and you must understand what is happening when you convert.

The *l*a*b* color space is an internationally accepted color model that many conversion utilities use to translate color from one color mode to another. The l*a*b space is device independent and is an ideal communicator between other color models. So, when you take an RGB color and convert it to CMYK, it passes through the l*a*b color space and the equivalent is found, defined, and then mapped to the closest corresponding color on the other side.

Approximately 16 million colors make up the RGB color gamut. You can create approximately 5,000 colors with CMYK, but the indexed color models associated with web graphic file formats limit your color palette to 256 colors. Going from 16 million to 256 is a big difference. There can be no doubt that colors will change throughout these transitions.

Add to that differences in manufactured monitors and monitor technologies, lighting, and computer platform specifications, and you can see how difficult color management can be to achieve.

Then there's the human factor. How we each interpret those light waves is another matter. I might see mauve and someone else might see purple. Many people have deficiencies that affect the way they see color. Color tests can ferret out those deficiencies, and anyone working in color should be color tested.

Having said this, if you want to evolve into a color-managed workflow, your Adobe products—including InDesign CS2—allow for color management by using color descriptions that are called *International Color Consortium*

(ICC) color profiles. ICC profiles are descriptions of color within the file based on specific devices, such as scanners, monitors, proofers, and presses. These profiles quantify the behavior of these devices so that printed outcomes can be predictable with proper quality control and calibration practices.

For example, say your print service provider is producing your image scans as well as creating final output from their printing presses. This vendor has taken great care and time to make sure these images will print consistently and predictably on their press. When you receive their scans to further work with them in Photoshop or place them in InDesign, you will likely get a message that the image has an embedded profile. You will need to keep and not discard the profile because this profile has compensated for the differences between the color the scanner has captured versus the color the press can print.

Optimizing Your Workflow with Templates

When planning for production, after you have your skill set in fine form, you need to start optimizing your workflow. You do this by making sure your tools are organized and that you understand the process for developing a specific publication. You can also develop shortcuts for certain processes in the form of keyboard shortcuts; plug-ins that can extend functionality; scripts that can optimize repetitive, mundane tasks or batch processes; and templates that contain everything you need for a common publication. Think of these templates as kits designed for easy construction. All the chapters in this book emphasize templates so that you can take this "practice" production and reuse it in a live business setting.

Many people confuse templates with master pages, but master pages are stored page formats or configurations. *Templates*, on the other hand, are dummy publications. They contain not only master pages, but also paragraph, character, and object style sheets; color swatches; and libraries. Additionally, because templates are dummy publications, they contain all the necessary master pages, document pages, and repeating elements on the pages that will appear in every edition or version of the publication. See Chapter 9, "Developing a Newsletter," for a classic example of a publication that lends itself to template generation.

Some templates are more sophisticated than others. If there is nothing to be stored in the template but you still want to store common sizes or styles of documents, consider using document presets, which enable you to save common sizes and basic page configurations that can be used repeatedly and shared with others.

Final Thoughts

Planning for production is well worth the time and attention you will spend on it. Creating and manufacturing content involves many tasks, and you will partner with several sources to produce your jobs. Professionals prepare. You often might be given little lead time, be tasked with coming up with resources, and be given extraordinary deadline goals. This makes it difficult to plan. However, if you don't take the time to plan, you will experience delays on the back end due to mistakes made on the front end. If you can find the time to correct errors, you should be able to find the time to plan. Having to correct mistakes at the last minute creates great stress for everyone in the creative and manufacturing workflow, which is impractical and unnecessary.

I once knew a prepress manager who, at the ripe old age of 35, was experiencing his third heart-related episode. By all appearances physically fit, the doctors put him on a treadmill, tested his heart, and found great stress. Perplexed, they finally sat him down in front of a computer with a database of the most stressful jobs on the planet. The number one most stressful manufacturing job? Printing. They were even able to rank the most stressful printing companies—and he had worked for 3 of the top 10. He is no longer in printing.

Do yourself, your stress level, and even your heart a favor—plan.

 NOTE

The previously mentioned checklists are also available at the publisher's website in Chapter 2's Zip file. There you will find InDesign files you can customize to fit your own needs and then export as PDFs.

The Switch

Even though I am making the assumption you've made the switch, I can't help but mention how well Adobe makes its case for the big conversion. For information addressing a switch from either PageMaker or Quark, visit Adobe's website address for key issues: http://www.adobe.com/products/indesign/conversion.html.

Here you will find information that addresses everything from ROIs and migration strategies to productivity benchmarks and conversion guides from both Quark and PageMaker to InDesign. This is an extremely useful resource.

Special Consideration for PageMaker Users

InDesign CS2 provides for a smooth transition for former PageMaker users by incorporating several popular PageMaker features into this new CS version. In addition to features and tools similar to PageMaker's, InDesign CS2 has training materials and special help files that should assist transitioning users to adapt to the new product while continuing to work in an environment that should feel familiar and comfortable to longtime users of PageMaker. Figure 3.1 shows the PageMaker toolbar for your review.

InDesign CS2 features that will look and feel familiar to PageMaker users include:

- ▶ PageMaker 6.0 publication converter
- ▶ InBooklet plug-in for document imposition
- ▶ Automated bullets and numbering
- ▶ Data merge
- ▶ Position tool
- ▶ PageMaker-compatible keyboard shortcuts
- ▶ PageMaker toolbar

Obviously, a great deal of thought and support has gone into protecting and preparing PageMaker users for their eventual conversion to InDesign.

FIGURE 3.1 The PageMaker
toolbar in InDesign CS2.

Conversion Features for Quark and PageMaker Files

For those of you who have made the switch and have a wealth of legacy files to consider, I offer the following advice:

First, determine how many legacy files you have. Then you need to consider who you typically share your files with. Will you still need to share those files with external users and, if so, will they be converting as well? Set aside assets that need to remain as they are, or static. For all other files that have the potential for conversion, determine how many of these will actually be reused. Finally, from this narrowed-down list, determine whether you will need to convert all the files at once, or a file at a time, as needed.

Then use this list to consider each file's internal resources. Do you have all the files (images) and fonts these legacy files require? This is very important and will help avoid conversion issues.

If a batch conversion is needed, take a look at Appendix B, "Resources." It includes plug-in sources that might assist you with your conversion requirements.

Finally, review some of the conversion specifications discussed in the next section. For a more thorough review, locate converting legacy InDesign, PageMaker, and Quark files in your InDesign CS2 user guide.

What InDesign CS2 Can Convert

InDesign CS2 can convert legacy InDesign files, PageMaker files, and even Quark files. The following versions will translate:

- ▶ Quark 3.3 or 4.1x documents or templates
- ▶ Quark Passport 4.1x

 NOTE

Later versions of Quark need to be saved down to 4.1x before you can convert documents.

- ▶ PageMaker 6.0 and later documents and templates
- ▶ InDesign legacy files, all versions

 NOTE

InDesign can recover most corrupt documents that PageMaker can't open.

How the Conversion Is Handled

InDesign CS2 converts the file formats discussed in the previous section, but what about the actual elements in the file? What happens to them, and how do they appear to you after the file is converted? When you open a file that is not native to InDesign, your application reports any issues it encountered during the conversion. This report is one you can read, save, and print, and it warns you about situations you might need to review or correct. Here are the conversion specifications:

- ▶ InDesign converts the original file (Quark or PageMaker) information to native InDesign information.
- ▶ Quark text boxes are converted to InDesign text frames.
- ▶ PageMaker threads are converted to InDesign text frames.
- ▶ Quark paragraph and character styles are converted to InDesign styles.

 NOTE

IDCS2 doesn't have a Superior type style: If you have a lot of Superior-styled dollar signs, for example, those become normal-size characters with a positive baseline shift.

- ▶ Quark color profiles are ignored, but PageMaker profiles are converted directly.
- ▶ Text and image links are preserved, with the exception of embedded graphics (that is, PageMaker files), which are not converted. There is no support for OLE embedded elements or Quark Xtensions.

Setting Your Composition Preferences

Text wrap options need to be set correctly for conversion to be accurate. Set your composition preferences in InDesign to Text Wrap Only Affects Text Beneath. Also, consider applying Adobe Single-Line Composer, found in the Paragraph palette, to affect paragraphs.

InDesign will treat each line separately, which can preserve the original line breaks.

Figure 3.2 shows the Text Wrap Only Affects Text Beneath preference setting. You will find this in the Composition tab of Preferences.

FIGURE 3.2   **Text wrap options in Preferences.**

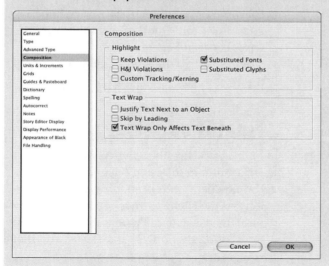

► Master pages and layers are converted for both applications.

► Master page objects and guides are converted.

► Grouped objects stay grouped, unless there are nonprinting items (PageMaker only).

► Strokes and lines are converted to the closest option in InDesign.

► Custom stokes and dashes are converted to custom InDesign strokes and dashes.

Colors are converted exactly, except for the following:

► Quark 3.3 HSB to RGB.

► Quark 4.1 HSB and LAB to RGB.

► Quark 4.1 colors from the color library are converted based on CMYK values.

► Multi-ink colors from Quark are mapped to mixed ink colors in InDesign, unless no spot colors are in use. If no spot colors have been used in a Quark multi-ink color, they are converted to process colors in InDesign.

Further Support for PM and Quark Users

In addition to InDesign shortcuts (many are the same in Illustrator and Photoshop), keyboard shortcuts are available for

PageMaker and Quark users as well. Open the Edit pull-down menu, select Keyboard Shortcuts, and explore the pop-up list under Sets. See Figure 3.3 as a reference for your keyboard shortcut options.

FIGURE 3.3   Keyboard shortcut sets.

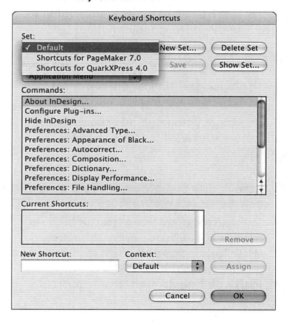

For more information about converting PageMaker and Quark files and the differences between PageMaker and Quark features, see the InDesign user guide or help file.

Final Thoughts

I have worked with many clients converting legacy files to InDesign 2.0 and CS. Overall, the experience has been fairly positive as long as the client sets her expectations appropriately. It is extremely important for you to understand that InDesign uses its own unique composition engine to flow text.

For this reason, the most prevalent challenge you will have is text reflow. So, for your longer documents, there is greater potential for text reflow. You therefore need to pay close attention to line breaks and wraps. As mentioned earlier, the Paragraph Composer controls found in the Paragraph palette can be employed to affect changes and improvements to the text flow.

Having said this, I can't imagine that this issue is more challenging or time-consuming than recreating your entire file. I have worked with page layout applications since the late 1980s (think Ventura Publisher) and have never been more excited by a product that delivers so many features and options that meet the demands of the marketing/ communications professional.

You will appreciate its robust typographical controls, rich creative tools and features, tight integration with the rest of the creative suite, long document publishing options, and cross-media and interactive features that allow for the repurposing of content. In the vernacular, it's the total package.

PART II: Projects

CHAPTER 4: Developing Business Collateral

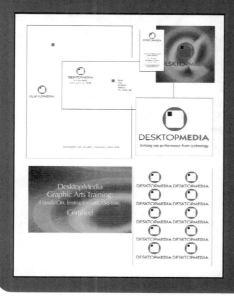

About the Project

In this project you will learn how to create various forms of business *collateral*, including letterhead, envelopes, business cards, and postcards. Optional projects such as a CD jacket, name tags, and a company t-shirt are covered at the end of this project.

Prerequisites

It would be helpful if you had a basic understanding of page layout, including using the Tool palette, formatting text, and performing basic page formatting.

@work resources

Please visit the publisher's website to access the following Chapter 4 files:

▶ Finished_Projects

▶ Art files [DMLOGO.eps, DMLOGOtag.eps, and DM_BGRD_DUO.eps]

Planning the Project

Company collateral is the first step, and an extremely important one, in establishing your company's image or brand. A lot of thought needs to go into not only how you will be using your collateral on a daily basis, but whether it accurately reflects your company's image, product, or service. Elements to consider include the budget, format, style, color, paper choice, bindery processes, finishing processes, and mailing processes.

Distribution Choices

When selecting stock and ink for your collateral project, you must consider how the collateral will be used and what type of devices it will be fed through. This can significantly affect which inks your printer will advise. As an example, one of my stock choices was vellum because it runs through laser printers but smears with inkjet inks:

- ▶ Will this collateral be used in conjunction with a laser printer or an inkjet, or both? Be sure you choose appropriate stock and ink for the output device you will be using.
- ▶ Will you be duplexing (printing on both sides) with your paper stock? Some stock is finished (coated) on one side only.

Orientation Choices

Although most formatting choices aren't really choices but are standard, I've seen some very creative interpretations of those standards. Please be advised that if you deviate from those standards, it can have a significant financial impact on your mailing costs:

- ▶ The format for letterhead is normally 8 1/2" × 11" (called portrait, or vertical, orientation).
- ▶ Envelopes are usually 9 1/2" × 4 1/8" (landscape, or horizontal, orientation).
- ▶ Business cards are typically 3 1/2" × 2" and are usually landscape; however, see my business card in Figure 4.1.

FIGURE 4.1 **This is a vertically formatted business card. Although it maintains the accepted dimensions of a business card, the orientation is atypical.**

DESKTOPMEDIA
Getting top performance from technology

Catherine Brosseau Indiano
Owner/President

P.O. Box 68801
Indianapolis, IN 46268
317.955.9300

cate@desktopmedia.biz
desktopmedia.biz

Paper Choices

Your substrate or paper is also another critical decision: Coated or uncoated stock and various finishes need to be considered in conjunction with the ink or foil stamping choices. If you have environmental concerns, you might prefer to work with recycled paper. However, recycled paper does have some limitations, including a higher absorption of ink and raster images that don't look crisp. Vellum smears with inkjet printers and doesn't fold well. Note that folding with a *paper's grain* is important and heavier stock choices make this problematic.

TIP

For an excellent reference to paper and ink, see a new publication offered via AIGA called *The SpecLogix Compendium of Paper & Printing.* You can find it on AIGA's website at https://www.aiga.org/onlinestore/ibo/orders/.

Now, for your company logo. Does one already exist? If so, review the next few paragraphs. If not, use the next few paragraphs as a guide when creating one or working with a graphic designer.

File Format Choices

Let's consider the digital file format of the logo. Is it *vector*? Remember, a vector format (an example would be files from Adobe Illustrator) for your logo is ideal because it allows you to scale (shrink or enlarge) your logo while maintaining its quality. In this way, you can use your logo for any number of purposes in a variety of publications. If it does not exist as a vector file, you can see whether your prepress service provider or printer will convert your *raster* logo for you (as long as the nature of the image lends itself to a conversion).

Color Choices

How many colors are in the logo, and are they *spot colors*? Remember, the greater the number of colors, the higher the cost. Many logos are two color: black plus a spot (PANTONE) color. This is economical (99.9%

of printed work uses black ink somewhere, typically in the text), and a second spot color avoids process *color separation*.

CAUTION

This color will appear repeatedly with your brand and should be selected with great care. Selecting an unusual color might affect future uses of the logo in additional marketing efforts, such as signage, website work, and so on.

Type Choices

When you create a logo for your company, you also might be making a decision about your company *typeface(s)*. These will be the typefaces you use consistently for all marketing efforts and, again, they need to be considered carefully. A good resource to start with is Adobe's website, www.adobe.com. Take a look at the font catalog. Which *type family* or families have you chosen? Do they include all the typefaces you will want (that is, italic, bold, bold italic, and so on)? Additionally, if you are in an industry such as finance or science, there are special characters you will want to make sure your type family includes, such as fractions, ordinals, and characters for scientific notation.

After a typeface(s) has been chosen, you must consider your choice of *font* technology. Fonts is the digital or electronic term for type families and faces. Who will need to use these typefaces? Which type of computer will they be using to generate marketing material? In my opinion, the best choice—both from a technology standpoint and a print production standpoint—is *OpenType*. The modern font standard is cross platform (it can be used on both PCs and Macs), is a single file structure (which simplifies its installation and transport), and supports extended character sets so special characters are easily accessed. I strongly recommend an investment in your company font selection. You will use these digital files repeatedly, and they are well worth the investment. Do not rely on free or "compatible" fonts because they are often problematic with your print provider's digital workflows and output devices.

 CAUTION

Font licensing is a serious matter and I advocate with my own clients that a periodic inventory should be taken to determine whether their font library is in compliance—meaning they own the fonts being used.

Mailing Choices

Planning for mailing your collateral is also important. Do any of your choices increase postage by nonconformance to postal standards? Will you be taking advantage of bulk mailing discounts by utilizing a mailing service? If so, care and attention to your envelope *template* and the placement of addresses are very important. For more information on postal regulations, visit the U.S. Postal Service at www.usps.gov.

Production Choices

How will you be producing your collateral? Most likely the method will be *offset lithography*. This printing method utilizes metal printing plates and the chemistry of oily inks and water. The image is transferred from a printing plate to a rubber blanket and then from the blanket to the paper, hence the term

offset. This is different from a direct impression from a plate to paper, which is called letterpress. Letterpress (one of the oldest methods of printing) actually uses a plate to strike the paper and is still used for printed pieces such as multipart invoices and ticketing.

After these decisions have been considered, arrived at, and preplanned with your print provider, it's time to put your files together and begin your first project.

Project: Letterhead

We'll be creating letterhead in 11 easy steps:

STEPS▼

1. Setting up your document format
2. Getting acquainted with the Control palette
3. Importing art files
4. Transforming placed art files
5. Creating a text element
6. Formatting text
7. Previewing your work with View commands
8. Drawing with tools
9. Applying color
10. Saving your work
11. Printing a composite proof

STEP 1▼
Setting Up Your Document Format

Launch InDesign, go to the File pull-down menu, and select New, Document. Fill out the New Document window, as indicated in Figure 4.2.

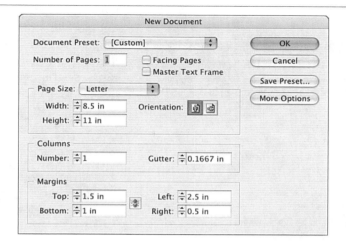

STEP 2▼
Getting Acquainted with the Control Palette

Orient yourself to the layout and check out the Control palette at the top of the window. You will be using the x,y coordinate to accurately position your elements. Your Control palette should look like Figure 4.3.

STEP 3▼
Importing Art Files

Go to the File pull-down menu and select Place. Navigate to your Chapter04\ 04Project_Files folder. Find the logo named DMLOGO.eps and double-click it to open it. An icon in the shape of a paintbrush appears.

Click anywhere on the page; the logo is shown at its actual size on the page in a selected state (with a blue frame outline and anchor points).

STEP 4▼
Transforming Placed Art Files

The logo will have to be scaled because it is too large to fit where we will be placing it. Because it is vector artwork, which is resolution independent, you can scale it without affecting its quality. However, caution should be exercised regarding strokes within the artwork because you might not want the strokes to scale. This is not the case with our logo, though. Make sure the logo is still selected and locate the X, Y fields in your Control palette (the first fields on the left side).

Make sure the *proxy* coordinate is set to the upper-left corner by clicking that dot.

Set the x coordinate to be .25 and the y coordinate to be 5. In the horizontal scale field, type **50%** (proportional scaling is on by default and will automatically set the vertical

scale equal to the horizontal scale). Note: If anamorphic scaling is required, unlock the proportional scale button next to the width and height fields and fill in the fields separately. See Figure 4.4 to identify the button directly to the right of your scale fields.

Let's take a look at the Swatches palette located under the Window pull-down menu. A new color has appeared in the palette, as shown in Figure 4.5. PMS 8322 was added to the Swatches palette when the logo was imported. Also notice that the icon to the right of the color has a dot or spot in it providing a visual indicator that you have imported a spot PANTONE color. If this color needs to be used again, perhaps in text on the letterhead, it can be used. In this way, color tags stay consistent throughout the

FIGURE 4.4 **Your coordinates and dimensions should look like this.**

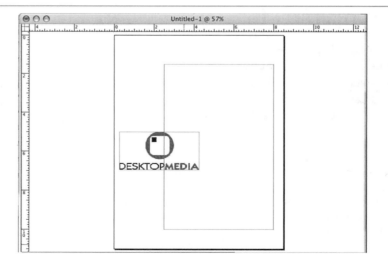

document. A problem that plagues prepress occurs when two spot colors named similarly are used throughout the document, with one created in InDesign and a similar one brought in with line art from another product, such as Illustrator. This creates an extra separation upon output.

 TIP

Always check to ensure that the number of colors and color definitions are accurate before giving a project to your service provider.

FIGURE 4.5 This is how your Swatches palette should look with an imported color.

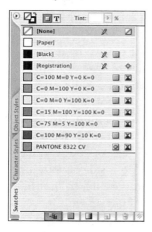

STEP 5▼
Creating a Text Element

Select the Text tool and position it on the bottom margin of your page so that the baseline of the I-beam lines up with the margin. Click and drag out a text box approximately the width of your bottom margin and deep enough to contain your footer, which will be the company contact information. Use your

control palette to tweak the width to 5.5" and the height to .25". Use your x,y coordinate to position the text box to 2 1/2, 10.

STEP 6▼
Formatting Text

Select your company font from the Type pull-down menu, and set the size to 14 points. In my example I am using Trebuchet, but feel free to use any font you own. Type **DesktopMedia • P.O. Box 68801 • Indianapolis, Indiana 46268**, or feel free to use your own company information.

After you type it, highlight the text and go to the Control palette. Make sure the Paragraph button is selected, and select Centered Alignment. With the text still highlighted, select the imported color from the Swatches palette. Use Figure 4.6 as a reference.

 TIP

To create a bullet, place your text insertion point where you want your bullet and select Type, Insert Special Character, Bullet Character. Take a look at all the special characters available!

If you want to slightly change the look of your text, try the following: Experiment with horizontal scaling (which affects the shape of the text) and tracking (which affects the space between all the letters in the high-lighted line). For horizontal scaling, a number greater than 100 increases the scale and does not affect the vertical height of the characters. For tracking, a number greater than 0 adds space between the characters in 1/1000 of an em.

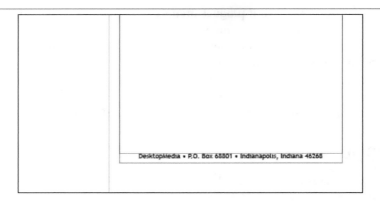

FIGURE 4.6 Draw your text box across the bottom of your layout to fit your margins, and tweak the coordinates in your Control palette.

DesktopMedia • P.O. Box 68801 • Indianapolis, Indiana 46268

 CAUTION

Scaling type should be used for special effect only, and it is not intended to replace extended or condensed typefaces.

 TIP

An *em space* is the size of the letter *m* in the typeface and point size currently selected. So, an em space would equal 10 points if you were using 10-point type.

STEP 7▼
Previewing Your Work with View Commands

Deselect the text and select View, Fit in Window. Review your work. It is helpful to turn off Frame Edges and Guides separately by going to the View pull-down menu. Or click the Preview button at the bottom of your Tool palette to turn off both Frame Edges and Guides at the same time. Click the Preview button when you need to see these visual boundaries again.

STEP 8▼
Drawing with Tools

Let's add one more graphical element to the letterhead. Select the Rectangle tool (not the Frame tool, no *X* should appear in the rectangle). Draw a square that is 1/4" (by holding down the Shift key while you are drawing, you can equally constrain the width and height—this applies to all tools that draw). Tweak the dimensions of the square in the Control palette. Drag a ruler guide from your vertical ruler on the left side of your window and line it up with the right side of your logo. Drag the square over to the ruler so that the right side of the square lines up with the guide. You will feel a pull or a snap from the guide if Snap to Guides in the View pull-down menu is turned on. The x,y coordinate for the square should be 2,1.5.

STEP 9▼
Applying Color

With the square still selected, let's add a color. Make sure your Swatches palette is displaying your swatches by name. To set this, click the triangle in the upper-right corner of your palette and select the view by Name. Make sure the Fill swatch in the upper-left corner of your palette is the active swatch (is on top) and click PMS 8322 in your swatch list. Your square should *fill* with color. If your square has a black *stroke* around it, click your Stroke swatch and click None in the Swatches palette. It should look like Figure 4.7.

FIGURE 4.7   **This is the square correctly colored and positioned.**

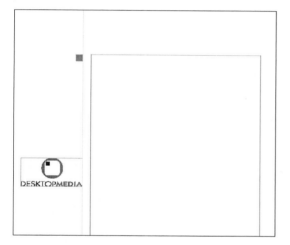

STEP 10▼
Saving Your Work

Let's save our work. Go to the File pull-down menu and select Save As. Next, navigate to the folder in the `04Finished_Projects` folder. Your finished layout should look like Figure 4.8.

STEP 11▼
Printing a Composite Proof

Let's print a content *proof.* Go to the File pull-down menu and select Print. Choose the appropriate settings for the printer that is available to you. Then go to the File pull-down menu and select Print. Again select the appropriate settings for the printer available to you. Under the general tab, select one copy. On the Setup tab select 8.5" × 11" and Vertical Orientation. Leave the Scale alone. On the Marks and Bleed tab, turn off all the options. On the Output tab, if possible, print color composite output for your work; if not, select Grayscale. On the Graphics tab, the default settings should work. The remaining tabs can be ignored for now. Print and review your proof. Make any necessary adjustments, and then save your changes. Print it again, using Figure 4.9 as your guide.

FIGURE 4.8   **Your finished, saved layout.**

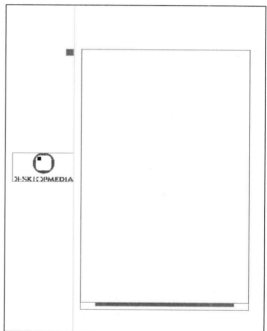

Close your file.

FIGURE 4.9 This is an example of how your print setting should look.

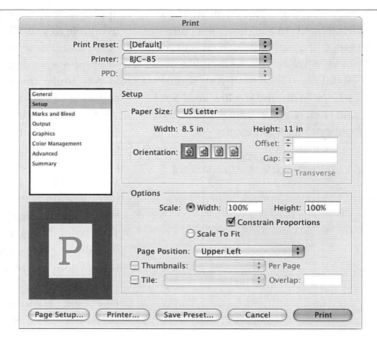

Project: Business Card

We'll be creating a business card in 10 easy steps:

STEPS▼

1. Setting up your document format
2. Importing art files
3. Positioning a graphic element
4. Transforming a graphic element
5. Placing a ruler guide and creating a text element
6. Formatting text
7. Viewing options
8. Saving your file
9. Printing a composite proof
10. Creating a template

STEP 1▼
Setting Up Your Document Format

Assuming InDesign is already launched, go to the File pull-down menu and select New, Document, as indicated in Figure 4.10.

 NOTE

If you enter the first number in the Top field and then click the icon with the broken link, InDesign automatically fills in the rest of the fields with the same amount. Click OK.

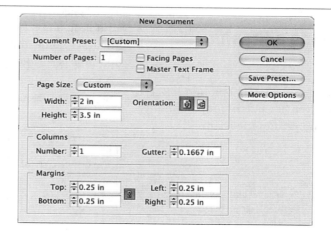

FIGURE 4.10 Please fill out your Document window as indicated and, yes, this will create a vertically oriented business card!

STEP 2▼
Importing Art Files

Go to the File pull-down menu and select Place. Then, navigate to your 04Project_Files folder. Find the logo named DMLOGOtag.eps, select it, and click Open. An icon in the shape of a paintbrush appears. Click anywhere on the page to make the logo, in its actual size, appear on the page (see Figure 4.11). Do not click and drag because that has a cropping effect on the logo.

STEP 3▼
Positioning a Graphic Element

Position the logo frame to fit the upper-left corner of the margins. Resize the frame to fit the right margin. The box should measure 1.5" wide by 1" high—use your control palette to type in the dimensions.

FIGURE 4.11 The initially placed image with the correct graphic frame size.

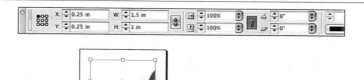

STEP 4▼
Transforming a Graphic Element

Go to the Object pull-down menu and select Fitting. Then select Fit Content Proportionally. Figure 4.12 demonstrates the results.

 TIP
You can use the Fit Proportional button on the right side of the Control palette to execute the same command.

FIGURE 4.12   You should see your logo resize.

STEP 5▼
Placing a Ruler Guide and Creating a Text Element

Click in the horizontal ruler across the top of your window and drag a ruler guide down to the 2" mark. You can monitor the ruler guide placement by watching the y coordinate in the Control palette. If you hold down the Shift key while dragging, the ruler guide will snap to the ruler increments.

Next, select the Text tool from the Tool palette and drag a text box to fit the intersection of the ruler guide and the left, right, and bottom margins (see Figure 4.13).

FIGURE 4.13   The ruler guide and text frame in place.

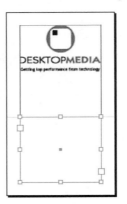

STEP 6▼
Formatting Text

Information on a business card is a subjective decision. How much should you include? What is necessary? The information on your business card is essentially a combination of a marketing tool as well as a tool to distribute contact information. I've included all my contact information, which required an adjustment of the type size to accommodate it all.

After I got all the information into the text box, I was ready to change the font and size of the characters. Choosing the font and size can be accomplished using the Type menu or using the type and size feature in the Control palette. Make sure the character button (the letter *A*) is selected on the left side of the Control palette. As with my letterhead, I selected my text and centered the text within the text box using the Paragraph button on the Control palette and then the Centered Alignment button. I chose Trebuchet for the font because it matches the company's tag line. I assigned a font size of 8 points for all the information (see Figure 4.14).

FIGURE 4.14   Add whatever information is appropriate as a marketing tool for your card.

STEP 7 ▼
Viewing Options

Go to the View pull-down menu (see Figure 4.15). Then select Actual Size. It is helpful to turn off Frame Edges and Guides on the View pull-down menu. Turn them on when you need to see these visual boundaries again.

 TIP

When evaluating type, it's extremely important to view the text at 100% or Actual Size. Sometimes, I print a test page to see the text on paper to evaluate the font choice, size, spacing, and so on. Zooming in to higher view percentages (or zooming out) can create deceptive spacing perceptions. Also note, 100% might not match the actual size if you were to put your card up to your monitor. Much depends on the screen resolution of your monitor.

STEP 8 ▼
Saving Your File

Go to the File pull-down menu and select Save As. Navigate to the 04Finished_Projects

folder. Name your file something appropriate and then click the Save button. Take a look at your finished product with guides and frame edges left on, as in Figure 4.16.

FIGURE 4.15   The View pull-down menu.

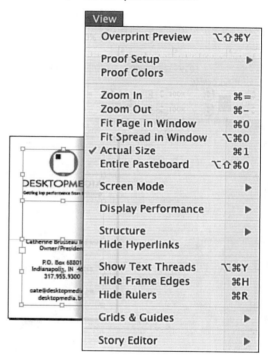

FIGURE 4.16   This is how your project should look when it's finished.

STEP 9▼
Printing a Composite Proof

Let's print a content proof. Go to the File pull-down menu and select Print. Choose the appropriate settings for the printer that is available to you. Then go to the File pull-down menu and select Print (see Figure 4.17).

FIGURE 4.17 Fill out the dialog box appropriate for your local output device.

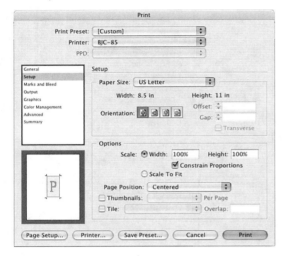

Similar to the letterhead project, choose the appropriate settings for the printer available to you; if possible, print a color composite output for your work. Additionally, for layouts that are smaller than letter size, it is also helpful to turn your page position under the Setup tab to Centered and to turn on crop marks, found under the Marks and Bleed tab. Review your proof, make any necessary adjustments, and save your changes. Then print it again.

STEP 10▼
Creating a Template

In this step, we introduce the concept of saving a template. Any of these collateral projects could benefit from creating a template. When a new business card needs to be produced, bringing up the template with all elements in place means you only have to type over and adjust the name and position of the employee.

To create your template, go to the File pull-down menu and select Save As. You should find that you are in the same folder you were just in during the previous save. Pull down the Format menu and select Template (see Figure 4.18).

FIGURE 4.18 Call your template something generic but memorable, such as company business card template.

Save and close your file.

Project: Envelope

We'll be creating an envelope in 12 easy
steps:

STEPS ▼

1. Setting up your document format
2. Creating a document preset
3. Importing art files
4. Transforming with tools
5. Creating a text element
6. Using a swatch to color a graphic element
7. Locking an element
8. Auto leading
9. Previewing your work
10. Saving your work
11. Printing a composite proof
12. Preflighting and packaging your files

 NOTE

It's imperative that you design and lay out your envelope with full knowledge of postal standards. Where
your return address is placed and how low you place the
addressee fields could greatly affect your ability to
receive discounts for bulk mailing (that is, taking advantage of barcoding). Please refer to http://www.usps.gov.
Additionally, some post offices conduct classes on this
subject as well as provide free templates you can place
over your comps/proofs to determine compliance.

Setting Up Your Document Format

Assuming InDesign is already launched, go to
the File pull-down menu and select New,
Document; then fill out the New Document
window as shown in Figure 4.19.

NOTE

This type of document lends itself to a *preset* because
envelopes are something you might create and address
repeatedly. We will discuss mail merges later in the
book.

Creating a Document Preset

Click Save Preset, and name the preset **Business
Envelope**. Click OK. Now when you need to
send an envelope, you will have a document
preset ready for you. When you choose a
document preset, all the fields in the New
Document window are filled out automatically for you! Click OK (see Figure 4.20).

TIP

Resize your window. Watch the envelope dynamically
resize with the window! When the view selected is Fit
in Window, InDesign automatically resizes the layout as
the window is resized.

FIGURE 4.19 **This is a standard business envelope setup.**

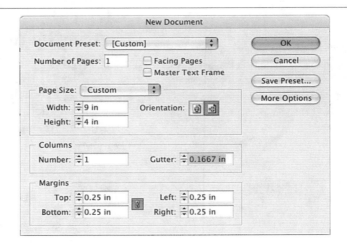

FIGURE 4.20 **Name your preset something generic, to be used repeatedly.**

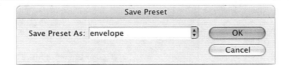

STEP 3▼
Importing Art Files

Go to the File pull-down menu and select Place. Then navigate to your 04Project_Files folder. Find the logo named DMLOGO.eps. Select it and click Open. An icon in the shape of a paintbrush appears. Click anywhere on the page and the logo appears on the page, shown at its actual size.

STEP 4▼
Transforming with Tools

Position the logo in the upper-left corner of the envelope's intersecting margin guides. Scale the logo with the Scale tool. With the logo selected, double-click the Scale tool in

the Tool palette; a dialog box appears. Turn on Preview and change the Uniform Scale to 50%. The dialog box remains present but the logo previews with the new scale dimensions. Click OK (see Figure 4.21).

STEP 5▼
Creating a Text Element

This version of the company logo does not include the address. Create a text box, select the Text tool, and drag out a text box that is 2" wide by 1" tall. Drag it to fit to the bottom of the logo box. Type in the address, highlight the text, and change the font to a sans serif font like Trebuchet, 12 pts. Center the text in the box. Your address should look like Figure 4.22.

STEP 6▼
Using a Swatch to Color a Graphic Element

Create a square that is 1/4" in size using the Rectangle tool. Open the Swatches palette if it isn't already open and fill the square with the PMS color that was imported along with the logo: PMS 8322 CV. Make sure there is no colored stroke on the box by selecting the Stroke swatch in the Swatches palette and clicking None. Position the box at 4" (x coordinate) by 1.5" (y coordinate). Figure 4.23 illustrates the progress of your layout.

STEP 7▼
Locking an Element

Create a text box to the right of your newly positioned square. The text box's coordinates should be at 4.5" (x coordinate) and 1.5" (y coordinate). The width of the box should be 4" wide by 1" deep. This will accommodate five lines of copy at 12 points and auto leading. Go to the Object pull-down menu and select Lock Position. Now your address text box will stay positioned correctly. See Figure 4.24 for a visual reference.

FIGURE 4.21 **This is how the logo should be positioned on the envelope.**

FIGURE 4.22 **This is the look and position of the company address.**

STEP 8▼
Auto Leading

Click the Text tool in the text box and type in the lines shown previously in Figure 4.24. Highlight the text and change the font to Trebuchet, 12 points.

 NOTE

Auto leading in InDesign is set to 20%, which is 20% of the point size currently in use. For example, 12-pt. type with auto lead has a lead measuring 14.4 pts. (120% of 12).

STEP 9▼
Previewing Your Work

Go to the View pull-down menu and select Actual Size. It is helpful to turn off Frame Edges and Guides under the View pull-down menu. Turn them on when you need to see these visual boundaries again.

STEP 10▼
Saving Your Work

Go to the File pull-down menu and select Save As. Then navigate to the folder in `Chapter04\ 04Finished_Projects`. Name this **company envelope**. If you want, you can select Save As again and save it as a template. Close your file.

STEP 11▼
Printing a Composite Proof

Let's print a content proof. Go to the File pull-down menu and select Print. Choose the appropriate settings for the printer that is available to you. Then go to the File pull-down menu and select Print. As with the letterhead and business card projects, select the appropriate settings for the printer available to you; if possible, print color composite output for your work. You might choose to print to an actual envelope or print the envelope layout to a letter size. It is also helpful to turn your page

FIGURE 4.23 **The square anchors the area where the addressee will be aligned and placed.**

FIGURE 4.24 **This locked box will allow you to type over the content, without the risk of moving the text frame out of position, and use this template repeatedly.**

position on the Setup tab to Centered. Also, you should turn on crop marks, found on the Marks and Bleed tab. Review your proof, make any necessary adjustments, and save your changes. Print it again (see Figure 4.25 for reference).

FIGURE 4.25 This is an example of how you might print a composite proof to your output device to a larger paper with crop marks turned on.

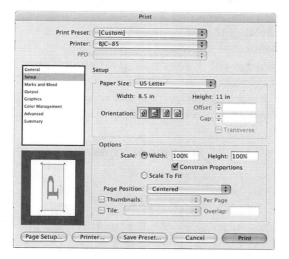

STEP 12▼
Preflighting and Packaging Your Files

Although this topic is covered in more detail later in the book, there is no doubt that you will send the letterhead, business card, and envelope to your printer. It is important that you include all the necessary files (layout and supporting linked images and fonts) as well as good documentation (instructions for processing the job as well as a final content proof, preferably color), which your print vendor will use to compare to the electronic file when processing your job. You should send your content proof at 100% or actual size. If you can't send it at actual size, be sure you clearly mark the proof as something other than 100% so as not to confuse your printer.

The Preflight command found under the File pull-down menu checks your work and alerts you to problems (see Figure 4.26). If problems exist, you can exit the window, fix the problems, and run your Preflight command again until no more errors exist.

FIGURE 4.26 The Preflight dialog box, reporting the status of the currently open file.

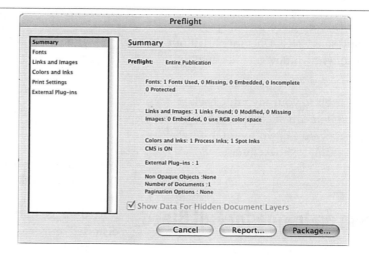

Project: Postcard

We'll be creating a postcard in 13 easy steps:

STEPS▼

1. **Setting up your document format**
2. **Placing an image for full bleed**
3. **Adding text**
4. **Creating breaks**
5. **Centering text horizontally and vertically**
6. **Creating a reverse or knockout**
7. **Navigating in an InDesign document**
8. **Creating ruler guides**
9. **Placing text**
10. **Positioning with the proxy**
11. **Constraining object moves**
12. **Spell-checking in InDesign**
13. **Printing a composite proof**

STEP 1 ▼
Setting Up Your Document Format

Launch InDesign, go to the File pull-down menu, and select New Document. Fill out the New Document window as indicated in Figure 4.27.

Orient yourself to your layout. Check to ensure that you can see your guides. If not, go to the View pull-down menu and select Grids and Guides, Show Guides.

STEP 2 ▼
Placing an Image for Full Bleed

Draw a rectangle graphic frame to fit the bleed guides on the front of your postcard.

This is called a *full bleed* because the image bleeds equally on all four sides. Go to the File pull-down menu and select the Place command. Navigate to your Chapter04 project files folder and open the DM_BGRD_DUO.eps file. After the file is initially placed in the picture frame, scale the image only (by selecting the image with the Direct Selection tool) *anamorphically* (disproportionately) to 350% wide by 150% tall. To do this, make sure you turn off the Constrain Proportions for Scaling option, which is the little link next to the Vertical/Horizontal fields in the Control palette. This type of scaling is unusual and beyond the normal acceptable scaling limits for standard production, but we are attempting to create a special effect.

FIGURE 4.27 Fill out the window as indicated.

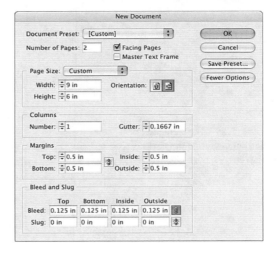

When you hover over this frame with the Direct Selection tool, the icon changes to the Hand tool. Using the Hand tool, drag the resized image in the frame so that the distorted ampersand symbol fits in the lower-left corner of the frame. See Figure 4.28 for a visual reference.

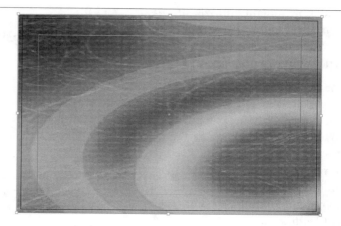

STEP 3 ▼
Adding Text

Now let's add the text to the front of the post-card. You are going to draw a text frame to fit the margins of the postcard by starting to drag a text frame with the Text tool, somewhere out on your pasteboard. The dimensions and coordinates of the frame should be as follows: w: 8", h: 5", x: .5", y: .5".

Begin typing with the Type tool. Feel free to use your company name and message; mine reads DesktopMedia Graphic Arts Training: Hands-On. Instructor-Led. On-Site. Certified.

Turn on Show Hidden Characters, found on the Type pull-down menu, to monitor the line breaks you are about to create.

STEP 4 ▼
Creating Breaks

To break a line without creating a new para-graph, create a *soft return*. To do this, hold down the Shift key and press Enter at the same time. Instead of creating a standard carriage return (signaling to any word

processing or page layout application that you want to create a new paragraph), the soft return simply creates a line break where you want it. I've inserted a soft return after the word DesktopMedia. I've placed normal, or *hard*, returns after Training: and Site.

 NOTE

Please note that, even though you can use a soft return to manually break lines for emphasis, readability, or controlling the *rag*, this type of a break is not discretionary. So, if your text rewraps, the soft returns will stay put, leading to strange breaks indeed.

STEP 5 ▼
Centering Text Horizontally and Vertically

After you have broken the lines the way you would like them to flow, select all the type and center the alignment horizontally (either by clicking the Paragraph button in the Control palette or by using the Paragraph palette itself). Next, center the type vertically by clicking the Vertical Alignment button to the right of the Control palette or by going to the Object pull-down menu and selecting Text Frame Options. See Figure 4.29 to make sure you have breaks in the correct places and that your type is aligned properly.

Highlight the text and format it as follows: For the text DesktopMedia Graphic Arts Training, I've chosen Optima, Roman, 50-point type over 52-point leading. For the text Hands-on. Instructor-Led. On-Site., I've chosen Optima, Roman, 38-point type over 52-point leading. For the last line, Certified., I've chosen Optima, Roman, 50-point type over 70-point leading. See Figure 4.30 to monitor your progress.

STEP 6 ▼
Creating a Reverse or Knockout

Finally, select all the type and open the Swatches palette if it's not already open. Then, with the Type swatch selected or clicked forward in the upper-left corner of the palette, select the swatch called Paper.

InDesign borrowed this concept from PageMaker and uses the color Paper (which really isn't a color at all) to convey the concept of *knockout* or *reverse* in the layout. Anything *tagged* or colored with the swatch paper creates a knockout (a reverse or hole)

FIGURE 4.29 Our text, with hidden characters turned on and the breaks in the correct positions.

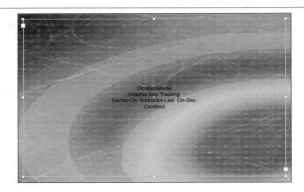

FIGURE 4.30 The front of the postcard so far.

in the color plates it sits on top of—in this case Black and PMS 8322 (the spot color found in the background image).

Take a moment to review your work so far by turning off the guides (found on the View pull-down menu) and turning off the Special Characters (found on the Type pull-down menu). See Figure 4.31 for the finished front.

STEP 7 ▼
Navigating in an InDesign Document

Let's navigate to the back of our postcard, page 2. To do this, you can use the navigation buttons at the bottom of the window by clicking the Next Page button, which looks like a right triangle. You can also use the Pages palette (double-click the page icon numbered 2) or the Next Page command, found on the Layout pull-down menu. Turn the guides back on.

It will be important to establish a visual aid to divide the back of the postcard in half. The left side will contain content, while the right side will be reserved for postal information, including the address and postage. To create a visual divide, you can place a ruler guide. I will offer two options.

STEP 8 ▼
Creating Ruler Guides

With the Selection tool, hover over the vertical ruler on the left side of the InDesign window; then click and drag out a ruler guide. Watch the ruler across the top of the window and drag the guide to the 4.5" mark. Let go of the ruler and you will see a new guide down the middle of the page.

Another method for placing guides can be found by using the Layout pull-down menu and the Create Guides command. Using this dialog box, insert two columns with a 0" gutter and click the preview box. A ruler guide will appear exactly down the middle of the page. See Figure 4.32 for the exact positioning of the ruler guide.

FIGURE 4.31 The finished front of the postcard with the type formatted and reversed out of the anamorphically scaled background image.

FIGURE 4.33 **The back of the postcard with the head line in place.**

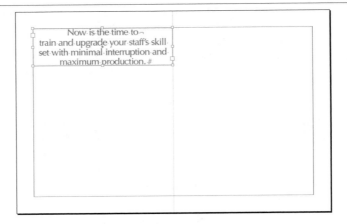

Now that you have a visual guide dividing the back of your postcard, let's add some content. Draw a text frame that is 4" wide by 1.125" deep and position it to fit the upper-left corner margins. Or, if you prefer, you can place it at the following x,y coordinate: x: .5", y: .5".

Type in the headline **Now is the time to train and upgrade your staff's skill set with minimal interruption and maximum production.**

Format this text as follows: Optima, Roman, 20-point type and 21-point leading, centered alignment. Tag the text with PMS 8322 from the Swatches palette. Remember that the spot color arrived in the Swatches palette when you imported the image on the front of the postcard. See Figure 4.33 to check your work.

STEP 9 ▼
Placing Text

Draw the next text frame as follows: x: .5", y: 1.75", w: 3.5", h: 3.25". Go to the File pull-down menu and import the text file named `training.doc`. This text file will flow into the text frame.

Highlight the text in the frame with the Text tool by clicking in the text box and using the Select All command, found on the Edit pull-down menu.

Format this text as follows: Trebuchet, Regular, 10.5-point type over 16-point leading. Place two hard returns after the word delivers. The following short paragraph will require two soft returns: one after contact us at... and another after e-mail us at.... Use Figure 4.34 as a visual reference and to compare your work.

Finally, we need to place the logo. Deselect everything on the back of the postcard either by clicking anywhere in the window that's not on an existing element or by using the Deselect All command found on the Edit pull-down menu.

STEP 10 ▼
Positioning with the Proxy

Go to the File pull-down menu and select the Place command. Select the DMLogo.eps file and click Open. Click the Paintbrush tool anywhere on the postcard, and you should see the logo appear. With the logo still selected, scale it to 50%. Click the center proxy point of your proxy in the Control palette and set the x coordinate to 4.5". This snaps the center of the logo to the center of the postcard. With the Selection tool, drag the logo straight down.

STEP 11 ▼
Constraining Object Moves

Holding down the Shift key while you are in motion *constrains* the movement of an option so that you do not accidentally move it off its axis. Drag the logo while holding down the Shift key until you feel the bottom of the logo snap to the bottom margin. Figure 4.35 shows the finished postcard back. Deselect all, hide the guides, and turn off hidden characters to review your work.

FIGURE 4.34 The back of the postcard with the imported text formatted.

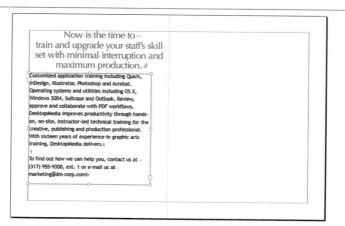

FIGURE 4.35 The finished back with all the type and the logo in place.

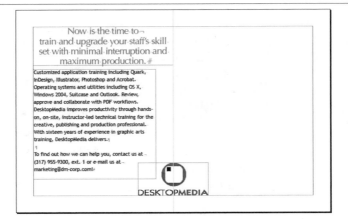

Save the postcard in your finished projects folder for Chapter04. Because this is the first project we've done together with some text, let's use the spell-checker in InDesign to make sure our typing doesn't contain errors.

STEP 12 ▼
Spell-checking in InDesign

You have several options for spell-checking in InDesign CS2. If you are a previous user, you will note the addition of Dynamic Spelling and Autocorrect. First, though, let's cover straightforward spell-checking.

Go to the Edit pull-down menu and select Spelling, Check Spelling. You will see a dialog box appear, ready to check your spelling. Click the Start button and spell-check begins examining the words in this document—if you have several documents open, you can have it spell-check all the open documents. The default option is This Document. As InDesign reaches an incorrect word, it suggests corrections. You can choose a correction from the list it offers, or you can type your own correction (see Figure 4.36).

FIGURE 4.36 The InDesign Check Spelling dialog box.

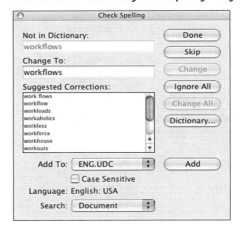

Options during spell-check include ignoring a word, including all instances of that word; changing a word, including all instances of that word; and adding a word to the dictionary of your choice. You can even include guidance on how you prefer to hyphenate a word.

Dynamic spelling allows you to spell-check using contextual menus. *Contextual menus* are pop-up menus you can access by either right-clicking with your mouse (if you are a PC user) or Control-clicking with your mouse (if you are a Mac user). When Dynamic spelling is enabled, InDesign underlines misspelled words directly in the layout. You then simply right-click or Control-click the underlined word in the layout and select the desired action from the context menu.

Finally, Autocorrect enables InDesign to automatically correct errors as you type. However, you have to train InDesign to do this. You set this option in Preferences (found on the Edit pull-down menu for Windows users and on the InDesign pull-down menu for Mac users). InDesign automatically corrects for capitalization errors if this preference is turned on. For all other misspellings, though, you need to first teach InDesign which words you typically misspell by telling it the common spelling mistake and then telling it the correction.

Spell-check your postcard with any of these methods before you generate your proof.

STEP 13 ▼
Printing a Composite Proof

Let's print a content *proof*. Go to the File pull-down menu and select Print. Select the appropriate settings for the printer available to you. On the General tab, select one copy. On the Setup tab, select Letter and Horizontal Orientation. Leave the Scale setting alone, but center the page positioning. On the Marks and Bleed tab, turn on crop marks. On the Output tab, if possible, print a color composite output for your work; if this isn't possible, select Grayscale. On the Graphics tab, the default settings should work. The remaining tabs can be ignored for now. Print and review your proof, make any necessary adjustments, and then save your changes. Print it again, using Figure 4.37 as your guide.

FIGURE 4.37   Fill out the window as indicated.

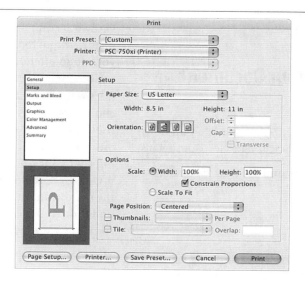

Project: CD Cover

This project covers a simple CD cover that you will create and insert into a simple jewel case. CD covers can be used for organizing your own CD archive of company files and images or a distribution of information to your sales force. This project does not cover the offset packaging production requirements for mass production and distribution of CDs such as you would find in software development or the music/gaming industry.

You will create this project in seven easy steps:

STEPS ▼

1. Setting up your document
2. Creating a picture frame
3. Fitting your image to the frame
4. Importing an art file
5. Aligning elements
6. Saving your work
7. Creating a composite proof

STEP 1▼
Setting Up Your Document Format

Launch InDesign and go to the File pull-down menu. Select New, Document (see Figure 4.38).

Click More Options and set your bleed to .125" on all four sides.

 TIP

You can ensure that all fields contain the same measurements by typing the measurement into the first field and clicking the Link icon, which fills in the remaining fields with the same information.

FIGURE 4.38 There is already a format for a compact disc insert.

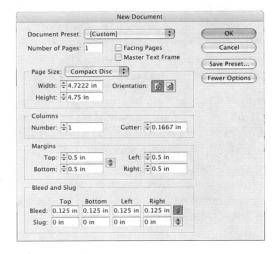

Click OK.

STEP 2▼
Creating a Picture Frame

Draw a picture frame with a rectangular picture frame tool to fit the bleed guides. If you let go prematurely or accidentally move the box, remember that you can always use the Control palette to reposition the box or change its dimensions. The x,y coordinate should be –.125" (that's a negative eighth of an inch) for both fields. Again we're assuming that your rulers have 0s starting in the upper-left corner of your layout. If not, click the 0 crosshair at the intersection of the rulers and drag and drop them onto the upper-left corner of your layout.

Make sure your picture frame is selected. A picture frame is different from an object shape because it's designed to be a container (note the universally accepted symbol of the X, a hold over from conventional paste-up days). Unlike Quark, InDesign does not require a frame or container to import an image; however, frames are a useful reference for area and positioning and the frame functions as the cropping agent (see Figure 4.40).

With your frame selected, go to the File pull-down menu and select Place. Navigate to the Chapter04\04Project_Files folder and select DM_BKGRD_DUO.eps.

FIGURE 4.40 This is what a picture frame looks like in InDesign.

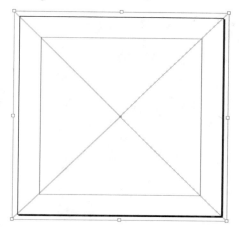

STEP 3 ▼
Fitting Your Image to the Frame

Select the Direct Selection tool (the hollow arrow) and hover your mouse over the image. Notice the tool turns into a hand, which enables you to position the image within the cropping frame. When you click and drag the image, a different vector (outline) appears representing the edge of the image. If you click and hold the mouse button down for a moment (a significant pause), you see the remainder of the image, dimmed, beyond the cropping frame. Drag the image to manually place it in the frame. Look at Figure 4.41 to make sure your image fits properly.

 TIP

In addition to manually positioning your image, another choice is to go to the Object pull-down menu and select Fitting, Center Content. Click off the image somewhere in negative space in your window to deselect your artwork.

FIGURE 4.41 **You should see two vectors: the vector of the picture frame and the vector outline of the image file.**

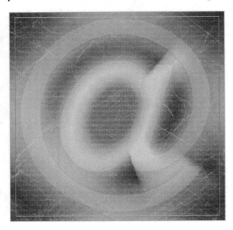

STEP 4▼
Importing an Art File

View your layout at actual size by selecting the View pull-down menu. Next, place the company logo and center it on the CD cover. Go to the File pull-down menu and select Place. Navigate to the 04Project_Files folder and select DMLOGO.eps. Click the Paintbrush icon and release the image.

 TIP

If the image pops into the CD cover frame, you did not deselect the picture frame before you placed the logo. Don't worry—just go to the Edit pull-down menu and select Undo. The Paintbrush icon will appear, allowing you to release the logo.

 NOTE

The negative space in the logo frame is clear or transparent, allowing the background image to show through. This is intentional and requires a little planning up front. When the logo was prepared in Illustrator, I wanted all the negative space to show up as clear rather than white, so when I saved the .eps file, I selected a TIFF preview with a transparent background.

STEP 5▼
Aligning Elements

Select both the background image and the logo (Shift-click with your Selection tool). As soon as you do, the Control palette changes (it is context sensitive) and presents alignment buttons on the right side. Center the objects both horizontally and vertically. The background does not shift because it is at the bottom of the stacked elements, but the top element (the logo) centers to the bottom element. Figure 4.42 shows the centered alignment.

FIGURE 4.42 **The aligning elements use the bottommost element in the stack as the primary reference.**

STEP 6▼
Saving Your Work

Go to the File pull-down menu and select Save As. Navigate to the folder in Chapter04\04finished_projects.

STEP 7▼
Printing a Composite Proof

You might choose to print this on slightly heavier stock. You will probably need to cut this down to size after you print it. Go to the File pull-down menu and select Print. Choose the appropriate settings for the printer that is available to you. Then go to the File pull-down menu and select Print. Again choose the appropriate settings for the printer available to you; if possible, print color composite output for your work. Additionally, for layouts that are smaller than letter size, it is helpful to set your page position on the Setup tab to Centered and turn on crop marks on the Marks and Bleed tab, using Figure 4.43 as a reference; then print it. Review your proof, make any necessary adjustments, and save your changes. Print it again.

If you are satisfied, save and close your file.

Creating Company T-Shirts

This project covers creating company t-shirts. They will be a wonderful touch when you are called upon to organize a special company event or the launch of a new product or service. This project does not cover the screen printing production requirements for mass production and distribution of T-shirts or other specialty promotional items. See Appendix C, "Printing Processes," for more information.

In this project you will create two InDesign files: One will be for the front of the t-shirt, which will be a small logo placed on the upper-right corner of your t-shirt (as you face the t-shirt) where most logos typically are placed. For this project, you will also learn how to create an *imposition*, or a step and repeat, of multiple logos to make the most from our iron-on transfer.

FIGURE 4.43 It's important to print this particular layout in color with marks and bleeds turned on.

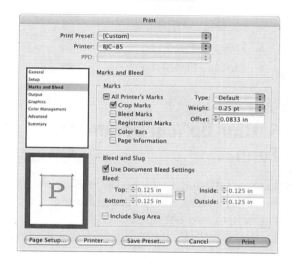

For the second file, we will create a much larger image for the back of the t-shirt, which will have a different orientation and scale. Of course, you can experiment with this project in any number of ways.

For those of you familiar with this type of work, an inkjet printer is required. You can't send iron-on transfer sheets through a laser printer because they would melt the substrate and damage your printer. Do not purchase fabric print sheets. A fabric sheet is simply a piece of fabric bonded to paper. You will need iron-on transfer sheets and access to an inkjet printer. For best results, choose paper that's indicated as being compatible with your brand and model of printer.

Project: T-shirt Front

You will accomplish this project in six easy steps:

STEPS ▼

1. Setting up your document format
2. Placing an art file
3. Copying an element
4. Stepping and repeating
5. Saving your work
6. Printing a flipped image

STEP 1▼
Setting Up Your Document Format

Launch InDesign; go to the File pull-down menu; and select New, Document using Figure 4.44 as a reference.

STEP 2▼
Placing an Art File

Go to the File pull-down menu and select the Place command. Navigate to the Chapter04\04Project_Files folder and select DMLOGO.eps. Click the paintbrush on your layout. Position the logo in the upper-left corner of the layout where the margins meet, and change the scale to 90%. Now we are going to duplicate the logo.

STEP 3▼
Copying an Element

With your graphic still selected, go to the Edit pull-down menu and select Duplicate. A copy of the logo appears on your layout. Drag it to fit the upper-right corner of your layout (see Figure 4.45).

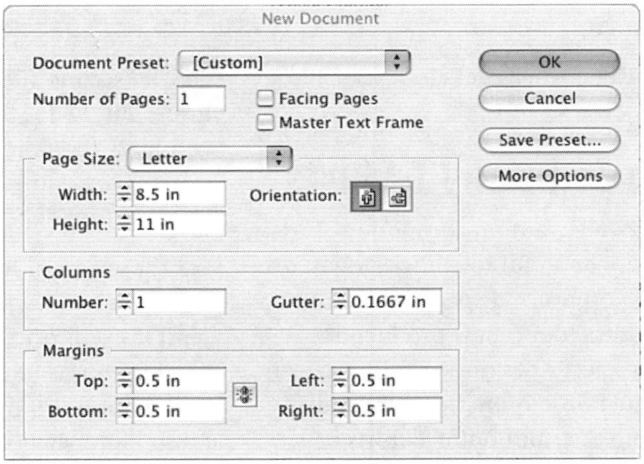

FIGURE 4.44 The front transfer can be imaged on a letter-size substrate.

FIGURE 4.45 These two elements, placed side by side, will be copied down the length of your page.

STEP 4▼
Stepping and Repeating

Now select both graphic elements by clicking the first element, holding down the Shift key, and clicking the second element. Now you will step and repeat the graphics to fill the page.

Go to the Edit pull-down menu and select Step and Repeat. The repeat count is 4. The horizontal offset is 0" and the vertical offset is 2". Click OK (see Figure 4.46 to fill out the window).

FIGURE 4.46 You do not want any horizontal movement, only vertical movement down your page.

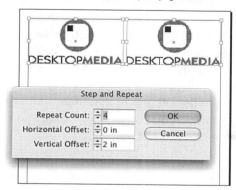

NOTE

Your layout is now filled with logos; this is called a multiple up imposition.

STEP 5▼
Saving Your Work

Let's save our work. Go to the File pull-down menu, select Save As, and navigate to the folder in `Chapter04\04Finished_Projects`. Call this **T-shirt Front**. Figure 4.47 displays the finished layout.

FIGURE 4.47 The multiple up imposition.

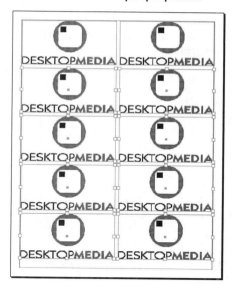

STEP 6▼
Printing a Flipped Image

Let's print a content proof to plain paper first. Go to the File pull-down menu and select Print. Choose the appropriate settings for the inkjet. Then go to the File pull-down menu and select Print. Again choose the appropriate settings for the printer available to you; if possible, print a color composite output for your work. Additionally, on the Setup tab, set the page position to Centered. On the Output tab, select Flip Horizontal. This is important to understand: Your image will come out backward after you iron it if you don't flip it when it is printed. Test print this to paper and hold the image up in a mirror to make sure it will iron on correctly. Review your proof, make any necessary adjustments, and save your changes. Print it again, this time to your iron-on transfer substrate. You will cut the logos apart and follow the manufacturer's directions for ironing. Use Figure 4.48 as your guide.

FIGURE 4.48 Make sure the Flip option is selected for horizontal or reversed output.

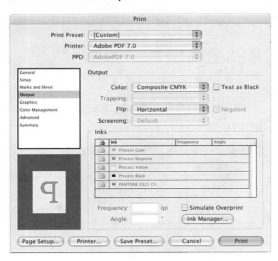

Close your file.

Project: T-shirt Back

This section works with the T-shirt back, which you create in four steps:

STEPS ▼

1. **Setting up your document format**
2. **Placing a graphic element**
3. **Saving your work**
4. **Printing a flipped image**

STEP 1▼
Setting Up Your Document Format

Launch InDesign; go to the File pull-down menu; and select New, Document (use Figure 4.49 to fill out your document window).

STEP 2▼
Placing a Graphic Element

Go to the File pull-down menu and select the Place command. Navigate to the Chapter04\04Project_Files folder and select DMLOGOtag.eps. Click the paintbrush on your layout. Position the logo in the upper-left corner of the layout where the margins meet, and change the scale to 250%. The logo should fit to the left and right margins. Move the logo down so that is centered visually on the layout (see Figure 4.50).

STEP 3▼
Saving Your Work

Let's save our work. Go to the File pull-down menu, select Save As, and navigate to the folder in Chapter04\04Finished_Projects. Call this **T-shirt Back**.

FIGURE 4.49 Because this transfer will be placed across the back of the t-shirt, a horizontal orientation is appropriate.

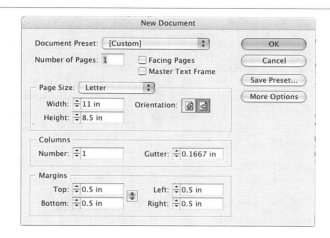

FIGURE 4.50 The back of the t-shirt should display the company logo prominently.

your work. Additionally, on the Setup tab, set the page position to Centered. On the Output tab, select Flip Horizontal. It is important that you flip your work when it's printed; otherwise, your image will come out backward after you iron it.

> **NOTE**
>
> If your printer driver doesn't offer a flip feature, you need to flip your artwork on the layout. To do this, select your artwork and go to the Transform palette. Select the Center Proxy dot and then go to the Palette menu and select Flip Horizontal.

STEP 4▼
Printing a Flipped Image

Let's print a content proof to plain paper first. Go to the File pull-down menu and select Print. Choose the appropriate settings for the inkjet. Then go to the File pull-down menu and select Print. Again choose the appropriate settings for the printer available to you; if possible, print a color composite output for

Test print this to paper and hold the image up in a mirror to make sure it will iron on correctly. Review your proof, make any necessary adjustments, and save your changes. Print it again, this time to your iron-on transfer substrate. You will place this image on the back center of your t-shirt and follow the manufacturer's directions for ironing (see Figure 4.51).

FIGURE 4.51   Creating mirrored output.

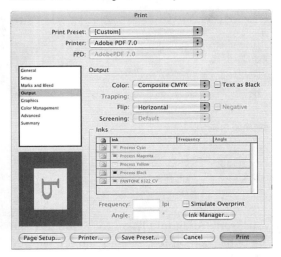

Close your file.

Final Thoughts

In this project you've begun to get acclimated to InDesign CS 2! These projects stepped you through basic page layout and text formatting skills, but more importantly, you've completed some of the most common and frequently requested publications.

Here are some important concepts to keep in mind:

▶ Vector artwork, particularly for your company's logo, will pay off dividends in the long run. It should be easy to use and scale so that it can be repurposed repeatedly.

▶ When creating collateral, you have to think about how people will use it—everything from what type of printer it will be put through to how a template will be used.

▶ Collateral is often mailed—after all, its primary use is word processing of letters. Make sure you clearly understand mailing requirements.

▶ Determine what type of information you want to include on your letterhead versus your business card. Are you simply trying to convey contact information, or more than that, such as marketing information?

▶ There's more to branding than letterhead and envelopes. Branding is all about delivering a consistent message anytime anyone encounters your company. So, everything from CD inserts to T-shirts must be considered.

▶ Communicating effectively with your print service provider is critical. Supplying them with everything they need to produce your work is a win-win for everyone. Always include a content proof so they can compare their work with yours.

CHAPTER 5: Creating an Advertisement and a Poster

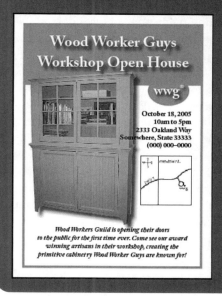

About the Project

In this chapter you will learn how to create an advertisement for placement in a magazine. You will then take that same advertisement and turn it into a poster.

Prerequisites

It will be helpful if you have a basic understanding of page layout, including the using Tool palette, formatting text, and performing basic page formatting.

@work resources

Please visit the publisher's website to download the following Chapter 5 files:

- ▶ 05Finished_Projects
- ▶ Art files [ed.tif, map.eps, pete.tif, and primativecab3.tif]

Planning the Project

Why would you need to place an advertisement in a magazine? or create a poster? These types of marketing pieces are event driven. To promote an event, you could place an advertisement in a magazine your customers might read. The date and time of your event should be prominent. An easy map to the location is also a good idea, as is a description of the event. You should explore the science of *demographics* in choosing the appropriate circular to place your ad. Who are your customers, and which publications do they read?

Most publications will send you a media kit with their demographic breakdowns, editorial and content calendar (in case you want to place an advertisement during an issue that might be discussing your industry), as well as their rates for advertising.

How large do you want your ad, and how many colors will drive the pricing structure? How many times you might want to run your ad will also affect the cost of your advertisement. Sometimes the placement of an ad within the publication (on the inside cover, as an example) is more expensive than an ad buried toward the back.

File Format Choices: PDF or PDF/X?

You are probably familiar with Adobe's Portable Document Format (PDF) file format. This format is designed to be platform independent and easily viewed by all users with Adobe's Acrobat Reader, which is free. Most applications support this file format, and it is very common in the graphic communications industry.

Even though generating a PDF is fairly simple, it is still possible to make mistakes in saving this file format. This can lead to problems processing these files with your print service provider. As with application files, PDF files made incorrectly cost everyone in the production process time and money.

Many publications have adopted the *PDF/X* file format for submission standards. This is explored in this chapter as well. PDF/X is a PDF that is certified to ISO standards, including font inclusion, CMYK or spot color inclusion, trim and media box information, and trapping acknowledgement. These publications insist that you submit a PDF/X of your layout that they will drop into place. They will not repair your layout. The whole point of submitting a PDF/X is to simplify a publishing workflow by certifying that this incoming digital file meets the publisher's standards.

Fortunately, InDesign makes this very easy to do. One of the features of exporting a PDF from InDesign is your choice of not only which version of PDF you want to make, but also which standard you want it to conform to. This will make your ad submission easy!

Now, the content of the ad should be timely, include important event information, motivate people to attend, and reflect your company's brand. The images might be consistent with a current campaign or shot specifically for the event.

Production Choices

The poster that will be based on the ad needs special preplanning consideration. Where will the poster(s) hang—inside or outside? The answer to this question will dictate the substrate and possibly the printing methodology. Thick *UV* inks on heavy weather-resistant substrate might be best screen printed, if the quantity you are printing will justify your setup charges.

If you are producing only a few posters and the environment is not a consideration, think about how and where the posters will be placed. Will they be hung and, if so, how? What about lighting? Will they be lit from the front or back? Quantity might dictate production choices as well: Wide format inkjets can offer short-run digital output as an efficient alternative to offset or screen printing, but cost can be a factor. You might need to involve an additional service provider if your offset printer doesn't offer these services. All these production considerations should be preplanned.

Transparency is an exciting feature for object-oriented programs such as InDesign and Illustrator. The effects are far reaching both creatively and from a production standpoint. Even the Drop Shadow command utilizes transparency to create the multiply blending effect that looks so realistic. It's important to note that the transparency feature can have unintended effects on your artwork and layout, so you need to consult your print service provider when contemplating the use of transparency features.

Color Choices

Is spot color involved? How important is the match? If it has to be exact, traditional separations are in order. If not, and you are working with a printer with a good *calibrated* and *characterized* device, perhaps you could consider a *wide format* digital output device for your posters.

Finishing and Distribution Choices

Because this chapter involves creating an ad that will appear in a local magazine, your finishing choices will be limited and the ad will be distributed based on the readership or circulation of the magazine.

You can request special finishing options for advertising—perhaps a spot varnish or a special die cut—but be prepared because it will significantly increase the cost of your ad and how it is placed and bound within the publication.

You can also affect the circulation of the magazine by requesting additional prints and distributing them yourself using your customer database.

The other project we will produce in this chapter is a poster. Depending on how it will be used, you have a few finishing options. Will it hang? If so, you might need to request grommets to accommodate hooks. Will it be displayed on an easel? If so, you might request that it be mounted on foam board. Will the poster be transported flat, or will it be rolled up in a tube? Be careful that your substrate choice won't curl on you. Again, all this should be planned in advance with your print service provider, even if that provider is an in-house partner. They can best advise you of your finishing choices based on how you will distribute the piece.

Project: Advertisement

We'll be creating a product sheet in 14 easy steps:

STEPS ▼

1. **Setting up your document format**
2. **Applying a stroke**

3. Inserting special characters
4. Placing raster elements
5. Creating drop shadows
6. Sampling color
7. Formatting text
8. Applying a drop shadow to type
9. Changing paragraph alignment
10. Scaling vector elements
11. Reviewing your work
12. Preflighting and packaging
13. Printing
14. Exporting PDF/X-1a

STEP 1 ▼
Setting Up Your Document Format

Launch InDesign and go to the File pull-down menu. Select New, Document and fill out the New Document window as indicated in Figure 5.1. Click OK.

STEP 2 ▼
Applying a Stroke

Orient yourself to your workspace. Select your Rectangle tool and create a rectangle to fit your margins. The x,y coordinate should be .25",.25", with a width of 4.25" and a height of 6.0".

Apply a 4-point stroke to your rectangle. You can do this by either using the Stroke palette found on the Window pull-down menu or from the collapsible bay on the right side of your workspace. In addition to these choices, you can stroke your objects from the Control palette as well.

For now, feel free to color your stoke black, but make sure there is a fill of None in your rectangle. We will change the color later.

Now, you are going to draw another rectangle in the same position, .25",.25", but the dimensions will be a width of 4.25" and a height of 1.5". Fill this rectangle with black, with no stroke (see Figure 5.2).

FIGURE 5.1   Fill out the window as indicated for this setup.

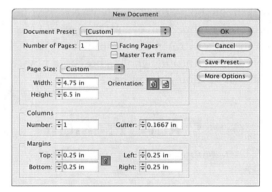

FIGURE 5.2   The wireframe should fit the margin guides.

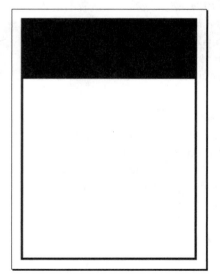

STEP 3 ▼
Inserting Special Characters

Let's re-create the logo. Make sure nothing is selected on your layout, and then draw an oval that has the following dimensions: width: 1", height: .75". With the oval selected, type in the following coordinates: 3.2" for the x coordinate and 1.5" for the y coordinate. Fill the oval with black, no stroke. Now, draw a text box out on the pasteboard and type in **wwg** and a registration mark (you can find it by selecting Type, Insert Special Character, Registered Trademark Symbol).

Highlight this text and format it. I've used Adobe Caslon Pro bold, 24-point type, but feel free to make your own type choices. Center the type horizontally (using the Control palette and the Paragraph button) and vertically by going to the Object pull-down menu and selecting Text Frame Options, Vertical Justification. Highlight the registration symbol and click the Superscript style button in the Control palette.

Highlight the text wwg. Make sure the Fill swatch is active (on top) in your Swatch palette, and then color your type with the Paper option. This creates a knockout or a hole in your color to let the color of the paper come through. Slowly drag the text box over the oval and visually align the two together.

 TIP

When you click, hold down your mouse button, pause for a second or two, and then start to drag slowly. You will get a live drag, meaning you see all aspects of your element as you drag—not just the outline of a box. Use Figure 5.3 as a reference.

STEP 4 ▼
Placing Raster Elements

Let's bring in your image. Deselect everything on your layout and go to the File pull-down menu and select the Place command. Navigate your way to the `Chapter05\05Project_Files` folder and select `primitivecab3.tif`. Click out on the pasteboard somewhere.

 NOTE

Clicking an element with the paint brush loaded places your image inside one of the boxes. If you do this accidentally, select Edit, Undo and your paint brush will load back up again with the image.

Place the image at .1", 1.05". Scale your image 50%. This image has a *clipping path* around it. The path outlines the foreground and clips, or removes, the background (see Figure 5.4).

FIGURE 5.4 The image appears to float on the page.

STEP 5 ▼
Creating Drop Shadows

With the image selected, go to the Object pull-down menu and select Drop Shadow. Fill in the Drop Shadow dialog box as shown in Figure 5.5.

FIGURE 5.5 Watch the drop shadow appear and blend with the background.

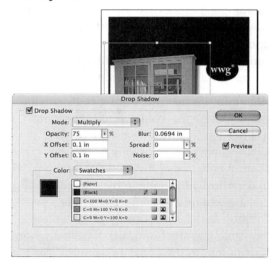

Raster Basics

Raster elements and resolution considerations are extremely important when publishing in a circular, such as a magazine. Most magazine work is at least 133lpi and more than likely 150lpi. Remember that *lpi* refers to the line screen at which your ad will be printed, meaning how close the halftone dots will be placed per inch. Ink, press, and paper all play a role in how fine and close this spot placement can take place. The higher the lpi, the finer looking the image. A good rule of thumb is to make sure your images have a resolution that is at least twice your line screen—for example, 150lpi × 2 = 300ppi.

This assumes there is no change in the size of the image itself. In other words, the size at which it is

scanned is the size at which it is printed. If the image will change size, great care must be taken to not distort the image. In a page layout program, when you scale something larger, the program can only spread the pixels farther apart, thereby reducing the resolution of the image. The converse is true as well: When you scale an image smaller, the program simply pushes the pixels closer together, thereby increasing the resolution. Scaling a raster image in a page layout program effectively changes the resolution of the printed image, which can lead to an undesirable, coarser image. My advice is to try not to scale raster images in your page layout programs. If you must, do so only in small amounts, and remember that decreasing scale is safer than increasing scale.

NOTE

You have just created a special effect in InDesign that invokes transparency. To accomplish the color blending modes selected, InDesign uses transparency. A checkerboard appears on this page in your Pages palette as a visual indicator as well. Transparency is covered in further detail in another step; however, it's important to note that this is a raster element, with a raster drop shadow, sitting on top of only the paper and there should be no flattening production issues.

STEP 6 ▼
Sampling Color

Let's sample a color from the image. Make sure that the fill swatch in the Tool palette is active, or selected. Select the Eye Dropper tool in the Tool palette and click a color in the image. Don't sample a color so dark that you won't be able to see the drop shadows you will make for your text. Notice that the color now appears in your fill swatch. Go to the Swatches palette and pull down the triangle in the upper-left corner of the palette; then select New Swatch Color. Your new color appears. Make sure the color type is process and the color mode is CMYK. Use Figure 5.6 as your guide.

Select the large rectangle you created. With the Stroke swatch active in your Swatches palette, select your new color. Select the smaller rectangle and make the Fill swatch active. Then click the new color. Now your framed ad and header box match the logo. Select the oval for the logo and with the Fill swatch active, click the new color. There should be no stroke on the oval (see Figure 5.7).

FIGURE 5.6 The swatch name is Sampled Color, and the Color Type should be process with a Color Mode of CMYK. If it is not, change the settings to match.

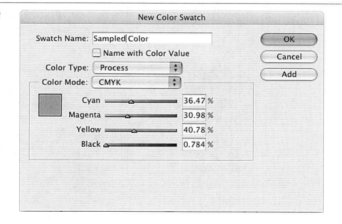

FIGURE 5.7   This is the advertisement thus far.

STEP 7 ▼
Formatting Text

Select the Text tool and create a text box on the pasteboard. Type in your ad headline. In the ad for this exercise, I typed Wood Worker Guys, clicked a carriage return, and typed Workshop Open House on the second line. Format the text as follows: Adobe Caslon Pro bold, 26-point type, 36-point leading, paragraph centered alignment.

Your box should be placed with the following coordinates: x: .25", y: .525", width: 4.25", height: .875" (see Figure 5.8).

STEP 8 ▼
Applying a Drop Shadow to Type

Now let's change the type a little. First, select your text with the Text tool and go to the Swatches palette. With the Fill swatch active in the upper-left corner of the palette, select Paper. Deselect your text and select the text box itself with your selection tool. Then go to the Object pull-down menu and select Drop Shadow. Fill in the dialog box as shown in Figure 5.9. Click OK.

FIGURE 5.8   **Your formatted ad headline.**

The color mode feature in InDesign functions the same in all Adobe products. This mode controls how colors combine. In Normal mode, colors do not combine but simply replace each other. Multiply mode does what it says—multiplies two colors together to form a third color, just like a real shadow. Opacity controls the transparency of an element and, in this case, by reducing the opacity setting to anything under 100%, you make the shadow more and more translucent.

TIP

If you want to see what your text will look like, check the Preview box and take a peek. If you don't like the effect, change your settings and your preview will update.

Repeat the procedure for the text in the oval.

NOTE

Let's talk about transparency when it's used in a mixed environment with both raster and vector elements. As in the case of a drop shadow on type with a colored background, a vector shape (the type) is sitting on top of the drop shadow (the raster), which is sitting on top of the fill of the oval and the rectangle (vector). When the file is output (printed or, depending on the version, made into a PDF document), a decision must be made regarding these elements. They have to flatten because you can't print in three dimensions, only two.

When that occurs, how will the raster and vector elements combine? If the elements are all raster, you don't have a problem because pixels simply merge and replace underlying pixels. If the elements are all vector you also don't have any problem because smaller vectors are created. But when there's a combination of the two, how will these elements combine? Feel free to consult with your service provider or refer to the Adobe website. Adobe has white papers on the subject, advising users about appropriate settings.

FIGURE 5.9 Another shadow should appear to the right and below your type. Feel free to experiment with other positions, modes, and blurs.

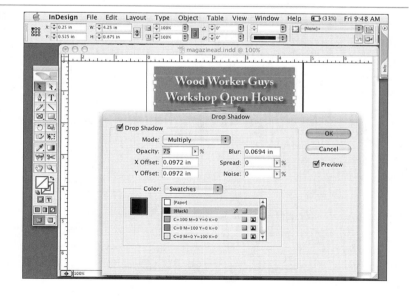

STEP 9 ▼
Changing Paragraph Alignment

All that's left now is your copy. Select the Type tool in the Tool palette and draw a box with the following dimensions: x: 2.375", y: 2.375", width: 1.875", height: 1".

Type in the date, time, address, and phone number of the event with a carriage return after each item. Select the text and format it as follows: Adobe Caslon Pro Bold, 12-point, auto lead, paragraph right alignment (which can be accessed from the Control palette or the Type and Paragraph palettes found on the Type pull-down menu, the Window pull-down menu, or the collapsible bays (the InDesign dock located down the right side of your desktop). See Figure 5.10 for an example.

FIGURE 5.10   The event time and location.

Create another text box at the bottom of the page by drawing it from the left margin all the way to the right margin. The coordinates should be as follows: x: .25", y: 5.25", width: 4.25", height: 1".

Type in the description of the event and format as follows: Adobe Caslon Pro, bold

italic, 12-point type, 15-point leading, paragraph centered alignment (see Figure 5.11).

FIGURE 5.11   The event description.

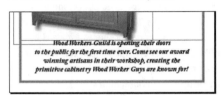

STEP 10 ▼
Scaling Vector Elements

Deselect everything on the page, go to the File pull-down menu, and select Place. Navigate to the Chapter 5 project files folder and select map.eps. Place the map below the text block containing the address. Place the map at the following coordinates: x: 3.25", y: 3.5" (see Figure 5.12).

FIGURE 5.12   See the following tips to tweak the map's appearance.

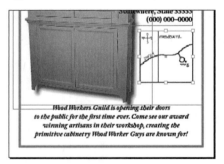

If you don't like the way a graphic looks (line art can look a little jagged because it's often a low-resolution preview) with the map selected, go to the Object pull-down menu and select Display Performance. Select High Quality and you should see the image improve (see Figure 5.13). Your other options include View Setting (however, your View menu is set for the entire layout), Optimized Setting (which sets your graphic to a gray box and speeds up onscreen display), and Typical (the default setting for all incoming images). If you scale the image again, the display performance resets to Use View Setting.

 NOTE

You might want to increase the scale of the map. This is a vector file and the guidelines for scaling vector files are different from those for scaling rasters. Vector art is resolution independent and there's no formula for scaling this type of file. The file simply stretches to the new scale and looks the same. All the elements scale, including fills and strokes, so be careful if you don't want your strokes to scale. Other than that caution, scaling vectors is easy and can be done freely by either enlarging or decreasing at will.

STEP 11 ▼
Reviewing Your Work

Review your work at 100% view. Turn off hidden characters, guides, and frames. Then save your file to the Chapter05/05Finished_ Projects folder. The finished ad should look like Figure 5.14.

STEP 12 ▼
Preflighting and Packaging

Make sure you have saved your work. Go to the File pull-down menu and select Preflight. The *preflight* process checks your file to ensure that it is in acceptable condition to submit to your print service provider. It checks for fonts, links, images, colors and inks, print settings, and any external plug-ins you might have used. All this information impacts your print service provider (see the sample in Figure 5.15).

FIGURE 5.13 The Object, Display Performance, High Quality Display command renders a more pleasing preview.

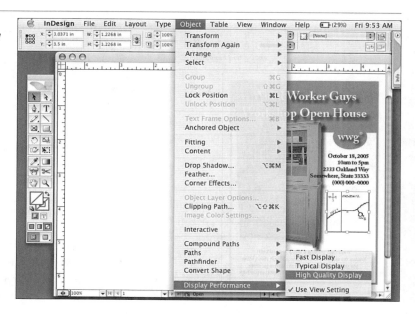

FIGURE 5.14   The finished project.

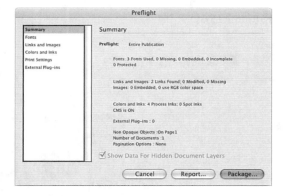

InDesgon uses a yellow caution or warning sign (the same for missing fonts or modified links) to indicate problems. When you are clicking through the Preflight dialog box, look for the yellow signs with exclamation points becasue they indicate a problem. You might find a problem such as a font used by the document is not turned on in your font management utility, you've moved or modified an image since you placed it in your document, or you have included an RGB image. If you see errors or warnings, you need to cancel out of this dialog box, fix the problem, and run the preflight again.

At the end of preflight, you can package up your files by clicking the Package button. You can then comment about the production of your file to your print service provider—don't rely on this as your only means of communicating or documenting your instructions, however. After you've typed any necessary instructions, you move on to the Create Package Folder window. Here you tell the program where to put the newly created folder with copies of fonts (with permission from the font developer) and your linked graphics. InDesign will even update the links after the graphics are copied into this folder so that when the recipient of your file opens it, all the images will be linked correctly for him.

Click Save and you have a copy of your layout and all the supporting resource files (see Figure 5.16).

STEP 13 ▼
Printing

You might want to print a copy of this and look at it on paper. Go to the File pull-down menu and select Print. Choose the appropriate settings for the printer that is available to you. Then go to the File pull-down menu and select Print. Again, choose the appropriate settings for the printer available to you. On the General tab, choose one copy. On the Setup tab, select 8.5" × 11", Vertical Orientation, and a page positioning of Centered. Leave the Scale setting as is. On the

Marks and Bleed tab, turn on crop marks. On the Output tab, if possible, print a color composite output for your work; if not, select Grayscale. On the Graphics tab, the default settings should work. The remaining tabs can be ignored for now. Print and review your proof. Make any necessary adjustments, save your changes, and print it again. Figure 5.17 shows potential print settings.

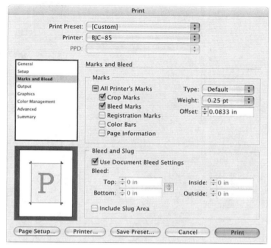

STEP 14 ▼
Exporting PDF/X-1a

With your document open and already proofed, go to the File pull-down menu and select Export. Navigate your way to your chapter05\05finished_projects folder and name your PDF. At the bottom of your window, make sure the format is Adobe PDF. Click Save.

At the top of the Export PDF dialog box is a Preset drop-down box; select the preset called PDF/X-1a (see Figure 5.18). All the settings necessary to make this PDF compliant with the /X-1a standard for publishing are already turned on, but let's take a tour. Note that the compatibility is automatically set to version 1.3, and the standard is set to PDF/X-1a. Notice that on the Compression tab, the images are set to 300ppi (twice the line screen of a typical 150lpi publication). InDesign can't make an image's resolution more than it is, but if you have images that exceed 450dpi, InDesign removes some of the resolution to comply with this setting. On the Advanced tab, the PDF/X setting uses a profile called U.S. Web Coated (SWOP) v2—most large circulation publications are printed on a web press using coated stock (SWOP stands for Standard Web Offset Press). See Figure 5.18 regarding the settings for PDF/X-1a.

Click Export.

FIGURE 5.18 **PDF/X settings.**

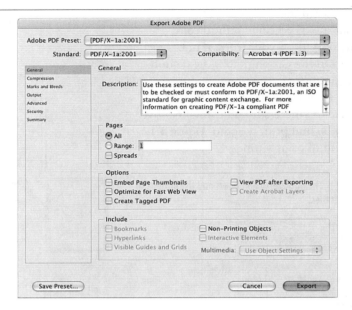

To check your PDF, double-click your file and your PDF should open in either Adobe Reader or (if you own a full version of Acrobat) Acrobat. Newer versions of Acrobat can actually verify and validate your PDF as a PDF/X-1a file, as well. Inspect your PDF and, if it looks correct, you can distribute it electronically. If it requires adjustment, go back to your InDesign document, make your corrections, save your document, and export it again.

Project: Poster

We'll be creating a poster in 17 easy steps:

STEPS ▼

1. Setting up your document format
2. Customizing the workspace
3. Adding a swatch
4. Creating a stroke
5. Aligning text horizontally and vertically
6. Creating a logo
7. Creating bullets
8. Creating indentation
9. Using the Transparency palette
10. Arranging elements
11. Constraining and copying while in motion
12. Placing images

13. Creating gradient strokes
14. Aligning elements
15. Reviewing your work
16. Preflighting and packaging
17. Printing

STEP 1 ▼
Setting Up Your Document Format

Launch InDesign; go to the File pull-down menu; and select New, Document. Then fill out the New Document dialog box, as indicated in Figure 5.19.

FIGURE 5.19 **The New Document setup window.**

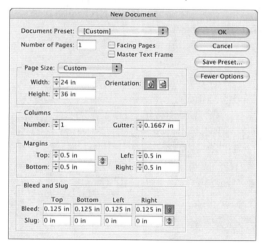

STEP 2 ▼
Customizing the Workspace

Orient yourself to your workspace. In fact, customize the workspace just as you would

like it. InDesign lets you arrange your interface the way you want it to appear and save the workspace. If you have a couple of different workspaces you would like to use, all the better. Let's say when you work intensively with type, you like all your Text, Paragraph, and Text Wrap palettes open. Arrange these palettes any way you like: as open, floating windows or in the collapsible bays. Now, go to the Window pull-down menu and select Workspace, Save Workspace. Give it a name, such as **text**, and click OK. Now toggle back and forth between the default workspace and the text workspace. You can have any number of workspaces—one for color, one for long document publishing, and so on. Figure 5.20 shows how I've saved my text workspace.

FIGURE 5.20 **My custom workspace.**

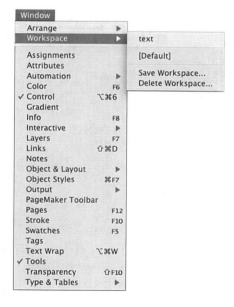

STEP 3 ▼
Adding a Swatch

Add a color to your swatches that will be the predominant color of the poster. You might want it to match your logo, as we did here for our exercise, but it could come from the picture you are going to use or reflect company colors. In any case, for this exercise, I added PANTONE 5767. Feel free to convert this to a process color if that is what you and your print service provider need. You can convert the spot color yourself by double-clicking the swatch and changing the color mode to CMYK and the color type to Process. Or, advise your print service provider that you would like them to convert it for you. Go to the Swatches palette and click the triangle found in either top corner (depending on how you accessed the palette). Select New Swatch, select Spot for the Color Type, select PANTONE Solid Coated for the Color Mode,

and then type **PANTONE 5767**, as shown in Figure 5.21. Click OK.

STEP 4 ▼
Creating a Stroke

Let's frame up the poster. Click the Rectangle tool and draw a rectangle. Use the following coordinates and dimensions: x: −.125, y: −.125" (for the bleed), width: 24.25", height: 36.25". Stroke the rectangle with 60 points, and select the align stroke to the inside button in the Stroke palette. Apply the spot color to your stroke, and deselect your item. See Figure 5.22 for how the poster should look so far.

Draw another rectangle inside the first with the following dimensions: x: 1", y: 1", width: 22", height: 10". Apply the spot color to your fill and deselect this new rectangle. Use Figure 5.23 as a guide.

FIGURE 5.21 **Adding a spot color to the Swtches palette.**

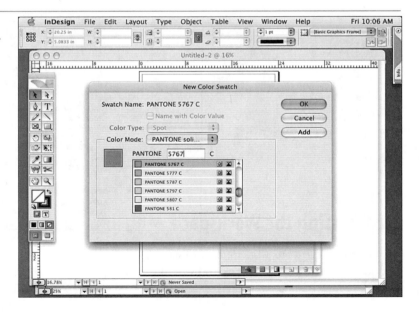

CHAPTER 5: Creating an Advertisement and a Poster

FIGURE 5.22   **Creating a border.**

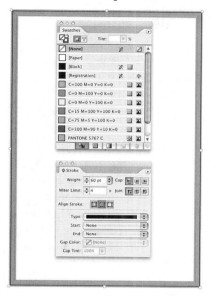

horizontally, using the Control palette; then center it vertically by selecting Object, Text Frame Options, Vertical Alignment, Centered. Highlight your copy and format it as follows: Adobe Caslon Pro Bold, 156-point type, 166-point leading. With the Selection tool, make sure the text box is selected and add a drop shadow by going to the Object pull-down menu and selecting Drop Shadow; use the coordinates shown in Figure 5.24. Finally, drag this box to the same coordinates as your first rectangle (align the upper-left corner).

FIGURE 5.24   **This will require flattening, which is part of the output or export process and is not the same flattening (or merging) you use with Photoshop layers.**

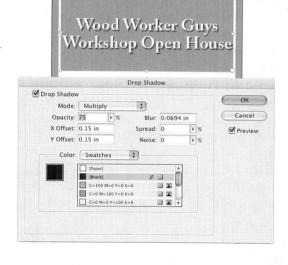

FIGURE 5.23   **The basic framework for your poster.**

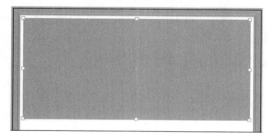

STEP 5 ▼
Aligning Text Horizontally and Vertically

Draw a text box matching the dimensions for the previous rectangle somewhere out on your pasteboard. With the Type tool, type in a two-line header. I've typed in WoodWorker Guys on the first line and Workshop Open House on the second line. Center the text

⊗ NOTE

The reason I chose to create a separate text box and not place the text inside the colored rectangle is because of the kind of drop shadow I wanted. I wanted the shadow on the text, not on the box, because drop shadows are a frame attribute.

STEP 6 ▼
Creating a Logo

Let's re-create the logo. Make sure nothing is selected on your layout and then draw an oval that has the following dimensions: width: 6", height: 4.5". With the oval selected, set the following coordinates: x: 17", y: 8.675". Color the fill with the spot color and apply a 20-point white stroke on the oval.

Now, draw a text box out on the pasteboard and type in **wwg** and a registration mark (you can find it by selecting Type, Insert Special Character, Registered Trademark Symbol). Highlight this text and format it as follows: Adobe Caslon Pro bold, 138-point type. Center the type horizontally (using the Control palette and the Paragraph button) and vertically (by selecting Object, Text Frame Options, Vertical Justification). Highlight the registration symbol and click the Superscript style in the Control palette. Slowly drag the text box over the oval and visually align the two together. Color the fill of the text white and, with only the text box selected, apply a drop shadow to the text using the same settings as mentioned previously. Use Figure 5.25 as a reference.

FIGURE 5.25   **The top of your poster should be completely formatted.**

STEP 7 ▼
Creating Bullets

Let's add the box at the bottom of the poster. Draw a rectangle with the following coordinates and dimensions: x: 1", y: 28.5", width: 22", height: 6.5". Color the fill of the box with your spot color. Select the Text tool and click inside your rectangle. Watch the I-beam's outer bounding outline bend because you are placing text inside an object. Type a bulleted list—you can find the bullet symbol by selecting Type, Insert Special Character, Bullet Symbol. After you insert the bullet symbol, press Tab. We'll come back and tweak the position of the tab stop later, but it's important to insert that hidden character (the tab) now. Type the description of the events; then highlight the text and format it as follows: Adobe Caslon Pro Bold, 72-point type, 86-point leading (see Figure 5.26).

STEP 8 ▼
Creating Indentation

Next, we should create an indentation. Go to the Object pull-down menu and select Text Frame Options, Vertical Justification, Centered. Now, zoom in on the left side of your text box. Then, with your text selected, open the Tab palette, found in the Type pull-down menu. Drag the bottom indent triangle on the left over (this will move the pair) and watch all your lines move to the right. You have set the general left indent value for the paragraph. The top triangle, by the way, is for setting the first line indent. Position your indent at .5" in from the left. Now, select a left tab and insert it at the 2" mark. Watch your text move and line up. Then deselect the text and compare your work to Figure 5.27.

FIGURE 5.26 The bulleted list with hidden characters turned on; note the tabs.

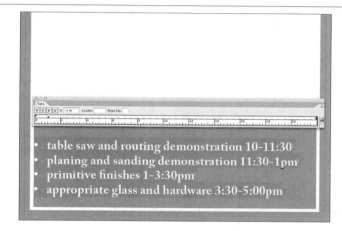

• table saw and routing demonstration 10-11:30
• planing and sanding demonstration 11:30-1pm
• primitive finishes 1-3:30pm
• appropriate glass and hardware 3:30-5:00pm

FIGURE 5.27 Our bulleted list, only better.

STEP 9 ▼
Using the Transparency Palette

Let's add some images. Go to the File pull-down menu and select Place. Navigate your way to the Chapter05\05Project_Files folder and select primitivecab3.tif. Position the image at x: 10.5", y: 10.5" and scale it to 200%.

 NOTE

I know I indicated you should not significantly enlarge your rasters, but in this case, I am deliberately doing so because I want the image to be soft and fuzzy. Bear with me and you'll see.

Let's make the image fade a bit by changing its transparency. Open the Transparency palette either under the Window pull-down menu or in one of the collapsible bays. There is an Opacity field that is probably set to 100%. Change that to 50% and watch your image fade. If you like, you can add a drop shadow to the image as well. This image has a clipping path around it; the path outlines the foreground and removes, or clips, the background (see Figure 5.28).

STEP 10 ▼
Arranging Elements

By now, you've realized the image is covering up the logo. Select the image with the Selection tool (the black arrow). Go to the Object pull-down menu and select Arrange, Send to Back (see Figure 5.29).

FIGURE 5.28 Note the checkerboard in the Pages palette indicating that transparency is in use by an element on this page. It's the result of the Opacity setting applied to the image, as well as the added drop shadow. Either effect alone triggers the checkboard appearance in the Pages palette.

FIGURE 5.28 Note the checkerboard in the Pages palette indicating that transparency is in use by an element on this page. It's the result of the Opacity setting applied to the image, as well as the added drop shadow. Either effect alone triggers the checkboard appearance in the Pages palette.

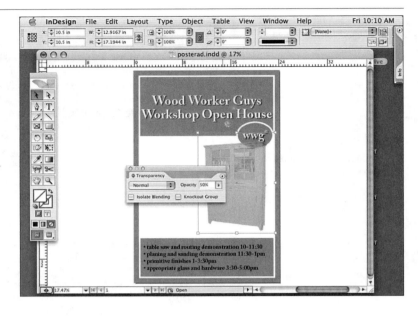

FIGURE 5.29 Sending an object to the bottom of the stack with the Send to Back command.

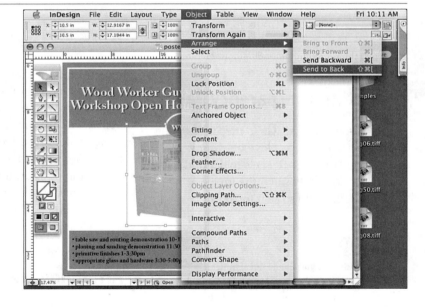

STEP 11 ▼
Constraining and Copying While in Motion

Draw a picture frame on the left side of your poster. The coordinates for the first box will be x: 1.5", y: 11.5", width: 5.25", height 7.25". Apply a stroke to the box of 20 points. With the Selection tool, drag the first picture box down. While dragging, hold down both the Shift key, which constrains, and the Option key (Alt on Windows), which duplicates, at the same time. This constrains the dragging motion straight down (no wiggling) and makes a copy of the box at the same time. Let go of the mouse before you let go of the modifier keys. Tweak the coordinates to x: 1.5", y: 20" (see Figure 5.30).

STEP 12 ▼
Placing Images

Select the first rectangle frame, go to the File pull-down menu, and select Place. Navigate to the chapter 5 folder, project files and select the image Pete.tif. With the Direct Selection tool, drag the image of Pete into position. Do the same with the other picture box, only this time use the image Ed.tif. See Figure 5.31 to approximate the positions of the images inside the picture frames. Align the left edges of the picture frames by using the Align Left

Edges button on the right side of the Control palette.

FIGURE 5.30   The result of our drag copy.

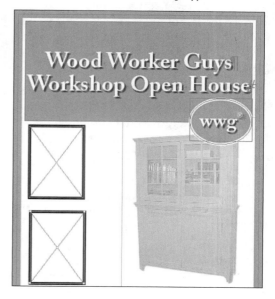

FIGURE 5.31   Remember that if you drag slowly, you can see the entire image (dimmed) for better placement.

STEP 13 ▼
Creating Gradient Strokes

Let's add a gradient to our stroked picture boxes. Open the Gradient palette by going to the Window pull-down menu and selecting Gradient. Notice there is already a black and white gradient (the default gradient) in the palette. Drag that large swatch into the Swatches palette. With the Stroke swatch active at the top of the Swatches palette, click the New Gradient swatch. The stroke of your picture box should change. To move the gradient around inside the stroke, select the Gradient tool and drag it across the selected picture box. I chose to drag from the upper-left corner to the lower-right corner, but feel free to play. Repeat this with the lower picture box selected. See Figure 5.32 for how the strokes should look.

FIGURE 5.32 **Try different angles and shift the gradient in the stroke.**

The final step is to create two text boxes describing the two images. With the Text tool selected, click and drag out a box off on the pasteboard—use my example as a visual guide. With Adobe Caslon Pro Bold, 36-point selected, type in the name of the person. Press Return and enter a brief description in 24-point

type. Then fill in the rest with 18-point type and 36-point leading. Fill the box with place-holder text found in the Type pull-down menu.

STEP 14 ▼
Aligning Elements

Drag your box to the right of the picture. Do this by clicking the far-right Alignment button in the Control palette. Repeat these last steps for the second image and text frame (see Figure 5.33). You can also drag the copy with the Shift and Option (Shift and Alt for Windows) keys held down. I suggest you align the left edges of the text frames, just as you did the pictures.

FIGURE 5.33 **Your two text boxes should be aligned with their respective images and vertically aligned to each other.**

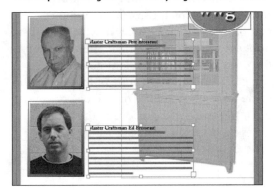

STEP 15 ▼
Reviewing Your Work

Review your work at 100% view—be sure to turn off hidden characters, guides, and frames. Save the file to your finished projects folder inside the Chapter 5 folder. Figure 5.34 shows the finished project.

FIGURE 5.34   **The finished poster.**

The Preflight command checks your file to ensure that it is in acceptable condition to submit to your print service provider. It checks for fonts, links, images, colors and inks, print settings, and any external plug-ins you might have. All this information impacts your print service provider.

InDesign uses a yellow caution or warning sign (the same for missing fonts or modified links) to indicate problems. When you are clicking through the Preflight dialog box, look for the yellow signs with exclamation points because they indicate a problem. You might find a problem such as a font used by the document is not turned on in your font management utility, you've moved or modified an image since you placed it in your document, or you have included an RGB image. If you see errors or warnings, you need to cancel out of this dialog box, fix the problem, and run the preflight again. Figure 5.35 shows a successful preflight report.

At the end of preflight, you can package up your files by clicking the Package button. You can then add a comment about the

STEP 16 ▼
Preflighting and Packaging

Make sure you have saved your work. Go to the File pull-down menu and select Preflight.

FIGURE 5.35   **Preflighting the poster.**

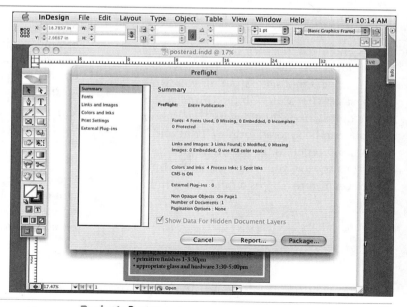

production of your file to your print service provider—but don't rely on this as your only means of communicating or documenting your instructions. After you've typed any necessary instructions, you move on to the Create Package Folder window, where you tell the program where to put the newly created folder with copies of fonts (with permission from the font developer) and your linked graphics. InDesign will even update the links after the graphics are copied into this folder so that when the recipient of your file opens it, all the images will be linked correctly for her.

STEP 17 ▼
Printing

You might want to print a copy of this and look at it on paper. Go to the File pull-down menu and select Print. Choose the appropriate settings for the printer that is available to you. Then go to the File pull-down menu and select Print. Again, choose the appropriate settings for the printer available to you. On the General tab, choose one copy. On the Setup tab, if possible, select 11" × 17", Vertical Orientation, and Scale to Fit. On the Marks and Bleed tab, turn on crop marks and bleed marks. On the Output tab, if possible, print a color composite output for your work; if not, select Grayscale. On the Graphics tab, the default settings should work. The remaining tabs can be ignored for now. Print and review your proof. Make any necessary adjustments, save your changes, and print it again. Use Figure 5.36 as a guide for printing options.

FIGURE 5.36 **The Print dialog box options.**

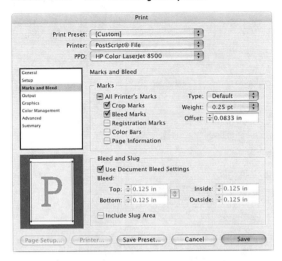

Final Thoughts

In this chapter you have added to your experience in basic page layout skills using InDesign CS 2. These two projects stepped you through basic construction and text formatting, as well as enhanced creative features.

Here are some important concepts to keep in mind:

▶ Producing an ad for placement in a commercially produced circular requires you to plan for the production specifications of the magazine or newspaper and for the circulation of your ad.

▶ Remember that more and more publications have moved to a PDF/X-1a standard for submission. You will see this become commonplace.

▶ I've introduced some additional production choices for your poster work—offset, screen, and digital—depending on how many you need, what type of substrate and ink are appropriate for the environment, and how the finished poster will be displayed.

▶ Transparency was introduced in this chapter, in a very basic way, to get your feet wet. We experimented with some transparency control. A wonderful effect, it has specific production considerations to achieve the best printed outcome.

▶ Raster basics and the importance of following a simple formula were introduced. Understanding resolution and scaling of raster images is essential to print production.

CHAPTER 6: Designing a Product Sheet

About the Project

In this chapter you will learn how to create a single-page marketing piece on a company product or service that can be distributed to your customers, sales force, and website.

Prerequisites

It would be helpful if you had a basic understanding of page layout, including using the Tool palette, formatting text, and performing basic page formatting.

@work resources

Please visit the publisher's website to download these Chapter 6 files:

▶ **Project06\Finished Project**

▶ **Art files [cabinet.tiff, wwglogo.eps]**

Planning the Project

Company marketing materials are one of the first ways you will express what your company does and what type of product or service your company offers. Aside from the material you will develop here, it is always important that you, or any representative of your company, be able to describe your company and products or services in a few brief sentences. One of my friends used to refer to this as the "elevator speech": Can you convey to someone in the time it takes to ride an elevator a few floors what your company is all about? This information should be included in any marketing piece.

In this exercise you will develop a single-page product sheet, front and back, which can be distributed in print form or as a *PDF*. It will convey information about a product or service and your company, and marketing/sales information that will define both the product or service and the company.

Production Choices

One of the first things to decide is how this piece will be produced and how often. This is the type of marketing piece that might need to be produced frequently. Will it need to be revised on a regular basis? Perhaps you have a small budget and prefer to produce it as it is needed, in house. Do you have a reliable device that produces consistent color with the finishing options you need? Or, perhaps you will order a large quantity to be printed with your print service provider and draw down on this *fulfillment* item throughout the year.

Distribution Choices

Distribution impacts production. Whether an item is produced in house or digitally and whether it is *duplexed* or perhaps three-hole punched or folded depend on the recipient. Perhaps it will end up in a binder for your sales force, be folded for direct mail in an envelope, be PDFed and sent as an email attachment, or be downloaded from a website.

Color Choices

If this product will be produced in house by a short-run, digital, on-demand output device, be careful about specifying a spot color. If your company collateral is two-color, trying to match that color with an in-house device will involve compromise and a lowering of expectations. It is very difficult, if not impossible, for a four-color printing process to match a spot color. PANTONE colors are not made from *process colors* (cyan, magenta, yellow, and black).

If this is a reality of your environment, invest in a PANTONE Process library, which will give you four-color equivalents of your *spot colors* so you can mix the closest color possible. Bear in mind that a four-color toner output device translates and renders color differently from how your print service provider's RIPs, proofers, and printing presses do. Some digital output devices print their own libraries of PANTONE swatches that they can reliably reproduce, so check with your manufacturer or vendor.

Stock choices also affect the way color appears on the page. A coated stock enhances and darkens the color, whereas an uncoated stock gives a dull appearance. In fact, PANTONE offers both a coated library of chips (like your paint store) and an uncoated library of chips so you can predict its appearance based on your stock choices. It is always a good idea to select your PANTONE color from a PANTONE swatch library and never from the swatches you see on your monitor. Remember, your monitor is an RGB device and your output device is more than likely CMYK. Only in offset printing can you specify a PANTONE chip and get that identical ink.

This exercise is designed as two-color, just like the collateral exercise previously. This choice allows for the enhancement of content without the expense of printing four-color work. Remember that the more colors you use, the greater the expense. For materials you will print frequently, this is always important to consider.

To make the most of this two-color job, you will create variety by adding tints of the same color. So, what would ordinarily be a black-and-white product with a grayscale image gains depth and interest with the addition of a single color.

Finishing and Binding Choices

As in our previous exercise, if folding is going to occur, make sure your paper choice will fold easily and not crack. Bear in mind that parallel folds can occur through an image and the results might not be satisfactory. Keep this in mind when you are putting your elements together on your page in InDesign. Additionally, if you'll use three-hole punching for distribution via a binder, be sure you have facing pages turned on and have an extra margin on the inside to accommodate the punch.

Project:
Product Sheet Front

We'll be creating the front of a product sheet (we tackle the other side in the second half of this chapter) in 18 easy steps:

STEPS ▼

1. Setting up your document format
2. Importing elements
3. Creating a text element
4. Creating a color swatch
5. Formatting text
6. Coloring type
7. Creating a shadow box
8. Grouping elements
9. Stepping and repeating
10. Creating columns versus threading text blocks
11. Threading text
12. Creating a style sheet
13. Creating a style sheet (alternative method)
14. Removing a style sheet and applying another
15. Filling with placeholder text
16. Positioning elements
17. Previewing your work
18. Printing a composite proof

STEP 1 ▼
Setting Up Your Document Format

Launch InDesign and go to the File pull-down menu. Select New, Document and fill out the New Document window as indicated in Figure 6.1.

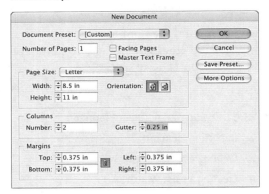

Orient yourself to the layout and check out the Control palette at the top of the window. You will be using the x,y coordinate to accurately position your elements.

STEP 2 ▼
Importing Elements

Go to the File pull-down menu and select Place; then navigate to the 06Project_Files folder and select cabinet.tiff. A paintbrush icon appears. Click the icon and the image drops onto your page. Set your proxy to the upper-left corner of the matrix. With the image still selected, type in the following x,y coordinate: x: .375", y: 1". Your image should snap into position.

 NOTE

How the image fades on all sides is called *feathering*, which can be applied to imported images as well a InDesign elements.

STEP 3 ▼
Creating a Text Element

Create a text box to fit the top of your page. The x,y coordinate should be .375",.375"; the width should be 7.75"; and the height should be .875".

STEP 4 ▼
Creating a Color Swatch

Open the Swatches palette found in the Window pull-down menu or check the *collapsible palette bays* that tuck along the edge of your window. Click the tab labeled Swatches and the palette will slide out.

NOTE

The collapsible bays are ideal for users with smaller monitors because they provide easy access but can be tucked away when not in use.

Let's add a swatch. If you are using the palette in the bay, pull down the menu from the triangle in the upper-left corner. If you are using the floating version of the palette, pull down the menu from the triangle in the upper-right corner of the palette. Select New Color Swatch and, from the Color Type menu, select Spot. From the Color Mode pull-down menu, select PANTONE Solid Coated. Type in the ink number you want (in our exercise, it's #5767) and click OK. Use Figure 6.2 for guidance.

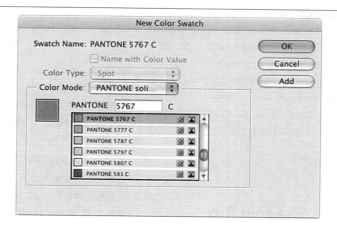

STEP 5 ▼
Formatting Text

With the Text tool, click in the text box across the top of your page (it should be slightly overlapping the image) and type **Wood Worker Guys: Custom Cabinets Since 1962**. Feel free to adjust this to your situation if you prefer. Highlight the text with the Text tool and format it as follows: Adobe Caslon Pro, italic, 30 points, −10 tracking, center aligned. Select the box with the selection tool, go to the Object pull-down menu, and select Text Frame Options. At the bottom of the window, select Centered Vertical Justification. Your text should look similar to Figure 6.3.

 TIP

All the text formatting for this exercise can be executed from the Control palette found just under the pull-down menus or via the Character and Paragraph palettes accessed via the Type pull-down menu, the Window pull-down menu, or the collapsible palettes found in the dock to the right of your window.

STEP 6 ▼
Coloring Type

With the text still highlighted, click the Swatches palette and click the Fill swatch so that it is selected (it will move forward or in front of the Stroke swatch). Click your newly added spot color, and the type should turn an olive green.

FIGURE 6.3 **The text should look as if it's floating in the box.**

Wood Worker Guys: Custom Cabinets Since 1962

Select the solid arrow or Selection tool. The text box itself should select; however, if you do not see the wire frame or anchor points around the text box, click to select it. Now, in the Swatches palette, with the fill swatch clicked to the forward position or selected and in front of the Stroke swatch, click the black swatch. The text box background should fill with black.

STEP 7 ▼
Creating a Shadow Box

On the pasteboard, draw a text box measuring 4″ wide by .5″ deep. Click the Selection tool (which is the black arrow) and apply a black fill (no stroke) using the swatches in the Swatches palette. Make a copy of the box (make sure the box is still selected) by selecting Edit, Copy. Go back to the Edit pull-down menu and select Paste in Place. A duplicate black box is placed on top of the original. Color this box PANTONE 5767. Apply a tint of this spot color after you have selected your swatch by going to

the top of the Swatches palette and typing **50%** instead of the usual 100%.

Select the Text tool again and click in the olive green box. Type **The Primitive**. The text should appear in black. Highlight the text with the Text tool and format it as follows: Adobe Caslon Pro italic, 30 points, centered alignment.

Go to the Object pull-down menu and select Text Frame Options. At the bottom of this resulting dialog box is the Vertical Justification option. Select Alignment, Centered so your text will be centered (*justi-fied*) both horizontally and vertically in your box (see Figure 6.4).

Select the Selection tool again and click the olive green box again. Now we will move the olive green box up and to the left ever so slightly. Rather than use the mouse, use your arrow keys to accomplish this. Each press of an arrow moves an element by 1 point. Move the box 4 points up and 4 points to the left. You have now created a basic shadow box; compare your work to Figure 6.5.

FIGURE 6.4 **Again, the text should look as if it's floating in the box.**

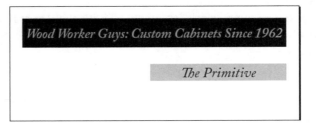

Wood Worker Guys: Custom Cabinets Since 1962

The Primitive

FIGURE 6.5 **This is an example of a very basic shadow construction.**

Wood Worker Guys: Custom Cabinets Since 1962

The Primitive

STEP 8 ▼
Grouping Elements

Select both boxes (green and black) and select Object, Group. The two boxes are grouped together, and the x,y coordinate for this group should be 4.125",1.75" (see Figure 6.6).

STEP 9 ▼
Stepping and Repeating

With the group still selected, you will step and repeat them twice down the side of your page. Go to the Edit pull-down menu and select Step and Repeat. Fill in the dialog box as shown in Figure 6.7. You now have two more groups, equally positioned down the right side of your page.

FIGURE 6.6 Grouping the two elements with the Object, Group command.

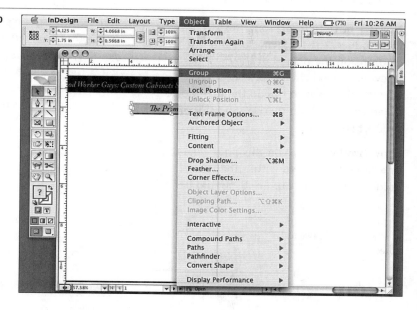

FIGURE 6.7 Make sure there is no horizontal movement, only vertical.

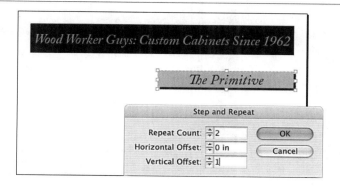

Select the Text tool, highlight the text in the second box, and type over it with different text. Do the same for the third box. Then adjust the type in both boxes to 24 points. I've typed in frame 2 Hand-planed, Maple Wood and in frame 3 Antiqued Nickel Hardware.

STEP 10 ▼
Creating Columns Versus Threading Text Blocks

Now we have to insert some text to describe the product. The text will flow into the two columns on the page, but they will be uneven. A good choice for columns of varying depths is to thread the text blocks together. We will do this on the front of the product sheet.

Draw two text boxes on this page. The first one should be drawn within the left column guide and the x,y coordinate should be .375",6"; the width should be 3.75"; and the height should be 4". The second text box should be placed and have an x,y coordinate of 4.375",4.75; a width of 3.75"; and a height of 5.25" (see Figure 6.8).

STEP 11 ▼
Threading Text

Now you are going to learn to *thread* text. With the Selection tool, click the first box. You will see little squares on the text box wire frame that look different from the anchor points. The little empty square in the upper-left corner is the in port, and the corresponding square in the lower-right corner is the out port. These squares facilitate the linking, or threading, of text boxes together. When they are both empty, they symbolize that the beginning and ending of this sequence of text begins and ends in that box alone (see Figure 6.9).

FIGURE 6.8   The two text boxes.

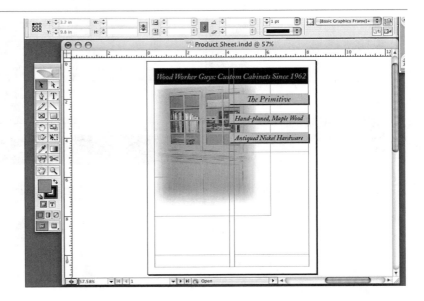

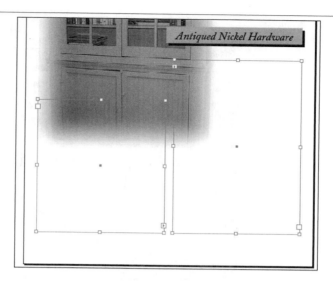

NOTE

For PageMaker users, the window shades that have loops in the middle and are found at the top and bottom of a text block serve the same purpose as the in and out ports in InDesign text frames. When they are empty, you know that is all the text in the block.

Now we will connect the two text boxes. With the Selection tool, click the out port of the first text frame. You might see the Selection tool turn into a miniature text block. Hover your mouse over the second text block, and the tool turns into a couple of links. Click the second block and your two blocks are linked together.

NOTE

The out port of the first text box has a triangle in it, and the in port of the second box also has a triangle in it, signifying the two are connected. If you want to see a physical connection, go to the View pull-down menu and select Show Text Threads.

With the Text tool, click in the first box and type in your product or service. In this exercise, I typed The Primitive. Format the text as follows: Adobe Caslon Pro, Italic, 30 points, left aligned, .1" space after, 1-point rule below, .05" offset.

NOTE

Paragraph rules can be accessed from the Control palette with the paragraph symbol selected. You will see a triangle on the far right of the Control palette. Pull this down and select Paragraph Rules. Select Rule Below and follow the previous instructions.

STEP 12 ▼
Creating a Style Sheet

Let's create a paragraph style based on the subhead you just created. With the Text tool, select the text the Primitive and, using the same pull-down menu from the Control palette, select New Paragraph Style. Name it **Product Subhead** (see Figure 6.10).

FIGURE 6.10 The definition
for Product Subhead.

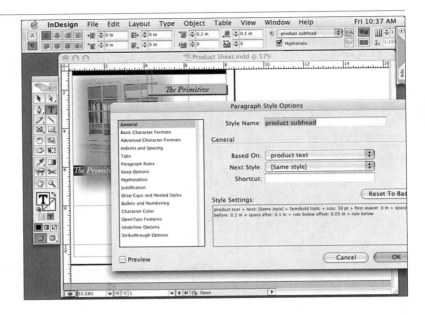

FIGURE 6.10 The definition
for Product Subhead.

NOTE

In the Style Settings box, you should see all the attributes associated with the formatting you just executed. Also note that to tag this text (The Primitive) with the paragraph style, you must be clicked somewhere in the text and then must select the style in the palette.

Click OK and go to the Paragraph Styles palette to see your new style sheet. You will use this style sheet on the back of this sheet.

If you haven't already created a paragraph return after your subhead, with the Text tool, place a return character after the Primitive to advance to the next line (see Figure 6.11) .

FIGURE 6.11 This subhead
will also be used on page 2.

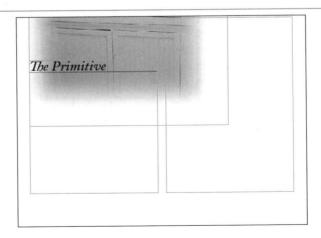

CHAPTER 6: Designing a Product Sheet

Now, type in some text that will reiterate the important features of the product or service this marketing piece is trying to promote. Highlight this text and format it as follows: Adobe Caslon Pro, regular, 20-point type, 40-point leading, centered alignment. Note the text has PANTONE 5767 applied to it via the Swatches palette. Make sure the type fill swatch, and not the type stroke swatch, is selected (clicked forward).

STEP 13 ▼
Creating a Style Sheet (Alternative Method)

Now you will make a basic style sheet for your body copy or paragraph text. But instead of it being based on something already on the page, you will make one from scratch. Let's explore the paragraph styles features. Access paragraph styles from the Control palette, the Type pull-down menu, or the Window pull-down menu. Select the New paragraph style and name it **paragraph text** (see Figure 6.12 to confirm the style definition).

A column down the left side of the window represents all the available categories of formatting. The General category offers the ability to base this style sheet on an existing style sheet. Make sure No Paragraph Style is selected in the Based on box and that Same Style is selected in the Next Style box. This means that this is an original style sheet. So, if you are typing in InDesign using this style sheet and you insert a carriage return, the text you type will continue to be formatted with this style.

Click Basic Character Formats and set the following: Adobe Caslon Pro Regular, 12-point size, 15-point leading. Click Indents and Spacing and select Left Alignment and a first line indent of .1". Click OK.

FIGURE 6.12 Creating a style sheet without basing it on something already on your page.

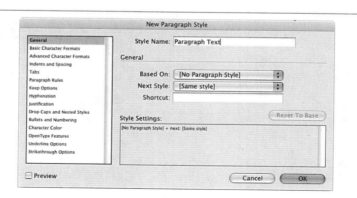

Removing a Style Sheet and Applying Another

With the Text tool, click at the bottom of your first text box. If you haven't entered a carriage return to take you to the top of the second box, you can also go to the Type pull-down menu and select Insert Break Character, Paragraph Break. Type some text, and you will notice that the text carries the same formatting as the previous paragraph. Highlight the few words you just typed and open the Paragraph Styles palette. Click No Paragraph Style with the Option/Alt key held down to strip away all the definitions and then click the new style you made in the palette called Paragraph Text. You should see your text formatted with the new style as in Figure 6.13.

TIP

If your text retains attributes from a former text style, you might see a plus sign appear next to a style sheet. This means something about the text has been modified or differs from the paragraph style definition. If you don't want this, hold down the Option key (Alt key in Windows) and click the paragraph text style again. You should see the text formatted exactly to the definition. This essentially removes any manual overrides.

STEP 15 ▼

Filling with Placeholder Text

To fill the box with *placeholder text*, go to the Type pull-down menu and select Fill with Placeholder Text. The rest of the box should fill with dummy text, formatted with your new style sheet. This command is useful because it allows you to create your marketing pieces without having to wait on copy from outside sources.

FIGURE 6.13 **This is how your project should look so far.**

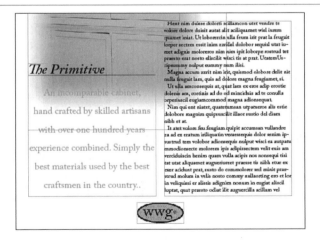

STEP 16 ▼
Positioning Elements

Deselect everything on your page, go to the File pull-down menu, and select Place. Navigate your way to the `06Project_Files` folder and select `wwglogo.eps`. Set your proxy to the center of the matrix and make sure the x coordinate is set to 4.25". With the down arrow, position the logo so that the baseline of the letters in the logo sits on the bottom margin (see Figure 6.14). Save your work.

STEP 17 ▼
Previewing Your Work

Review the front of your product sheet by turning off both the guides and frame edges on the View pull-down menu and by turning off hidden characters on the Type pull-down menu. Figure 6.15 shows how the front page of the product sheet should look.

STEP 18 ▼
Printing a Composite Proof

You might want to print a copy of this and look at it on paper. Go to the File pull-down menu and select Print. Select the appropriate settings for the printer that is available to you. Then go to the File pull-down menu and select Print. Again choose the appropriate settings for the printer available to you. On the General tab, select one copy. On the Setup tab, select 8.5" × 11" and vertical orientation (see Figure 6.16).

Leave the Scale setting alone. On the Marks and Bleed tab, turn off all the options. On the Output tab, if possible, print a color composite output for your work; if not, select Grayscale. On the Graphics tab, the default settings should work. The remaining tabs can be ignored for now. Print and review your proof. Make any necessary adjustments, save your changes, and print it again.

FIGURE 6.14 **The placed logo with centered proxy.**

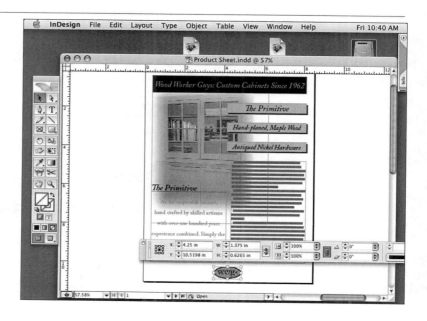

FIGURE 6.15 **The finished front.**

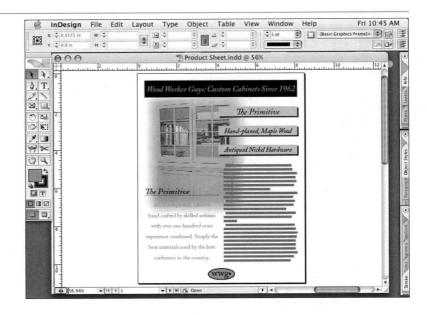

FIGURE 6.16 **The Print dialog box.**

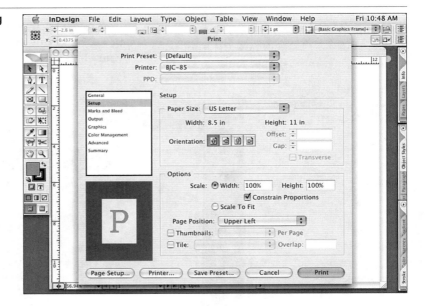

CHAPTER 6: Designing a Product Sheet

Project:
Product Sheet Back

We'll be creating the back side of the product sheet now, which will explain, in greater detail, the specifics of the product or service you will be marketing. You will execute this project in 13 easy steps:

STEPS ▼

1. Using the Pages palette to add a page
2. Tinting an element
3. Copying from one page to another
4. Creating multiple columns inside a single text box
5. Creating a drop cap
6. Aligning elements
7. Using the Glyphs palette
8. Using OpenType
9. Grouping and text wrap
10. Managing file links
11. Preflighting your project
12. Creating a color composite proof
13. Creating a PDF for alternative distribution

STEP 1 ▼
Using the Pages Palette to Add a Page

Assuming the file is already open, you will now add another page, the back of the sheet, to your file. You will do this with the Pages palette, which is accessed from the Window pull-down menu, from a floating palette, or from the dock on the right side of your window (by clicking the Pages tab). Click the triangle on the left or right of the palette (depending on how you accessed the palette) and select Insert Pages. Insert one page after page 1 and click OK (see Figure 6.17).

FIGURE 6.17 Inserting a new page using the Pagrs palette menu.

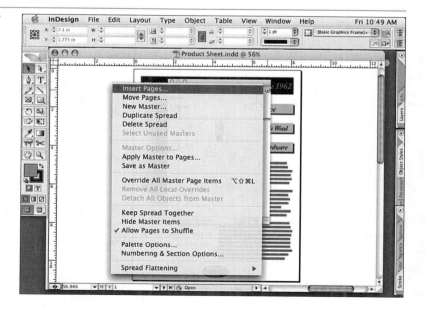

On the Pages palette, you should now see a second, miniature page with a number 2 on it. Double-click the miniature page and InDesign will take you to your new page 2. (You can also navigate to page 2 by using the page indicator at the bottom of your window.)

STEP 2 ▼
Tinting an Element

Make sure the proxy is set to the upper-left corner of the matrix. Create a vertical rectangle with the following coordinates: x: .375", y: .375", width: 2", height: 10.25". With the rectangle still selected, go to the Swatches palette and select the PANTONE fill, but this time apply a 50% tint at the top of the Swatches palette (see Figure 6.18).

FIGURE 6.18 This vertical element will anchor the left side of the page.

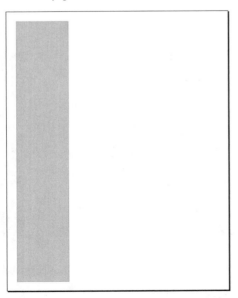

STEP 3 ▼
Copying from One Page to Another

Navigate back to page 1 and select the header across the top. Select Edit, Copy; navigate back to page 2; and select Edit, Paste. Drag the header to the upper-left corner, where the margins intersect. Highlight the text and type over it with your product or service specifications. For this step, I suggest you type **The Primitive Specifications** as I have done. Use Figure 6.19 as your guide.

FIGURE 6.19 Another shortcut to formatting is copying and pasting a similar element, highlighting it, and typing over it.

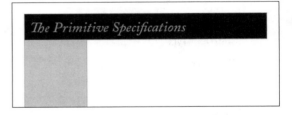

STEP 4 ▼
Creating Multiple Columns Inside a Single Text Box

Create a text box across your entire page with an x,y coordinate of x: 1", y: 1.5", width: 7.125", height: 9.125". Because both of these columns will be of equal size and there are no more pages in the file, you will take this single text box and make it a two-column text box. In the Control palette, with the Paragraph button selected, look to the far right, where you will see the Column button followed by an open field with the number 1 in it. Highlight the number 1 and change it to a 2 (see Figure 6.20).

With the Text tool, click at the top of the first column and go to the Type pull-down menu. Select Fill with Placeholder Text. Highlight the text and apply (or *tag*) the Paragraph Text style found in the Paragraph Styles palette.

FIGURE 6.20   Another way to create multiple columns, this is especially suited for columns that have consistent dimensions.

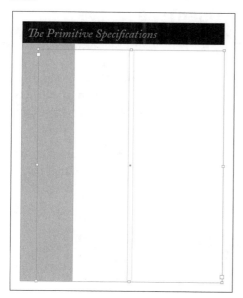

STEP 5 ▼
Creating a Drop Cap

Click anywhere in your first paragraph. Click the paragraph button on the left side of the Control palette. Remove the first line indent by editing the field in the Control palette and resetting this option to 0. Now, let's add a

drop cap. In the middle of the Control palette, you will use the Drop Cap fields. Create a drop cap that is three lines deep by one character, and then click OK to activate the fields. Use Figure 6.21 as a visual guide.

Type some random subheads in both columns. You could add **hardware**, **installation**, **warranty**, and **Contact us** by clicking in your text and making sure you place a paragraph (carriage) return before and after each subhead.

FIGURE 6.21   You can format your drop cap any way you like. Experiment with a different typeface or color.

Apply the Subhead style sheet to the new subheads you have created.

Under the subhead Contact Us, I added some generic contact information. Feel free to highlight the remaining placeholder text and type over it with your company contact information as well.

STEP 6 ▼
Aligning Elements

Let's create a special graphic and learn how to use *text wrap*. Off on your pasteboard (the area on either side of your sheet), you will compose a graphic. Create a rectangle that is .75" wide by 1" deep. Apply your PANTONE color to the fill, with no stroke. Create another rectangle, smaller than the first, with a white fill and a black 2-point stroke. Align the two to each other using the Control palette's two rows of alignment buttons—click the middle button of the first row (align horizontal centers) and click the middle button of the second row (align vertical centers). Group these two rectangles together by selecting them both and selecting Object, Group. See the results in Figure 6.22.

STEP 7 ▼
Using the Glyphs Palette

Draw a small text box, about the same size of the last rectangle you drew, somewhere on your pasteboard but away from your rectangles. Go to the Type pull-down menu and select the Glyphs palette (see Figure 6.23).

FIGURE 6.22 With InDesign's drawing tools, you can supplement your art files by creating graphic elements without having to use an additional program.

STEP 8 ▼
Using OpenType

OpenType is the new font file format developed by both Adobe and Microsoft. Two key benefits of it are its cross-platform compatibility and support for extended character sets. These character sets are accessed in InDesign by selecting Type, Glyphs.

Make sure Adobe Caslon Pro, or your company typeface, is selected at the bottom of the

FIGURE 6.23 The Glyphs palette displays every character of any typeface of every type family you have installed.

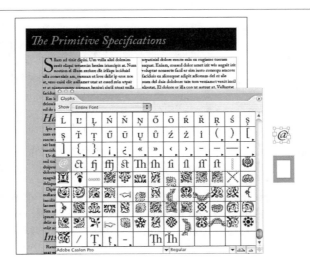

palette. Scroll down through the glyphs until you find a symbol you would like to use. I chose the at symbol (@), as in "Contact us at…".

Highlight the symbol and make it 36 points. Drag the text box over your two existing rectangles and, with the arrow keys, move the symbol visually into position (see Figure 6.24).

FIGURE 6.24 I've chosen a special character in this glyphs set.

FIGURE 6.25 Note the additional vector that creates the wrap. It can be reshaped like any other vector to create unusual wraps.

Save your work; turn off your guides, frame edges, and hidden characters; and review your work.

> 🚫 **CAUTION**
>
> Why can't you center this box to the others? Because of spacing considerations, including kerning and leading, centering the box doesn't center the type.

STEP 9 ▼
Grouping and Text Wrap

Group this box to the others and drag it under your contact subhead. Access the Text Wrap palette by selecting Window, Type and Tables, Text Wrap. With your grouped elements selected, click the third icon, Wrap Around Object Shape. Your text should wrap around your group. Feel free to use the arrow keys again to position the box. The left edge of the group should align with your column guide, but slide your group up and down until you get your first line of text to align with the top of your group (see Figure 6.25 for the positioning of the icon to the text).

STEP 10 ▼
Managing File Links

To manage a *file link*, open the Links palette under the Window pull-down menu. You should see the image `cabinet.tiff` and `wwglogo.eps` represented in the list on the Links palette. Next to the filenames are the pages on which these images are placed. Both should be labeled page 1. If you double-click either file in the palette, you will see information about the image, its status (that is, whether it's up-to-date, embedded, modified, or missing), and its current location on a physical drive. The up-to-date status is the preferred status. Any other status displays a symbol: Missing is indicated by a stop sign, modified is indicated by a yellow caution symbol, and embedded is represented by simple geometric shapes. To demonstrate these symbols, I've created a screen capture, shown in Figure 6.26, specifically displaying the missing, modified, and embedded symbols, respectively.

STEP 11 ▼
Preflighting Your Project

Make sure you have saved your work; then go to the File menu and select Preflight. The preflight command checks your file to ensure it is in acceptable condition to submit to your print service provider. It checks for fonts, links, images, colors, inks, your print settings, and any external plug-ins you might have. All this information impacts your print service provider (see Figure 6.27 for an example of the preflight dialog box).

InDesign uses a yellow caution or warning sign (the same for missing fonts or modified links) to indicate problems. When you are clicking through the Preflight dialog box, look for the yellow signs with exclamation points because they indicate problems. You might have a problem such as a font used by the document is not turned on in your font management utility, you've moved or modified an image since you placed it in your document, or you have included an RGB image. If you have errors or warnings, you need to cancel out of this dialog box, fix the problem, and run the preflight again.

FIGURE 6.27   Your dialog box should reflect an error-free summary.

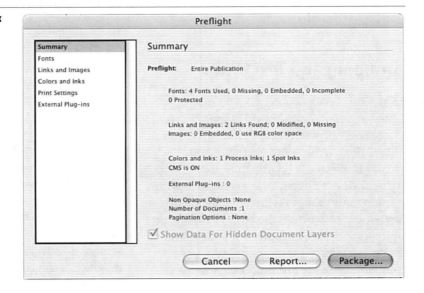

STEP 12 ▼
Creating a Color Composite Proof

Let's print a content proof. Go to the File pull-down menu and select Print. Choose the appropriate settings for the printer that is available to you. Then go to the File pull-down menu and select Print. Again choose the appropriate settings for the printer available to you. On the General tab, select one copy. On the Setup tab, select 8.5" × 11" and Vertical Orientation (see Figure 6.28).

Leave the Scale setting alone. On the Marks and Bleed tab, turn off all the options. On the Output tab, if possible, print a color composite output for your work; if not, select Grayscale. On the Graphics tab, the default settings should work. The remaining tabs can be ignored for now. Print and review your

proof. Make any necessary adjustments, save your changes, and print it again.

STEP 13 ▼
Creating a PDF for Alternative Distribution

You can make a *PDF*, which stands for Portable Document Format, and distribute the file via email, a website, or an FTP site. This is a file format developed by Adobe that allows for document distribution without the recipient of the document needing the software used to create the original document. Adobe distributes Acrobat Reader for free, allowing anyone to open a PDF. You can make a PDF from virtually any software application you might use. Adobe products, such as InDesign, natively support the creation of PDFs via the Export command.

FIGURE 6.28 The Print dialog box.

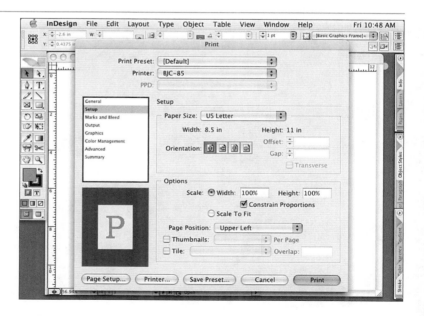

Benefits of the PDF structure include cross-platform compatibility, with images and fonts self-contained, and a prerendered form of PostScript that practically ensures printability. Anyone can make a PDF, receive a PDF, and distribute a PDF. A PDF can be made one-way, for viewing only (low resolution), or it can be made for the purpose of a printing press. We will make a simple PDF for easy distribution as an attachment via email.

With your document open and already proofed, go to the File pull-down menu and select Export. Navigate your way to Chapter 6\ 06Finished_Projects and label and save the file as a PDF. At the bottom of the window, make sure Adobe PDF is selected in the Format drop-down box; then click Save (Figure 6.29 shows the Export dialog box).

This first PDF we will make will be very simple. At the top of the Export PDF dialog box, select Print in the Preset drop-down box. Then click Export (see Figure 6.30).

NOTE

Presets are explored more thoroughly throughout the book, but put simply, they are predefined settings. The preset called Print is designed for basic laser printing.

To check your PDF, double-click your file and your PDF should open in either Adobe Reader or (if you own a full version of Acrobat) Acrobat. Inspect your PDF and, if it looks correct, distribute it electronically. If it requires adjustment, go back to your InDesign document, make your corrections, save it, and export it again.

FIGURE 6.29 **Make sure the PDF file format is selected. You should probably store your PDF with your InDesign production file.**

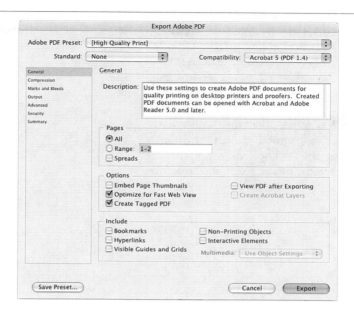

FIGURE 6.30 **Presets make creating PDFs easy.**

Final Thoughts

In this chapter you created a two-sided marketing piece that can be used to promote either a product or a service. You created a two-color product sheet using not only basic page layout skills, but also advanced text formatting and creative object formatting.

Here are some important concepts to keep in mind:

- How will this piece be used, and will the product information change or be updated frequently? Answers to these questions will likely dictate whether you will choose longer run lengths and therefore offset printing or whether you will need smaller batches printed with frequent updates, which lends itself to digital printing. If these product/service sheets will be organized along with others, consider a three-hole punch.

- Alternative distribution methods, such as creating a printable PDF, will save you the cost of printing altogether. This file format and size can be flexible enough to allow you to email this marketing piece, assuming you have such data, or post it on a website or FTP site so that anyone with access can download it.

- Flowing text throughout a document is a useful skill, and you will use it for many marketing pieces. In this project you created the forward flow of text by threading, utilizing in ports, outports, and multiple column text boxes.

- In this chapter, you learned some advanced text formatting skills, including creating paragraph styles, creating a drop cap, and using the Glyphs palette for accessing any character you have available on your system.

- Finally, learning to manage your resource files with the Links palette is very important. In most cases, InDesign creates a link to the placed image file and displays a preview when you place your image. Unless you embed your placed file (which copies the entire file into the InDesign layout), the Links palette keeps track of all placed files and where they are stored. Learning how to interpret the Links palette and its symbols enables you to manage your workflow more efficiently. It also helps you make a smooth transition when you use the Package command to gather your layout, fonts, and resource files for your print service provider.

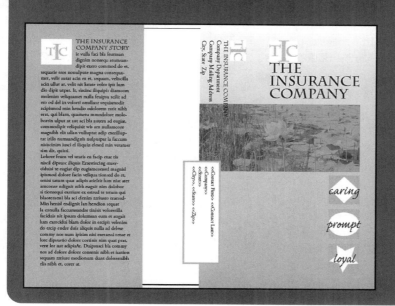

About the Project

In this chapter you will learn how to create a *trifold* brochure (three panels with two folds that cross over each other) on a company product or service that can be distributed to your customers by inserting it into a folder, including it in a business-size envelope, or sending it as a *self-mailer*.

Prerequisites

It would be helpful if you had a basic understanding of page layout, including using the Tool palette, formatting text, and performing basic page formatting.

@work resources

Please visit the publisher's website to access the following Chapter 7 files:

▶ **finished projects**

▶ Art files: **lilly1gray.tif, logo.eps**

Planning the Project

This project is an extension of the previous project: creating a product/service sheet. The product sheet focuses on a specific feature of the company and is more technically oriented. The brochure, while more sophisticated in layout, structure, and production, will be more general in content. Whether you are involved in marketing business-to-business products/services or are a consumer-oriented manufacturer or service provider, having a nice printed piece to leave behind is an important part of your marketing portfolio.

You can approach this project with a specific purpose or goal, such as "we need to promote or sell x," or you can approach this project with the idea that this will serve as the template for a variety of products and services. It's up to you. Nonetheless, there are always planning considerations to think about. By now, you will have answered questions such as "Who is our audience?" and "What kind of style will best convey our message?"

Production Choices

The style of the piece, coupled with your target distribution and budget, will affect your production choices. Do you intend to mass mail this to a database of your customers? Compare the cost of digital production versus *offset*. Past a certain count, offset becomes the less expensive option. Is this piece going to change frequently, or do you see this brochure being distributed for a significant time into the future? This will affect how many you might order and therefore which production method you choose. If you don't want to keep many on hand and

you're not certain you will need this printed piece again, consider digital options.

Distribution Choices

If this is to be mailed in an envelope, you need to make sure that the dimensions of the piece will insert or fold correctly into an envelope. If the piece is a self-mailer, you need to ensure that the back panel adheres to postal regulations. Also, if you are going to seal the piece with some type of adhesive (sticker), make sure it can be easily removed or torn through so your customers can open the mailer without destroying the content and, if possible, the finish. If the piece is simply meant to sit on a table at a trade show or on a counter in a stack, make sure that when it's folded, it lies flat.

Color Choices

As always, consider what the budget will allow for, who your audience is, and what they will want to see. In this project, I've constructed a conservative, two-color brochure. Of course, you can take it from there and move to four colors. But I thought it was important to demonstrate what you can do with a limited number of colors.

Stock and Binding

Considerations here include folding; consult with your print or paper vendor to discuss folding concerns. Remember that you might not want to place images such that they will have a fold through them if they are meant to be referenced in the foreground or contain a caption that will be difficult to read through a crease. If there's a lot of ink coverage, surface cracking along the fold might not be too attractive. Depending on the stock choice and extensive ink coverage, you might want to discuss fingerprints left behind on the surface. See the following section, "Finishing," if this is the case. The heavier the stock, the more difficult it is to fold, and *scoring* the paper might be recommended. Keep in mind that unusual folds increase the bindery cost, which is the area of print production that folds stock (among many other bindery operations).

Finishing

If there's a lot of ink coverage on your printed piece, and it ends up in the direct mail stream, your print service provider might recommend some type of liquid coating to prevent damage such as fingerprints. Such a coating can also improve the appearance of the printed piece. You have a few choices, such as *varnish*, *aqueous coating*, and *ultra-violet (UV)*. It's important that you discuss all the distribution possibilities with your service provider when *planning* the piece to avoid costly mistakes on the back end of production.

Project: **Trifold Brochure**

We'll be creating a brochure in 16 easy steps:

STEPS ▼

1. Setting up your document format
2. Placing guides
3. Adding a swatch
4. Creating a gradient
5. Directing a gradient
6. Importing a logo
7. Creating the title for the brochure
8. Placing an image and coloring it
9. Creating graphical elements
10. Transforming elements
11. Creating text wrap
12. Fitting content to frame
13. Creating and linking text blocks
14. Using the pen tool
15. Printing a composite proof
16. Data merging

STEP 1 ▼
Setting Up Your Document Format

Launch InDesign and go to the File pull-down menu. Select New, Document and fill out the New Document window as indicated in Figure 7.1. You will be creating a two-page landscape layout with bleed, which will visually assist you in placing your background image for the CD cover.

FIGURE 7.1 Fill out the window as indicated.

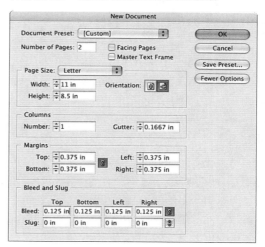

STEP 2 ▼
Placing Guides

Let's create some guides and position them along the *fold lines*. Check with your print service provider to find out whether they want actual stroked lines (often they are dashed lines) or whether the guides alone will suffice because the printer will add fold marks during production. Often, fold indicators are placed outside the trim edge of the page, just like crop marks.

First, go to the master page by double-clicking Master A in the Pages palette. Go to the Layout pull-down menu, select CreateGuides, and fill out the resulting dialog box as indicated in Figure 7.2.

Now, let's set margins for the individual columns. Click the first guide you just created and take note of its x coordinate, which should be about 3.667".

Drag a ruler guide from the left ruler and drop it just to the left of the first guide. With it still selected (click it and it should change color to indicate it is selected), go to the x coordinate box and type in **3.667-.375"**. Your new ruler guide will snap to 3/8" from the left of the guide.

 TIP

The Control palette enables you to execute mathematical equations using all the units of measure supported.

Drag another rule to the right of your fold guide and, with it still selected, type **3.667+.375"** in the x coordinate box. Your new rule should snap 3/8" to the right of the fold guide! Repeat these steps with your other fold rule. Double-click page 1 in your layout; the results should look like Figure 7.3.

FIGURE 7.2 Fill out the window as indicated for this three-column setup. The rules you are creating will act as fold rules or guides.

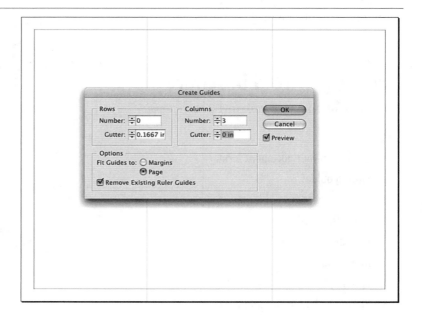

CHAPTER 7: Creating a Brochure

FIGURE 7.3 The finished
results! Experiment with math
in the control palette; try adding
inches and picas together—for
example, 1.24 " + 3p0.

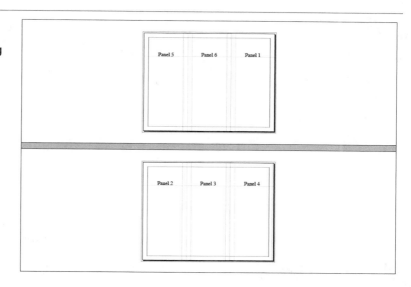

STEP 3 ▼
Adding a Swatch

Let's add a swatch. This will be the second color for the brochure. You might use your company's color or choose a color complementary to a product or service line. For this project, I've chosen PANTONE 8321. Go to the Swatches palette, pull down the Swatch palette menu (triangle), and fill out the dialog box according to Figure 7.4.

FIGURE 7.4 Choose a spot color. Note that I have chosen a coated spot color because I am going to use a coated stock.

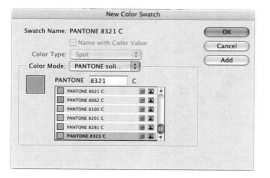

Always choose your colors based on printed samples. PANTONE offers swatch fans with PANTONE colors printed on both coated and uncoated stock.

STEP 4 ▼
Creating a Gradient

Go back to the Swatches palette and pull down the menu once again, except this time select New Gradient Swatch. Give the new gradient a name, such as **brochure gradient**, and click the first stop (the little square) on the gradient color ramp (the bar at the bottom of the screen containing graduated color). If PANTONE 8321 isn't already selected, click it and the stop will fill with that color. Click the other stop to assign a different color, scroll through your list to Paper, and click it (see Figure 7.5). Click OK. You should see a new gradient swatch in your palette.

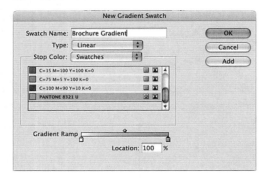

STEP 5 ▼
Directing a Gradient

Let's create a rectangle with the following coordinates: x: 5.5", y: –.125", width: 5.6375", height: 8.75". Tag the fill of the box with your new gradient swatch. Select the Gradient tool in the Tool palette and drag it vertically, starting at the bottom of the box straight up (hold down the Shift key) to the top of the box (see Figure 7.6).

FIGURE 7.6   This is how your layout should look so far.

STEP 6 ▼
Importing a Logo

Go to the File pull-down menu, select Place, and navigate to the Chapter 7 project files folder. Select logo.eps and drag the logo to the far right panel. Tuck it into the upper-left corner intersection of your margin guide and ruler guide (the x,y coordinate should be 7.705,.375).

 NOTE

To see the logo at its best, with the logo still selected, go to the Object pull-down menu and select Display Performance, High Quality Display.

STEP 7 ▼
Creating the Title for the Brochure

Draw a text frame to line up with the left margin of panel one, line up under the logo (approximately y: 1.215), and line up on the right margin with a height of 1.25. Type in your headline with whatever font you choose. I have used Charlemagne Std, Bold, 32-point type and 30-point leading. Use Figure 7.7 to monitor your progress.

FIGURE 7.7   Here's how your logo and title should look.

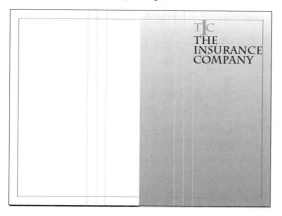

FIGURE 7.8   The image should extend all the way to the bleed.

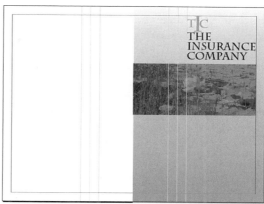

STEP 8 ▼
Placing an Image and Coloring It

Now let's place an image and do something different. Draw a picture frame with the following coordinates and dimensions: x: 5.5", y: 2.475", width: 5.625", height: 2.25". Go to the File pull-down menu and select Place. Navigate to the Chapter 7 project files folder and select lilly1gray.tif. Use the Direct Selection tool and click and hold your mouse down over the image. You should see another vector and a dimmed image representing the entire picture as well as the frame you drew representing the cropped area. Position the image so the lily is somewhat centered in the frame.

Now, let's apply color to the background. With your rectangle frame tool selected (not the picture itself), go to the Swatches palette. With the Fill swatch selected (clicked forward), click your spot color. The background of the picture box should change. This is a nice effect—not quite a duotone, but a nice effect nonetheless (see Figure 7.8).

STEP 9 ▼
Creating Graphical Elements

Somewhere off on your pasteboard (the area on either side of your pages), we are going to make some graphical elements that will repeat through the layout. They will anchor the cover panel and be used again to distinguish three areas of your company, service, or product. Let's start by making a square 1" in dimension. Color the fill of this square with your spot color. Make two more by dragging your square and holding down the Option (Mac) or Alt (PC) key. This is known as a *drag copy*. Let go of your mouse before you let go of the Option key and you will create a copy. Your goal is to create three squares.

Let's create different graphics to layer on top of these squares. I have chosen a diamond, an oval, and a star, but feel free to experiment and draw your own using your Rectangle, Ellipse, and Polygon tools. To make the diamond, I drew a square and then rotated it. The oval is self-explanatory. I created the star by first double-clicking the

Polygon tool found in the same place you also found the oval and then setting the star attributes to 5 points and 40% inset. We'll refer to these three graphical elements as *icons* now. Select each pair of objects (icons) and align their centers using either the Control palette or the Alignment palette.

Next, I drew a text frame across the middle of each icon and typed in three action words to describe the company or service. They will serve as subheads on the inside of the brochure. Choose whatever type you like. I've used Caflisch Script Pro Regular, 34 points. After you tweak the three elements of each icon, group them together by selecting the multiple elements (Shift-clicking) and selecting Object, Group.

Stack the icons down the right side of your front panel, and align the right sides of your icons with the right margin. Your front panel is done! You can use the Alignment palette, select all three icons, and choose to align their right edges. You can also use the Distribute Vertical Centers option. Review your work by comparing it to Figure 7.9.

FIGURE 7.9   **The logos, stacked down the right side of the front panel.**

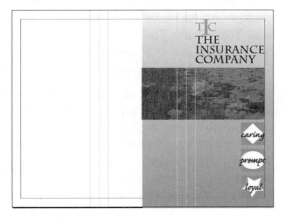

STEP 10 ▼
Transforming Elements

If you want to make this brochure a self-mailer, the next few elements will be important. As I've indicated in previous chapters, it's extremely important that you understand postal regulations and ensure that the placements of the return address and the addressee are compliant. Make sure your addressee area is not so low that the post office's automated postal readers can't scan the address or barcode. If this is not going to self-mail, design this panel vertically with the company logo and contact information.

Let's place another logo. Go to the File pull-down menu, navigate to your projects folder, and select logo.eps again. Click your cursor on the middle panel. Scale the logo to 75% by using the Scale fields in the Control palette. Now rotate the logo –90° and fit it to the intersection of the top margin and the leftmost of the three vertical guidelines on the right.

Draw a text frame 2.75" wide and 1" high. Type in the company name and address—again, choose whatever font you want. Rotate this box –90° and tuck it under the logo.

Create the last element on this panel by creating a text box with a width of 3.5" and a height of 1.25". Stroke the box with 4 points and color the stroke with your spot color. Rotate the box –90° and place the addressee box slightly overlapping both the image and the gradient. Again, the position should be in keeping with your postal regulations.

As an optional exercise at the end of the chapter, I cover the great new feature of InDesign CS2: mail merge. So, if you want to produce a piece such as this in house, you can merge this file with your own data. See the completed middle panel in Figure 7.10.

FIGURE 7.10   **The completed panel.**

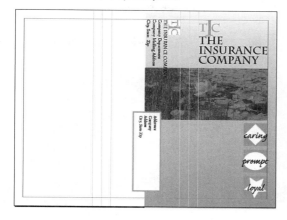

wrap. Feel free to tweak the wrap by changing the values in the Offset fields or moving the bounding box with the Selection tool. Review your work with Figure 7.11.

FIGURE 7.11   **The company story.**

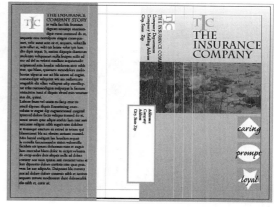

STEP 11 ▼
Creating Text Wrap

The last panel of the brochure tells the company story. Create a frame that fits from the bleeds on three sides to the first fold line and fill it with your spot color. Draw another frame, a text frame, to fit the margin guides for this panel. Go to the Type pull-down menu and select Fill with Placeholder Text.

Type in a subhead at the beginning of this text box for this panel, such as **The Company Story**, and format it in larger type.

Draw another rectangle that is 1" wide and .75" high. Fill it with paper and move it to the upper-left corner of your brochure to fit the margins. Place another copy of the logo on top of this white box and center these two elements to each other using the alignment buttons found in the Control palette. Group these elements together.

Let's wrap the text around it. Go to the Window pull-down menu and select Type & Tables, Text Wrap. A new palette appears. Choose the second icon, Wrap Around Bounding Box, and you should see the text

Save your work in your finished projects folder.

STEP 12 ▼
Fitting Content to Frame

Let's move on to the inside of the brochure. Advance to page 2 (either by clicking next to the page number at the bottom of the window or using the Page palette and double-clicking page 2).

Draw a picture box to fit the entire inside of the brochure, including the bleed. Place the `lilly1gray.tiff` image inside this rectangle frame. With the frame selected, go to the Object pull-down menu and select Fitting, Fit Content to Frame. Don't worry about distorting the image—that's intentional.

Open the Swatches palette and drag and drop the spot swatch on top of the lily picture. Unlike the cover panel, where the background was colored and the image itself remained black, the image will change to the spot color. The image will look faded and will become the background of the inside of the brochure (see Figure 7.12).

FIGURE 7.12 The inside panels.

corner of each margin intersection of each panel (see Figure 7.13).

FIGURE 7.13 The inside panels with background image, icons, and placeholder text.

STEP 13 ▼
Creating and Linking Text Blocks

Draw three separate text frames to fit the three columns, each with a y coordinate of 1.5" and a depth of 4.25". Link them together by clicking with the Selection tool, the out port from text box 1 to anywhere in text box 2. Click the out port of text box 2 and anywhere in text box 3. Click in text box 1 with the Text tool and select Fill with Placeholder Text from the Type pull-down menu. Select all the text and format it with your chosen typeface, using 12 points and a first line indent of 12 points.

Make sure guides and frame edges are turned on under the View pull-down menu. Go back to page 1, select all three icons, and copy them to the Clipboard. Move back to page 2 and paste the three icons down onto the page. Position each icon in the upper-left

STEP 14 ▼
Using the Pen Tool

If you are up to the task of creating a wavy vector, select the Pen tool and click and drag a wavy line across the inside spread beginning on the left bleed and ending on the right bleed. Format the line to 20 points, using a dotted style. Tag the line with your spot color, go to the Object pull-down menu, and apply a drop shadow.

If you are not up to the pen work, simply create a straight line across the inside spread and format it in the same way. Position this rule around y 6".

Below this rule draw a text box all the way across the bottom of the brochure from margin to margin. The coordinates and dimensions are as follows: x: .375", y: 6.625", width: 10.25", height: 1.125". Fill the box with placeholder text and format the text with your company typeface (I've used Adobe Garamond Pro, semibold, 12 points).

The last element is another text box. Draw it below the last line from the far left margin to far right margin. Type in one headline referencing the copy above. Format the text. I have used Caflisch Regular, 40 points, centered. With your arrow keys, move the box down so that the baseline of the text sits on the bottom margin. Figure 7.14 shows the inside panel finished.

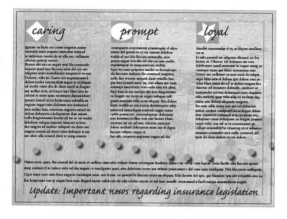

Save your work.

STEP 15 ▼
Printing a Composite Proof

You might want to print a copy of this and look at it on paper. Go to the File pull-down menu and select Print. Choose the appropriate settings for the printer that is available to you. On the General tab, go to the File pull-down menu and select Print. Again, choose the appropriate settings for the printer available to you. On the General tab, choose one copy. On the Setup tab, select 8.5" × 11" and vertical orientation. If your brochure has images or elements that bleed and you want to see that, print to something larger than

8.5" × 11". Leave the Scale setting as is. On the Marks and Bleed tab, turn on crop marks. On the Output tab, if possible, print a color composite output for your work; if not, select Grayscale. On the Graphics tab, the default settings should work. The remaining tabs can be ignored for now.

If you cannot print to a tabloid size paper, you have to reduce the layout in the Setup Tab using the Scale to Fit feature. Be sure to mark the composite proof as "scaled" so your service provider understands that the proof does not represent your job as the actual size.

Print and review your proof. Make any necessary adjustments, save your changes, and print it again.

STEP 16 ▼
Optional Exercise: Data Merging

Go back to page 1 and look at the middle panel. Assuming you intend to create a self-mailer, look closely at the box you've created for the addressee. If you were going to produce this piece in-house, wouldn't it be nice if you could merge your list of addresses with your InDesign document? Now, in CS2 you can!

Your data source for this exercise can be a comma-delimited file or a tab-delimited file, meaning your data is separated by commas or tabs. This can be accomplished in most database or spreadsheet applications when you save the file—look for file format options and choose accordingly. For this exercise, we'll use a file called text.txt.

Zoom in on the middle panel of page 1 and remove any copy inside the addressee text box. Go to the Window pull-down menu and select Automation, Data Merge (see Figure 7.15).

The Data Merge palette actually steps you through the process because the directions are housed right in the palette window. Follow the instructions by first selecting the *data source* file from the palette menu (click the triangle and select Data Source) making sure that you choose the tab-delimited option for your text.

Navigate to text.txt in the Chapter 7 project files folder, select the file, and click Open.

You will see a list of all the headings from the file appear in the palette (see Figure 7.16).

FIGURE 7.15 **The new Data Merge palette.**

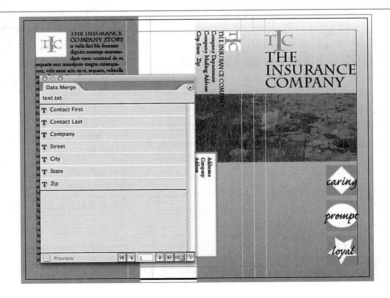

FIGURE 7.16 **The Data Merge palette with your imported data source data fields.**

Make sure there is a text insertion point in your box and click on the first data field in the Data Merge palette (in our project example, that's Contact First). Press the space-bar and click Contact Last; then press Return and click Company. Press Return again, click Street, press Return, and click City, State, Zip until your text box looks like Figure 7.17.

Now you are ready to merge. If you want to see a preview of the merge, select Preview from the Palette pull-down menu.

Now you are ready to create a *merged document*. Go to the Palette menu and select Create Merged Documents. For the purpose of this exercise, merge all the records and leave the rest of the settings at their defaults. Click OK. InDesign creates a separate untitled file, which is the merged document with a new page generated for each record. Your original is preserved and is referred to as the *target document*. After you've inspected your merged document for any errors, you are ready to send your file to your output device. Figure 7.18 illustrates a sample merged document.

Final Thoughts

In this project you have executed a common marketing layout: the brochure. Although a brochure can take different forms, you have created a two-fold, three-panel marketing piece you will be able to use repeatedly. Important concepts to remember include

- ▶ One of the key features of this project includes making the most of two colors. Not only is this discussed from a production/cost perspective, but it also is accomplished by tagging images (both the foreground, which is the image itself, and the background of an image).

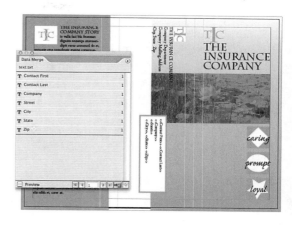

FIGURE 7.17   Your text box with the data fields in place.

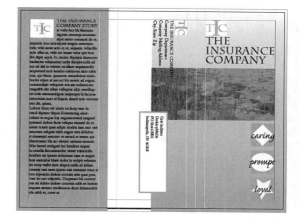

FIGURE 7.18   The finished merged document.

- ▶ You've used InDesign CS to create simple icons with InDesign by combining basic shapes together with color and text. You can then reuse them throughout the layout or even add them to a company library.

- ▶ Planning for distribution increases the success of your project and one of the considerations we discussed is the self-mailer, for both postal standards and the potential for mail merges.

▶ Finally, I introduced creative features such as the text wrap for flowing text around other elements in the layout, drop shadows for creating perspective and depth to your images, and gradients for creating two-color backgrounds.

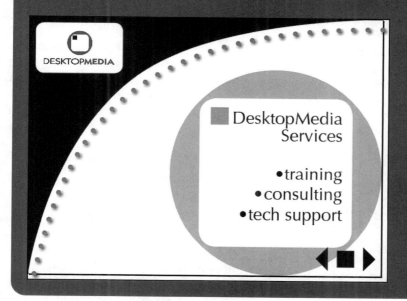

About the Project

In this chapter you will learn how to create an *interactive* presentation that might be created for some type of company presentation, a sales presentation for a product or service, a training module, a financial review, or an introduction of a new benefits plan. This layout might be delivered as a slide presentation, an interactive communiqué via email attachment, or a printed piece.

Prerequisites

It would be helpful if you had a basic understanding of page layout, including using the Tool palette, formatting text, and performing basic page formatting. It would also be helpful to have an understanding of PDF navigation.

@work resources

Please visit the publisher's website to access the following Chapter 8 files:

▶ **finished projects**

▶ Project_files [DM_BGRD_DUO.eps, DMLOGO.eps, DMintro_01.swf, DESKTOP_Cate.mov]

Planning the Project

The presentation you will create with this project will serve a variety of purposes. First, it will serve as a slide presentation, so there will be some production discussion centering around projectors, color, and navigation. Second, this will also contain interactive elements, so that when distributed to individuals, they can engage with the layout and experience rich content including sound, movies, and *hyperlinks*. Finally, these pages can be printed and distributed as companions to a presentation.

Workflow Considerations

One approach is to build the layout for print (CMYK), but export it to PDF (RGB) to create the slide presentation and the interactive PDF for electronic distribution. This is particularly logical if your image assets are already saved as CMYK. If, on the other hand, you work in an RGB workflow, building in RGB might be the best option and you could convert it to CMYK on-the-fly when printing. Again, keep your color expectations low because moving back and forth between these color spaces can cause changes to color. RGB has a color *gamut* of approximately 16 million colors, whereas the CMYK color space has a limited gamut of approximately 5,000 colors.

Content and Audience Considerations

When creating a presentation, your approach to content should center on "talking points." In other words, you're not trying to cram detail into a slide presentation, but broad bullet points from which to talk from. The content must be visual in nature and consistent from slide to slide (or page to page). Think about the audience and how they will see the presentation. The graphics should be consistent with branding, and the visual content should be able to be clearly seen by anyone in a room when projected onto a screen or wall.

Navigation Considerations

Navigating through the slide presentation should be easy—in fact, invisible to the audience. We've all attended presentations in which the presenter spent a great deal of time fumbling with the presentation itself, or the equipment, and it distracts from the content. So, be sure that navigating through the slides is easy. Universally accepted symbols for *last*, *next*, and *home* are strongly advised for the content (see Figure 8.1).

Because this is also an interactive presentation, you are planning to distribute this to individuals who can open this, take a tour through the presentation, and experience a variety of content. Be sure that the interactive elements are easy to understand and play and won't require advanced knowledge of usability. If you want users to play the movie, direct them with a caption under the movie frame with something like `Click the movie poster to start the movie`, as illustrated in Figure 8.2. Don't assume they understand what to do.

Equipment Considerations

If you plan to distribute this in a number of ways, you must accommodate all distribution methods. For slide presentation purposes, you will be using a projector, which is an RGB device. You might consider using RGB colors to reliably predict the projected color. Several types of projectors are available on the market, and resolution and color go hand in hand with expense. Smaller doesn't necessarily equate with better, but portability might win out over resolution and color. So gauge your expectations accordingly.

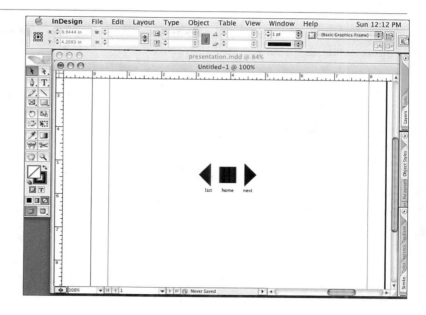

FIGURE 8.1 Universally accepted navigation symbols

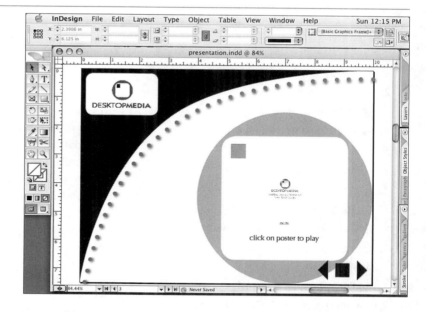

FIGURE 8.2 Example of instructions to play an interactive element.

Bear in mind that recipients of the digital file do not necessarily possess the same equipment you do, such as the same size monitor and video card, so try to format the presentation assuming an average size device and a limited color palette. Be prepared to handle technical support questions such as, "I can't hear the sound, so what should I do?" or "How do I get to the next slide?" If you are distributing this file as an email attachment, you might consider offering some directions and minimal desktop configuration standards for running the interactive presentation.

Printing Considerations

Finally, you might want to print the slide presentation as companion hand-outs or as part of a media kit. This presentation is 10" × 7.5" and can easily be centered on standard letter-size stock. As long as color expectations are realistic, you should print it on a color output device for greater impact.

Project:
An Interactive Presentation

We'll be creating a presentation in 15 easy steps:

STEPS ▼

1. Setting up your document format
2. Setting up master pages
3. Creating multiple masters
4. Tagging elements with color
5. Working with the pen tool
6. Adding more pages
7. Working with libraries
8. Creating layers
9. Adding a heading and bulleted text
10. Creating style sheets
11. Adding library elements
12. Adding animation and movies
13. Creating hyperlinks for icon navigation
14. Printing a composite proof
15. Exporting a PDF

STEP 1 ▼
Setting Up Your Document Format

Launch InDesign and go to the File pull-down menu. Select New, Document and fill out the New Document window as indicated in Figure 8.3. You will be creating a landscape layout.

FIGURE 8.3   Fill out the window as indicated.

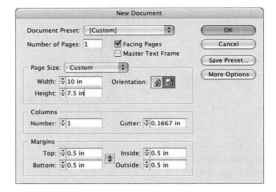

Orient yourself to the layout, and set up your workspace as you would like. We will be creating master pages for the title slide as well as the basic slides that follow the title. Additionally, we will be creating icons that will assist individuals navigating through the presentation. To accommodate these goals, we will work with the Pages palette and the Library palette. Let's start with the Pages palette.

STEP 2 ▼
Setting Up Master Pages

Go to the Window pull-down menu and open the Pages palette. You are going to modify your *master page*. Double-click Master A at the top of the palette. This will be your master for the opening or title slide as well as your closing slide. Create a graphic frame that fits the entire page and select File, Place. Then navigate to your project files and select `DM_BGRD_DUO.eps`. You will notice immediately it doesn't fit the frame. Go to the Object pull-down menu and select Fitting, Content to Frame. Because this will become a muted background, we will not be concerned about raster resolution considerations.

Now let's create a rectangle with the following dimensions: w: 4.5", h: 3.5". Fill the object with the color swatch called Paper; this is the mechanism InDesign uses to convey the status of white or knockout. With the rectangle still selected, go to the Object pull-down menu and select Corner Effects. Select the Rounded effect and enter a size of .5". Click OK.

Go to the File pull-down menu, select Place, navigate to your projects folder, and select `DMLogo.eps`. Select all three elements (by holding down the Shift key and clicking each element, one at a time) and align them vertically and horizontally using the alignment buttons in the Control palette or the Alignment palette (see Figure 8.4).

FIGURE 8.4   **The finished master page A.**

STEP 3 ▼
Creating Multiple Masters

Now that you've edited master page A, let's create another master. Go to the Pages palette, access the palette menu, and select New Master. Fill out the window as indicated in Figure 8.5.

FIGURE 8.5   **Fill out the window as indicated and click OK.**

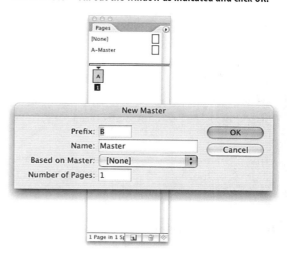

Double-click Master B at the top of the Pages palette. We will use Master B for the majority of the slides in this presentation. We will create a border on Master B to visually anchor the slide as well as a repeating graphical element to anchor our content or media.

Create a large circle with these dimensions: w: 6", h: 6". Tuck it into the lower-right corner at the following x,y coordinate: 4,1.5.

STEP 4 ▼
Tagging Elements with Color

Open the Swatches palette; at the bottom of your list, you should see a newly imported spot color. Apply the spot swatch color that was imported with the logo, PMS 8322, to the large circle and apply a tint of 50% so that it looks faded.

Draw a square from the center out by positioning your cursor over the center point of the large circle and holding down the Option key (Mac) or Alt key (Windows) and Shift key as you draw. You will create a perfect square from the center out. Stop short of the circle's edge, and then fill this square with the color Paper. Go to the Object pull-down menu and select Corner Effects, Rounded, .5". Select the circle and the square and center these objects both horizontally and vertically to each other.

Draw a small square, .5" on all sides, positioned at 5.15, 2.6. Fill it with black and tint it 50% as well.

This element will frame the content of each slide. See Figure 8.6 to gauge your progress so far.

FIGURE 8.6   **The faded logo.**

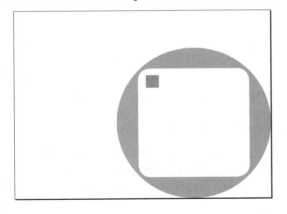

STEP 5 ▼
Working with the Pen Tool

Create an element in the upper-left corner to anchor the opposite side of the slide. I did

this by taking the Pen tool and clicking the lower-left corner of the slide, clicking the upper-left corner, clicking the upper-right corner, clicking and dragging a curve point between the two corners, and then closing the shape by clicking the original starting point. Fill this with black. Use Figure 8.7 as a guide for creating this element.

Create a rounded rectangle at the following coordinates and dimensions: x: .15", y: .15", w: 2.5", y: 1.5". Fill it with white, and place the DMLogo.eps on top of this rectangle. You will have to scale it 50% for it to fit. Select both the rectangle and logo and align the elements by centering them both horizontally and vertically.

I have added one more sweeping element. Select the Pen tool and click and drag a curve point in the lower-left corner of your slide. Click and drag another curve point in the upper-right corner of your slide. Stroke this vector with 10 points, dot style; tag it with the spot color; and apply a drop shadow using the default settings.

Your master page B should look like Figure 8.8.

STEP 6 ▼
Adding More Pages

You can add more pages to your layout a couple of ways. You can drag and drop a master into the main body of the Pages palette, or you can go to the palette menu and select Insert Pages. Use either method to insert six pages after page 1, based on the B master. Then add an eighth page based on the A master. Figure 8.9 shows what the Pages palette should look like when you're done.

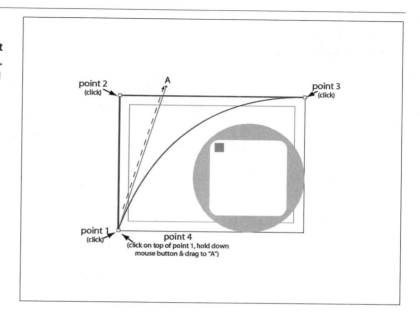

FIGURE 8.7   1. Click to start the shape. 2. Click (don't drag) for the second point. 3. Click (but don't drag) for the third point. 4. Click and drag on top of point #1 to create the curvature.

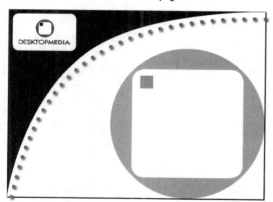

FIGURE 8.8   The finished Master page B.

STEP 7 ▼
Working with Libraries

Let's turn our attention to repeating graphical elements, namely the navigation icons we will use. We'll create a *library* for these elements and introduce you to this interface.

Go to the File pull-down menu and select New, Library. Give it a name such as **navigational icons** and place it in your projects folder for Chapter 8. A new, floating palette named navigational icons should appear in your window, as shown in Figure 8.10. Now let's make some icons

Select the Rectangle tool and click with it somewhere on your pasteboard. A dialog box will appear; type *.5"* for both the width and height and fill this square with black. Select the Delete Anchor Point tool, hidden under the Pen tool in the Tool palette and delete one of the points on your square. You now have a triangle! Rotate the triangle so that it points to the left. Drag and drop this icon onto your library and name it **previous page**.

 NOTE

To name a library item, double-click the small thumbnail in the Library palette to open the Item Information dialog box. Name your item and click OK.

FIGURE 8.9 The Pages palette after adding the necessary pages based on the corresponding masters.

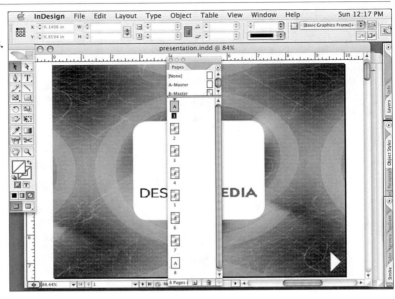

FIGURE 8.10 The empty Library palette.

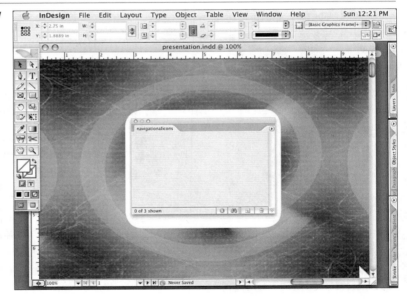

Go to the Edit pull-down menu and copy your triangle. Next, go back to the Edit pull-down menu and select Paste in Place. Go to the Window pull-down menu and select Object & Layout, Transform. Using the Transform palette menu, select Flip Horizontal. Drag and drop this triangle into your library and name it **next page**. Finally, create a .5" black square, drag and drop it into the Library palette, and name it **home**. You now have navigational icons you can drop into place (see Figure 8.11 for the finished page). Later we'll create hyperlinks for them.

FIGURE 8.11   Your navigation icons in the Library palette.

STEP 8 ▼
Creating Layers

Now, we're going to manage the elements on our slides with *layers*. Open the Layers palette and you will see Layer 1. Double-click Layer 1 and rename it **background**. Let's create a new layer called content by either using the Palette menu or clicking the new layer icon at the bottom of the Layers palette. Finally, create another new layer and name it **navigation** (see Figure 8.12).

FIGURE 8.12   This is how the Layers palette should look.

 TIP

Layers are an organizational tool. People are often intimidated by layers or unaware of their existence. The Adobe InDesign CS2 Layer palette is easy to use and allows you to gather like elements together in a stack. I often create layers such as background, type, and images. When I don't want to see some of them, I turn off the eyeball in the respective layer. If I have things just the way I like them, I lock the layer. They are useful because you can create them at any time and move elements to them to separate and organize the elements.

STEP 9 ▼
Adding a Heading and Bulleted Text

Double-click page 2 in the Pages palette; it should look like the master page B we just finished.

 NOTE

All page 1s are tagged with master A. Even if you never use master pages, page 1 will always be formatted with master A.

Click the content layer and then draw a text frame large enough to fit the rectangle with rounded corners on your page 2 layout.

Type a title beside the 50% black square and format it as you see fit. The font should be consistent with your company standards. I've used Optima, 36 points, right-aligned. I am leaving the text black. Insert a return or two. Check your work against Figure 8.13.

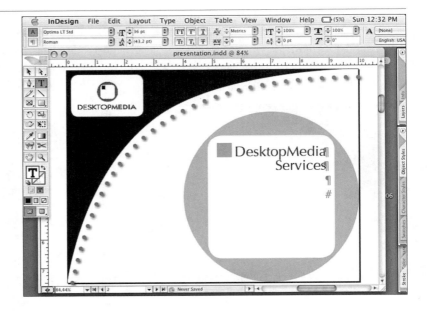

FIGURE 8.13 The slide width heading and returns; note that the carriage returns are red because the content layer is red.

For the body of the slide, the content should probably reflect the upcoming slides. Like an outline, these main bullets will become the headings of the subsequent slides. We will make a bulleted list, but you could also make it a numeric list if you want.

STEP 10 ▼
Creating Style Sheets

You can find a bullet you like by going to the Glyphs palette and selecting a typeface you want you use for your headings. Again, I've chosen Optima 36-point type, 36-point leading, right-aligned. Type some headings—I've used the services of my company. If you like the way this looks, you can create a style sheet. Select the formatted text, go to the

Paragraph Style palette, select New Style, give it a name, and click OK. You've now created your own new style sheet (see Figure 8.14). Now for future slides, you can simply type your text and tag it!

STEP 11 ▼
Adding Library Elements

Navigate to page 1, click the navigation layer, and then drag and drop your next page library element down to the lower-right corner of your slide. It will probably be difficult to see, so apply a fill of Paper to this triangle. Your title slide is complete and should look like Figure 8.15.

Navigate to page 2 and add all three icons to the bottom-right corner of your slide. See Figure 8.16 for the completed slide.

FIGURE 8.14 The new paragraph style sheet.

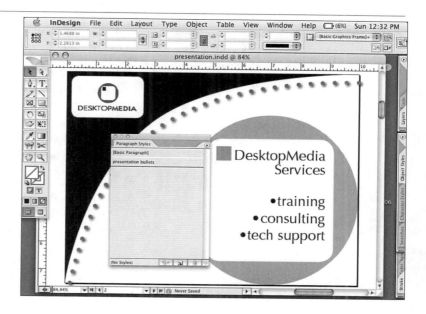

FIGURE 8.15 Slide one completed.

STEP 12 ▼
Adding Animation and Movies

Navigate to page 3. Now we are going to add a brief Flash animation. Click the Content layer, go to the File pull-down menu, and select Place. Navigate to your project files

folder and select DMintro_01.swf from the list of files. Click somewhere on your pasteboard to work with the movie. Later you'll move it into position on the page. Scale DMintro to fit in the opening on the right side of the slide. With the movie selected, go to the Object pull-down menu and select Interactive, Movie Options.

FIGURE 8.16 Slide two completed.

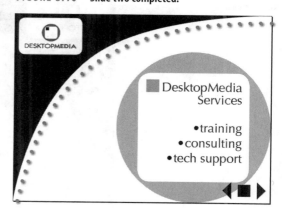

Here you can control how the movie looks, control how it is played, or replace it with another movie. First, select Movie Frame As Poster under Options; then browse for a frame. See Figure 8.17 to fill out your remaining options for slide three.

FIGURE 8.17 **Fill out your movie options as shown.**

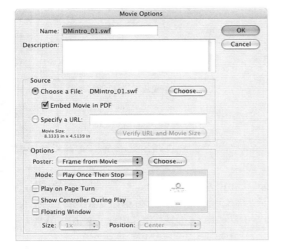

Now you need to add a little instruction so that the recipient will know what to do once inside the PDF. Create a caption under the movie with a text box and tell the audience to click the movie to play it.

You have just placed an interactive element on your page, and although you can't play the movie in InDesign, you will be able to after you make this layout a PDF. Add your three navigation icons to the lower-right corner of your slide (see Figure 8.18 for the completed slide).

Slides one, two, and three are now complete. The next four slides should be constructed as follows:

> **⊗ NOTE**
>
> Be sure that, before you place content on the slide, you select the content layer. Before you place a navigation icon on your layout, select the navigation layer.

▶ Slide four will contain information about our training. Create a text box to approximately fit the rounded white square. Type in the heading **Training** and format it as Optima, Roman, 36 points,

FIGURE 8.18 **Slide three completed.**

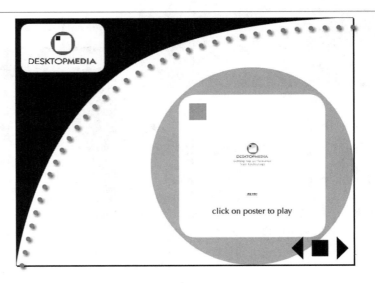

CHAPTER 8: Putting Together an Interactive Presentation

right aligned. Add a carriage return and type in training topics on the next seven lines. Each should start with a bullet and include the following topics: **Digital Workflow**, **CSR Bootcamp**, **Preflight**, **InDesign**, **Illustrator**, **Photoshop**, and **Acrobat**. Format these lines as Optima Roman, 24 points, right aligned.

► Slide five will contain a QuickTime movie of a presentation. Place the movie, DESKTOP_Cate.mov, somewhere out on the pasteboard and then drag to the inside of the large opening of the logo and place it under the 50% gray square. You might choose to scale to fit, but this can affect the quality of the playback. Go to the Object pull-down menu; select Interactive, Movie Options; then fill out the window according to Figure 8.19.

FIGURE 8.19   The Movie Options settings.

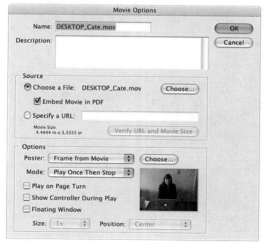

Again, make sure, via a text box caption, that you instruct the viewer how to play the movie by clicking it. Simply draw a text box on your pasteboard and type **Click on image to play movie!** Format the text with Optima Roman, 16

points. Drag the box and place it to the right of the 50% grayscale square.

► Slide six will contain more information, this time on our consulting services. Format slide six as you did slide four. Create a text frame that will fit, approximately, within the large square with rounded corners, but initially draw the text frame somewhere out on the pasteboard. For the heading, type **Consulting** and format it with Optima Roman, 36 points, right aligned. Type a carriage return and add the following items on the next six lines: **workflow**, **skills assessments**, **technology assessments**, **software selection**, **best practices**, **pdf**. Format each of these lines with Optima Roman, 24 points, right aligned.

► And slide seven contains content about our tech services. It will look like slides four and six. Create a text box on the pasteboard. Type in the heading **Tech Support** and format it as before. The following lines should include **onsite**, **Remote support**, **Desktop: mac & pc**, **Server: osx & windows**, **Infrastructure**, **Application**, **Output devices**.

Slides two through seven should have all three library elements lined up as follows: previous page, home, next page. Navigate to slide two and line up these icons in the lower-right corner. Select all three icons and copy them to the clipboard. Navigate to the next slide and paste text in place from the Edit pull-down menu. Execute this for each slide. On slide eight (the last slide), execute the paste in place but delete the last triangle (next page) because there is no next page. Select the remaining two icons and fill them with Paper swatch.

Click through all eight slides and make sure that everything looks consistent.

Creating Hyperlinks for Icon Navigation

After all the slides are in place and will not be moved around, it's time to add the hyperlinks to the navigation icons. Navigate to the first page in your file and open the Hyperlinks palette. With the icon on page 1 selected, either select New Hyperlink from the Hyperlinks palette menu or click the New Hyperlink button at the bottom of the palette and fill out the window as shown in Figure 8.20.

FIGURE 8.20 **Hyperlink options.**

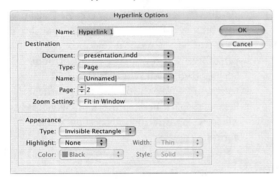

 NOTE

When the user clicks the icon, you want the presentation to advance to the next page (page 2) and fit that next page in the window, no matter what the size.

Click OK. One hyperlink down, 20 to go!

Navigate to page 2, which will have three hyperlinks. Select the first icon (previous) and

create a new hyperlink—only this time you want it to hop back to page 1 and fit in the window.

Select the middle icon (home) and create a new hyperlink. Home will always link to page 1.

Select the last icon; create a new hyperlink; and select page 3, Fit in Window.

Repeat these steps for the next five slides, with the previous icon hopping back a page, the next icon hopping forward a page, and home always hopping back to page 1.

The last slide will have only a previous icon and a home icon. See Figure 8.21 for the finished Hyperlinks palette.

FIGURE 8.21 **The finished Hyperlinks palette.**

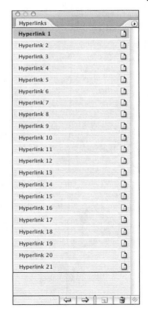

Save your work.

At this point, your presentation is complete.

STEP 14 ▼
Printing a Composite Proof

You might want to print a copy of this and look at it on paper. Go to the File pull-down menu and select Print. Choose the appropriate settings for the printer that is available to you. On the General tab, go to the File pull-down menu and select Print. Again choose the appropriate settings for the printer available to you. On the General tab, choose one copy. On the Setup tab select 8.5" × 11" and Horizontal orientation. Center your output, but leave the Scale setting alone. On the Marks and Bleed tab, turn on crop marks. On the Output tab, if possible, print a color composite (CMYK) output for your work; if not, choose Grayscale. On the Graphics tab, the default settings should work. The remaining tabs can be ignored for now. Print and review your proof, make any necessary adjustments, and save your changes. Then print it again.

When everything meets with your approval, it's time to export your presentation as a PDF, open the PDF, and test your interactive elements.

STEP 15 ▼
Exporting a PDF

Go to the File pull-down menu and select Export. Make sure that the format choice is for PDF, name the resulting file, and navigate the file to your finished projects folder. Fill out the dialog box per Figure 8.22.

🚫 CAUTION

Exercise caution when using the Flash file in this project or any project because you must have Acrobat or Reader 6.0 or above for the animation to play properly. Also, when you include interactive elements in your PDF, you should embed (as shown in the screen capture) those interactive elements for portability's sake rather than linking them and having to carry around movie and animation resource files.

Open your PDF and inspect it for both content and interactive elements. You should be able to click the icons and move through your slides as you intended. You should also be able to play the movies by clicking them.

❈ NOTE

If you own a full version of Acrobat, experiment with the full-screen view (slide presentation mode). You can make it self-running as well with page transition options.

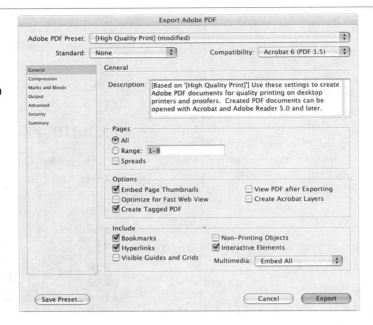

Final Thoughts

In this project you've picked up some unique and intermediate layout skills. You've worked with some new InDesign features as well. Most importantly, you've constructed a common presentation using the same tool you would use for page layout—how efficient!

Important concepts to keep in mind include

▸ Remember to keep your slides simple and graphic in nature. You are only creating content for talking points, not detail.

▸ If this presentation is to be distributed, interactive elements can engage the recipient, so think about enriching the experience with sound, animation, or movies.

▸ Hyperlinking can add to the interactive experience by taking the end user through the presentation in a nonsequential way, and they are extremely useful navigational elements in any independent presentation.

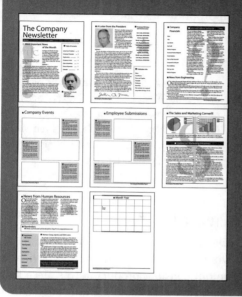

About the Project

In this chapter you will learn how to create a newsletter for your company. You will create it in such a way as to develop a template for reuse. You will be able to deliver it printed offset using a commercial print service provider, printed in-house using a digital output device, or via PDF.

Prerequisites

It would be helpful if you had a basic understanding of page layout, including using the Tool palette, formatting text, and performing basic page formatting skills.

@work resources

Please visit the publisher's website to access the following Chapter 9 files:

▶ **finished projects**

▶ **Project_files [Chart1.eps, Chart2.eps, Logo.eps, Pete.tif, Ed.tif]**

Planning the Project

The newsletter you will create in this project can be delivered in a variety of ways. It serves an internal communications purpose, but it could also be used to acquaint a potential customer with your company or acquaint investors to your company culture. Obviously, you will construct your company newsletter with your primary customers in mind: your fellow employees.

You need to consider not only content, but also style. A company newsletter is often the primary way a company communicates a lot of information all at once. It can also be placed on the company *intranet*, or portions can be doled out via email.

The newsletter you will construct will deliver information on all aspects of your company, but feel free to adapt your template to content that is most appropriate for your company. I have included information from HR, sales and marketing; product development and engineering; the president or CEO; and important dates and reminders.

Remember that, when developing your newsletter, it is more than likely a repeat publication. You should therefore develop a format with icons that are readily recognizable, a format and icons that give it character and that are unique to your company and this publication. So, in addition to logos, you will probably use the library you created for your brochure project. Additionally, in this chapter, we will cover the new feature of InDesign CS2—*object styles*. Object styles, like all saved styles, give your publication consistency of formatted elements throughout. Whether you use libraries or object styles, both features assist you in developing consistent-looking objects throughout your publication.

Because different areas in the newsletter are devoted to different departments, you will likely be working with contributing writers for the newsletter. You will have to work with these contributors to ensure that you receive appropriate text files.

> ### ⊗ NOTE
>
> You will have a couple of choices for this project. You can use the Fill with Placeholder Text command, or you can ignore those steps, opting to import a text file and formatting them with the style sheets you will develop. We will discuss the unique steps you have to take to clean up imported text.

Production Choices

Depending on the number of newsletters and your available internal output devices, you might consider producing this piece in-house. If you have a device capable of folding and stapling, this eight-page newsletter could be accomplished by printing on two tabloid-size pages, folded in half and stapled. I have deliberately avoided bleeding elements so that it could be produced in-house. Be mindful of the fact that, if you choose to print this in-house as suggested, you will have to rearrange your pages into *printers pairs* so they print in the correct sequence for binding.

In addition, you can export this document out as a PDF and give it to your webmaster to post on your company intranet. If this is the case, consider some navigational elements for the recipients (for example, hyperlinks for moving through the document).

Although the project you will construct assumes in-house digital, keep your color expectations realistic. If you'll be distributing it via PDF, there's no telling how your newsletter might be read or printed, but more than likely it will be grayscale. If you're producing it with a commercial printer and budget is a consideration, reduce your layout to two colors.

Distribution Choices

Odds are, this will be delivered via internal mail, the least expensive of your hard copy options. If this is to be mailed via the USPS, I have provided guidance for a self-mailer with a data merge on the back self-cover. Again, if this is to be distributed via PDF, keep your resolution set to 72ppi (small file size and low-quality output); however, if it is to be printed by the recipient, laser (print, not press) quality should be sufficient.

Stock, Binding, and Finishing

Your paper choice should fold and staple easily. Remember that a coated stock makes colors more vibrant. To keep things simple, don't place images through the fold.

Project: Newsletter

We'll be creating a newsletter in 20 easy steps:

STEPS ▼

1. Arranging windows
2. Setting up your document format
3. Creating the masthead
4. Creating tabs
5. Using the Glyphs palette
6. Creating text wrap
7. Formatting master pages with auto page numbering
8. Creating object styles
9. Using display performance
10. Creating a table
11. Importing and cleaning up copy from text files
12. Back to the layout
13. Creating type outlines
14. Creating tab leaders
15. Creating a color composite proof
16. Managing horizontal space with kerning
17. Managing horizontal space with tracking
18. Managing horizontal space with justification
19. In-house digital production
20. Creating a PDF for alternative distribution

STEP 1 ▼
Arranging Windows

These last few projects are going to get more complicated. You might want to navigate to the finished projects folder and open my version of the finished newsletter as a reference alongside your project file, as well as use the screen captures throughout this chapter. When you eventually have two windows open (my file and yours), go to the Window pull-down menu and select Arrange (see Figure 9.1). Experiment with your options based on your available workspace/monitor size.

STEP 2 ▼
Setting Up Your Document Format

Launch InDesign and go to the File pull-down menu. Select New, Document and fill out the New Document window as indicated in Figure 9.2. You will be creating an eight-page portrait layout with a three-column grid.

FIGURE 9.1   Open the layout
using the Window, Arrange,
Tile command.

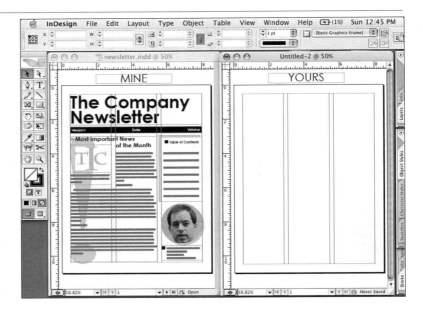

FIGURE 9.2   Fill out the window as indicated.

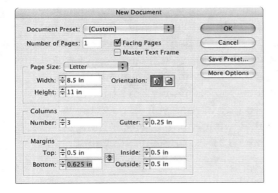

We're going to start by laying in the structure of your document, specifically the repeating elements. When I say *repeating elements*, I'm not just referring to elements placed on the master pages, but also elements that will repeat in every issue.

Those elements include the masthead, the table of contents, the letter from the editor, financials, a calendar of events, mailing information, and so on.

STEP 3 ▼
Creating the Masthead

Let's start with the *masthead*. Create a text box with the following coordinates and dimensions: x: .5", y: .5", w: 7.5", h: 1.8125". Type in your company newsletter masthead. I've used The Company Newsletter formatted in Century Gothic bold, 72 points, and 64-point leading. Note: I created a soft return (Shift-Return) so that my masthead takes up two lines.

Below the masthead, you will create a slug for publication information, including volume, date, and version. See Figure 9.3 for an example. Create a text box with the following coordinates and dimensions: x: .5", y: 2.425", w: 7.5", h: .375".

FIGURE 9.3   **The masthead and slug.**

STEP 4 ▼
Creating Tabs

Let's create tab stops in this text box. Double-click inside the box to switch to the Type tool and then go to the Type pull-down menu and select Tabs. Drag the left indent to the .25" mark. Then click a center tab stop and click it at the 3.75" mark (or type **3.75"** for the x coordinate and press Return) to set the first tab. Now, select a right tab stop and click it at the 7.25" mark. Now close the Tab window and type **Version 1**; then tab to the center and type **Date**. Finally, tab to the right and type Volume **Volume 1**. Highlight the text and format it. I have chosen Century Gothic, 14 points, vertically centered. Color the text Paper and the background of the text box Black (or create spot company color and use it for the accent color throughout this project).

Your first page should look like Figure 9.4.

FIGURE 9.4   **Your progress on page 1.**

STEP 5 ▼
Using the Glyphs Palette

Now let's create the text box for the main story on the front page. Create a text box starting at x: .5", y: 3" and spanning the first two columns on the page; draw it to fit the bottom margin. I've used the headline Most Important News of the Month, but feel free to improvise. Likewise, I experimented with an element that would anchor every feature with a *dingbat*. You can find your character by using the Glyph palette and selecting a dingbat font. I've used a square Zapf Dingbat, followed by a space, followed by the headline formatted in Century Gothic Bold, 24 points (see Figure 9.5).

> **NOTE**
>
> Later in the project you can either use the Fill with Placeholder Text command found on the Type pull-down menu or import a supplied text file from any number of your contributors at the text insertion.

STEP 6 ▼
Creating Text Wrap

Draw a graphic frame to fit the upper-left corner of your text box, just below the headline, to fit the first column with the following coordinates x: .5", y: 3.5". Set the width to fit the column and set the height to 2.5". Place a text wrap around this picture box with a right offset of .25", but no offset on the top, bottom, and left offsets (use Figure 9.6 as a reference).

Create a text frame in the last column at the same y: 3" and with a height of 3.75". Type a square Zapf Dingbat and then type **Table of Contents**.

FIGURE 9.5   Using the Glyphs palette to insert a dingbat.

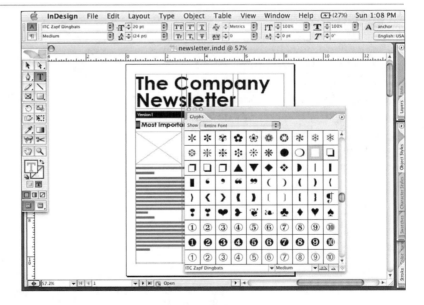

FIGURE 9.6   Your continued progress on page 1.

FIGURE 9.6   Your continued progress on page 1.

Just below the `Table of Contents` text, draw a circle graphic frame to fit the column. Below it create a text box for a caption and type **Employee of the Month**. I've formatted my text in Century Gothic, 12 points. Page 1 is shown in Figure 9.7.

FIGURE 9.7   Page 1 so far.

STEP 7 ▼
Formatting Master Pages with Auto Page Numbering

Go to the Pages palette and double-click Master Page A. Draw a text frame across the bottom of the left master with the following coordinates and dimensions: x: .5", y: 10.375", w: 7.5", h: .25". Use Century Gothic, 12 points and type **The Company Newsletter**. Add a comma and a space after `The Company Newsletter`. With the text insertion point next to the word `Page`, go to the Type pull-down menu and select Insert Special Character, Auto Page Number. You should see an *A* appear. Now we will create a rule above by going to the Paragraph palette menu. You can also select the Paragraph Control palette, pull down the menu to the far right of the Control palette, and select Paragraph Rules. Select Rule Above, 1 pt, and an offset of .15". Do the same thing for the right master, but change the paragraph alignment to right aligned. Your finished master page should look like Figure 9.8.

Go back to the Pages palette and double-click Page 1. Notice the new footer.

> ◎ **TIP**
>
> If you don't want a page number on the first page of your newsletter, remove that master item from page 1. You can't just select a master item on a regular document page by clicking it. You must hold down the ⌘ and Option keys (Mac) or Ctrl and Alt keys (Windows) and then click the master item and delete it.

FIGURE 9.8   Master page A
formatted.

Let's rough in the rest of the pages. Page 2 should contain a letter from the CEO, president, or editor. Create a text frame that fits the first two columns and from the top and bottom margins. Type **A letter from the President** (or CEO or Editor) using Century Gothic bold, 24 points. Press Return.

> ### ✖ NOTE
>
> Later in the project, you can either use the Fill with Placeholder Text command found on the Type pull-down menu or import a supplied text file from one of your contributors at the text insertion. Format this text as 12 points.

Create a picture frame to fit the first column, roughly 2 1/2" in height. Place the picture, Pete.tif, in the frame. With the Direct Selection tool, select the image and scale it to 50%. Using the Direct Selection tool, drag the image into position—the Direct Selection tool turns into a hand when you hover over the image.

The last column should contain two text boxes: Employee Birthdays and Anniversaries and Publication Info. Use Century Gothic bold, 12 points for this text. Use Figure 9.9 as a reference.

FIGURE 9.9   A roughed in page 2.

On page 3, the first column will contain the text Company Financials. Use my example and add text such as sales, profit, stock stats, new initiatives, and so on.

Create a text box across the top of the last two columns .5" high. I've used this area for new product/service information and have titled it Advanced Product or Service Concepts, formatted Century Gothic, 16 points, centered text (horizontally and vertically), with paper text, and a black fill. Underneath this box, create another text box across the last two columns, 6" deep. Make this text frame two columns, with a gutter of .25" by going to the

Object pull-down menu and selecting Text Frame Options.

Finally, create a text frame across the bottom of the page, starting at y: 7.265 " and fitting all the margins. I've titled this section News from Engineering, formatted it in Century Gothic bold, 24 points. Press Return, and change the type to Adobe Garamond Pro, 12 points. Fill the box with placeholder text, select the first paragraph, and create a drop cap using the Control palette. Use Figure 9.10 as a reference.

FIGURE 9.10   A roughed-in page 3.

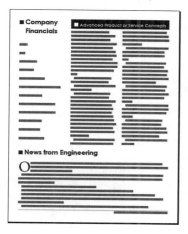

Pages 4 and 5 are the *center spread* of the newsletter, and I've devoted them to pictures, with page 4 for company events and page 5 for employee submissions. Because most shots are horizontal in orientation, I've drawn three graphic frames on each page with corresponding caption boxes.

STEP 8 ▼
Creating Object Styles

Let's explore a new feature with InDesign CS2. We are going to create an object style for the caption boxes. Drop in your graphic frames as I have done in Figure 9.11. Essentially, each graphic frame is two columns wide and approximately 2 3/4 " deep. There are three frames on each page—don't worry about being exact. Create a caption box to the right of the first picture box and format it as you would like.

I've filled it with 20% black and created a text inset using Text Frame options in the Object pull-down menu. I developed the text using Adobe Garamond Pro italic, 12 points and have saved that text as a paragraph style called Caption.

Creating Nested Styles

If you look at Figure 9.11, you'll notice a dingbat character at the beginning of each caption. You can insert a glyph each time you need one, or you can create a nested style to accomplish this. Highlight your first dingbat and create a character style; call it Caption Intro. Now go to the Paragraph Styles palette and double-click your caption style. Click the Drop Caps and Nested Styles option. Select Caption Intro from the pull-down option. Select through 1 and then pull down to Character. Now, the next time you want to add the dingbat, click in your caption and apply the caption paragraph style.

Next, with the frame selected with the Selection tool, go to the Object Styles palette. Select the Palette menu, and then select New Object Style. Make sure all your options are turned on and label this new style **spread caption boxes** (see Figure 9.12 for guidance).

FIGURE 9.11 The inside spread of your newsletter roughed in.

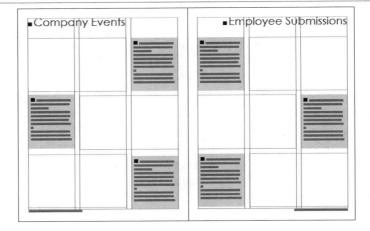

FIGURE 9.12 The New Object Style window.

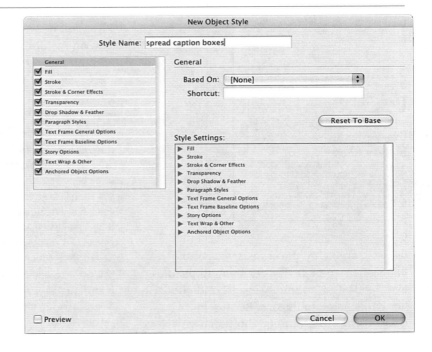

 NOTE

This new feature allows you to develop styles for your graphic elements, much like the Graphic Styles palette in Illustrator—but note all the different characteristics you can capture!

To test your new object style, create another text frame and, with it selected, choose your new style from the Object Style palette and watch the frame reformat. Draw four more frames aligned with the graphic frame on the spread for pages 4 and 5.

Finally, draw two text frames, one across the top of each page. On page 4, the coordinates and dimensions should be x: .5", y: .5", w: 7.5", h: .85". On page 5, the coordinates and dimensions should be x: 9", y: .5", w: 7.5", h: .85". Type **Company Events** on page 4 and **Employee Submissions** on page 5, both formatted Century Gothic Regular, 40 points. Text should be left aligned on page 4 and right aligned on page 5. Refer to Figure 9.11 for reference.

Page 6 will be devoted to sales and marketing. Across the top of the page create a text box that fits the top, left, and right margins and is .5" deep. Choose a title for the page (I used The Sales and Marketing Corner!!!) and format it Century Gothic, 30 points.

STEP 9 ▼
Using Display Performance

Below the title, create two graphic frames side by side. Each graphic frame should measure 3.5" × 2.35" with a y coordinate at 1.15". Import chart1.eps from the Chapter 9 projects folder into the first box and chart2.eps into the second box. For each box, use the Fit Content Proportionally command on the Object pull-down menu. Stroke the graphic frame with 1-point, black. Create a caption text box that spans from the left margin to the right margin. Fill it with placeholder text and apply the caption paragraph style you made previously.

 NOTE

Remember that, if your important images don't display very well, with the element selected, go to the Object pull-down menu and select Display Performance, High Quality.

Next, create a text frame that spans the width of your page from margin to margin with the following coordinates and dimensions: x: .5", y: 4.5", w: 7.5", h: .5". I've used the title Update on Marketing Initiatives. Highlight the text and format it Century Gothic bold, 24 points, horizontally and vertically centered aligned, fill with paper swatch. Fill the text frame with black.

Below this headline, create a two-column text frame with a .25" gutter. Fill it with placeholder text. Select the first paragraph and create a drop cap three lines deep. Your finished page should look like Figure 9.13.

Page 7 will be devoted to human resources. Create a text frame across the top of the page that fits the top, left, and right margins. Its coordinates and dimensions should be x: 9", y: .5", w: 7.5", h: .5". I've used the title News from Human Resources, Century Gothic Regular, 36 points. Create a text box with three columns, .25" gutters, and the following dimensions: x: 9", y: 1", w: 7.5", h: 3.5". With your text insertion point, select Adobe Garamond Pro, 12 points. Fill the box with placeholder text and create a drop cap for the first paragraph three lines deep.

Create a text box that spans the middle of your page with these dimensions: x: 9", y: 4.5", w: 7.5", h: 1". Use the Object pull-down menu and Text Frame Options and create a text inset .125" on all sides.

FIGURE 9.13   The roughed-in page 6.

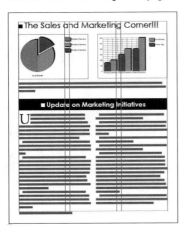

Note: This might be another good object style to create.

For the headline, type **Reminders:** formatted with Century Gothic Bold, 24 points. Press Return and change it to Adobe Garamond Pro bold, 12 points. In this area, I've added the location of the HR forms on the website. Stroke the box in 1-point, black.

Draw the next box in the first column with the following dimensions: x: 9", y: 5.75". Tag this box with your Spread Caption Boxes object style and then type the title **Important HR Dates**. Highlight the title and format it with Century Gothic Regular, 18 points. Press Return, change the point size to 14 points, and type some HR topics with 32-point leading.

Add a text box to the right two columns with the following dimensions: y: 5.75", h: 3.4". I've used the headline Workers Comp, Injuries, and OSHA news formatted Century Gothic Regular, 16 points. Press Return.

NOTE

Later in the project you can either use the Fill with Placeholder Text command found on the Type pull-down menu or import a supplied text file from one of your contributors at the text insertion.

Finally, add a frame just below the Workers Comp article to fit the two columns and fit the bottom margin. I've used the text Inspirational or Motivational Thought of the Month: formatted in Century Gothic Regular 14 points, paper, centered. On the next line of copy, the thought itself is formatted in Adobe Garamond Pro, 14 points, paper. Fill the box with black. Use Figure 9.14 as a reference and compare your own layout accordingly.

FIGURE 9.14   The roughed-in page 7.

STEP 10 ▼
Creating a Table

On the last page, or back self-cover, we'll create a calendar using the table feature. First, drag and drop a horizontal ruler guide to the 5.5" mark. This represents your fold mark should you self-mail. Click and drag a text frame that fits the left, top, and right margins and the fold rule. Go to the Table menu and select Insert Table. Fill out the window as shown in Figure 9.15.

FIGURE 9.15 The initial Insert Table window as described in the screen capture.

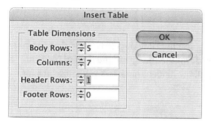

Select the first row of your new table and set the row height to .5". To do this, go to the Window pull-down menu and select Type & Tables, Table. With the row still selected, type .5" in the height field. Highlight the next five rows and set the row height to .875" in the Table palette. Highlight the first row (header row), open the Table Palette menu, and select Merge Cells. Click in the header row with the Text tool, center the text insertion point horizontally and vertically, and then type **Month Year**. Format the text Century Gothic bold, 26 points. Use Figure 9.16 as your reference.

> ⊗ **NOTE**
>
> If you're producing a self-mailer, use the area below the calendar for the return address and mailing address. You might even use the data merge feature we used earlier. This area will also contain the USPS indicia. If it's not a self-mailer, use this area for article overflows!

Congratulations, you've just roughed in your eight-page newsletter. Now we're going to fine-tune all the pages by adding graphical elements, developing style sheets, and discussing supplied text files and horizontal spacing strategies.

FIGURE 9.16 The last page roughed in.

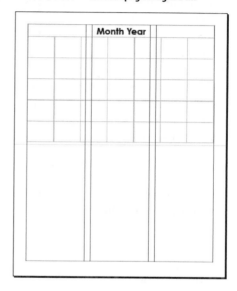

Move back to page 1. Let's create a couple of style sheets. The first paragraph of a published article or story typically does not contain an indent. Assuming you've filled the frame with placeholder text, select the first paragraph in your main text and create a new paragraph style using the Palette menu; name it **first paragraph**. Select the second paragraph and create a first-line indent of 12 points. With the paragraph still highlighted, create another new style sheet called **body copy**. Highlight the remaining copy and tag it with body copy. Go through the remaining pages, highlight each page's first paragraph, and tag it with the first paragraph style sheet. Highlight the remaining paragraphs throughout the rest of the pages and tag them with the body copy style sheet.

STEP 11 ▼
Importing and Cleaning Up Copy from Text Files

If you are importing copy from an outside source, you are virtually at the mercy of your supplier. What am I referring to? Specifically how well they created their text file. Ideally, you would like your supplier to type in their copy with no formatting, except for a carriage return between paragraphs and a spell check. That's it. However, this is not realistic. So what follows are some tips to assist you in cleaning up the text.

Import your copy into a text box using the File, Place command. Turn on Show Import Options and review your choices. I recommend the following setup, shown in Figure 9.17.

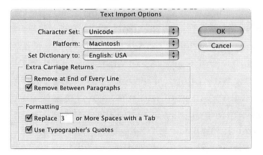

Turn on Show Hidden Characters on the Type pull-down men, and then examine the imported copy. Common errors include double carriage returns between paragraphs, spaces or tabs for indentation, and double spaces at the end of each sentence (which is correct for word processing but incorrect for typesetting).

These *hidden characters* can be found and replaced using the Find/Change command on the Edit pull-down menu. You find and change not only normal text, but hidden characters as well. For example, instead of filtering them out through import options, you can use the Find/Change command and find every double return and change it to a single return (see Figure 9.18).

FIGURE 9.18   Use the Find/Change command on the Edit pull-down. Pull down the triangle to the right of the Find field and view all the hidden characters you can search for and change.

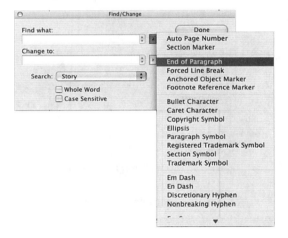

STEP 12 ▼
Back to the Layout

Create a text frame below the rectangular graphic frame on page 1—it will hold the caption for the image. Create a text wrap around the caption box just like the text wrap of the logo itself. Set no offset in the top, bottom, and left fields, but set a .25" offset on the right side. Tag this new text frame with your caption style sheet; then type in anything relevant.

Move to the last page, 8. Let's create a couple of styles for the calendar—one for the dates and one for the descriptions. Feel free to play around with one in an individual cell.

My date style is Century Gothic bold, 12 points. Save the style and name it **calendar date**. Now create another style with Century Gothic Regular, 10 points; save it as a new paragraph style; and name it **calendar description**.

STEP 13 ▼
Creating Type Outlines

Finally, you'll create some finishing touches to the layout using type outlines as modified graphics. You'll choose a text character, sizing it very large. Then you'll convert that character to vector art, which you'll add as graphical elements throughout the layout.

Throughout the newsletter, you are going to place oversized characters in 20% black placed behind significant stories. Let's take page 1. Out on the pasteboard, draw a rather large, vertically oriented text box. Type in an exclamation point and format that character as Adobe Garamond Pro, bold, 240 points. Select the frame itself, go to the Type pull-down menu, and select Create Outlines.

NOTE

If you still have the exclamation point selected when you create outlines, the result will be an anchored object within a text frame. Consequently, the shape will respond to text wrap situations. Instead, select the frame itself when creating outlines; then you'll have a freestanding element and the text frame will go away. You still have the ability to easily transform because it's grouped and has a group bounding box.

Now you can stretch the exclamation point to any size because it's no longer type but a graphical element. Fill the shape with 20% black and drag it over the main story. Go to the Object pull-down menu and select Arrange, Send to Back. Create two more elements for page 1—they will look like drop shadows. Create a rectangle slightly offset to the top and left of the table of contents (TOC) box. Fill with 20% black and send it to the back, behind the TOC. Create a circle slightly offset from the initial circle down and to the right. Fill it with 20% black and send it to the back. Check your work against Figure 9.19.

Go to page 2 and place a star behind the birthdays and anniversaries. Again, fill it with 20% black and send it to the back. Create another rectangle similar to the publication information one, only offset this one to the left and above the publication information box. Fill it with 20% black and send it to the back.

Go to page 3 and, like page 1, create a long, vertically oriented text box on the pasteboard. Type in a question mark and format it Adobe Garamond Pro, bold, 240 points. Create outlines, fill it with 20% black, and stretch it into a shape. Place the question mark between the last two columns and send it to the back.

Go to page 6 and draw a text frame on the pasteboard that is rather large and vertically oriented. Type in a dollar sign and format it as Adobe Garamond, bold, 240 points. Create outlines, stretch it into shape, position it in the middle of the page, and send it to the back.

Go to page 7 and draw a horizontal rule through the middle of the three-column story. Apply an 80-point stroke, a dot style, and 20% black. Drag it into position and send it to the back.

**FIGURE 9.19 The
exclamation point and circle.**

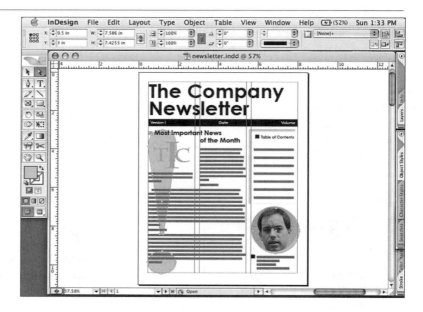

FIGURE 9.19 The exclamation point and circle.

STEP 14 ▼
Creating Tab Leaders

When all the elements are in place, just where you want them, you can go back to page 1 and fill out the table of contents. For the purposes of this short document, we'll create one manually. For the longer publications in the upcoming chapters, we'll use InDesign's TOC feature.

So, for now, insert a carriage return or two after the Table of Contents title. Set the paragraph alignment to left-aligned, reduce the type size to 12 points, and reduce the leading to 30 points. Go to the Type pull-down menu and select Tabs. You are going to create a tab stop with a dot *leader*. Select a right tab and click it at the 2" mark. In the Leader field, type a period and press Return to activate the field. Close the Tab window and begin typing the TOC items. First, type **Letter from**, and then

press the Tab key and type the page number. You should see the dot leaders appear and fill up to the page number. Press Return, type the next topic, press Tab, and then type in the page number. Do this for the remaining TOC items.

I've added the following thumbnails so you can see the finished pages collectively. Use Figure 9.20 to view the finished project pages.

Prior to printing, always save your document. In this case you might want to save it twice—once as a document and once as a template.

⊗ NOTE

The key elements of a template (which you can think of as a dummy publication) are the average number of pages, master pages, style sheets, colors, and repeating elements in every publication. When you open a template, all the necessary elements should be available to you so all you really need to concentrate on are importing text, tagging it, and placing images.

FIGURE 9.20 **The finished pages in sequential order.**

FIGURE 9.20 The finished pages in sequential order.

STEP 15 ▼
Creating a Color Composite Proof

Let's print a content proof. Go to the File pull-down menu and select Print. Choose the appropriate settings for the printer that is available to you. Then go to the File pull-down menu and select Print. Again choose the appropriate settings for the printer available to you. On the General tab, choose one copy. On the Setup tab select 8.5 " × 11 " and Vertical Orientation; leave the Scale setting alone. On the Marks and Bleed tab, turn off all the options. On the Output tab, if possible, print a color composite output for your work; if not, select Grayscale. On the Graphics tab, the default settings should work. The remaining tabs can be ignored for now. Print and review your proof, make any necessary adjustments, and save your changes. Print it again.

STEP 16 ▼
Managing Horizontal Space with Kerning

One of the last things you can tweak is the type, particularly after you create a proof and see your publication in print at the actual size. *Kerning* is typically executed on large type when pairs of characters look awkward. In the Kerning field either in the Control palette or Character palette, positive numbers add space between characters (see Figure 9.21) while negative numbers take space out (see Figure 9.22). The numbers are expressed in 1/1000 of an em space. An em space is the width of the letter *m* in the typeface and point size with which you are currently working. In the case of our masthead, the em space is a 72-point character. By doing nothing, you allow InDesign to automatically kern (called font metrics) using the kerning tables supplied by the font vendor. To override the metric setting, you can select Optical Kerning to allow InDesign to visually kern the pair of letters in question, or you can type your own number to override InDesign completely and kern to your own amount.

STEP 17 ▼
Managing Horizontal Space with Tracking

Essentially, *tracking* should be used only for special effect and not for horizontal space management. Typically, you will see it used to spread letters far apart or bring them close together. But it should never be used for copy fit, which is when you need to get that last line of text to fit in the box, which is currently overflowing, and you track it all to squeeze it in. See the effect of tracking on letters in Figure 9.23. Do you want the recipient to read the content? If so, don't make it more difficult! Tracking is a monospaced command, so it does not distinguish letter spacing from word spacing. It's therefore better to use letter and word spacing: Select Justification from the Paragraph palette's pull-down menu.

FIGURE 9.21 **The letters *M* and *P* have positive manual kerning.**

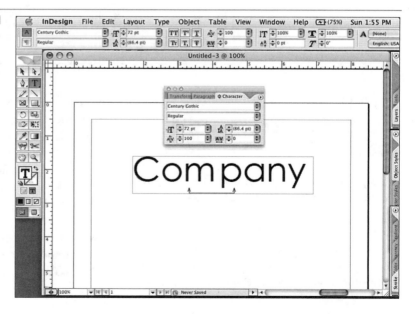

CHAPTER 9: Developing a Newsletter

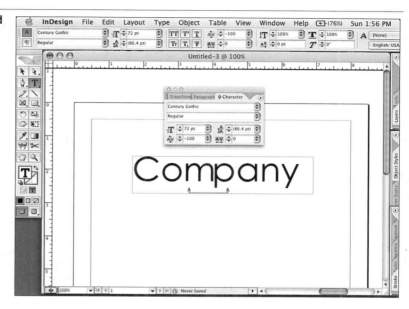

FIGURE 9.22 The letters *M* and *P* have negative manual kerning.

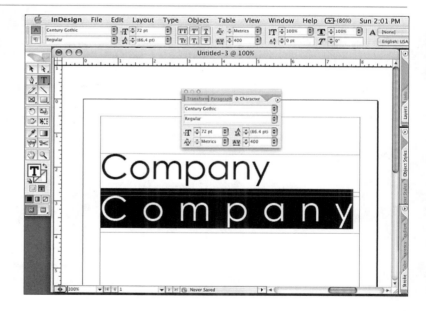

FIGURE 9.23 *Company* without tracking, and *Company* with tracking of 400, for special effect.

You can see the differences between unadjusted spacing, word spacing, and letter spacing in Figures 9.24–9.26

FIGURE 9.24 Paragraph spacing unadjusted.

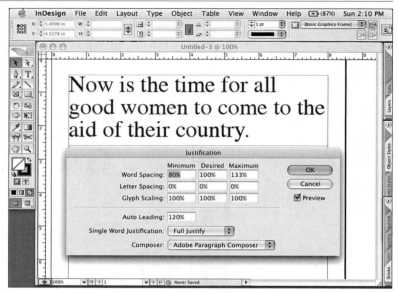

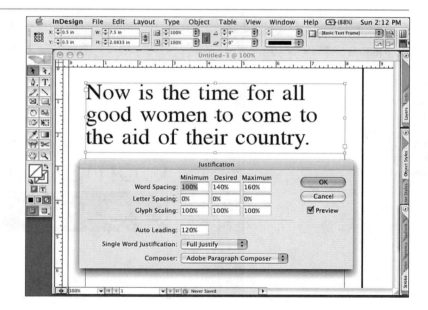

CHAPTER 9: Developing a Newsletter

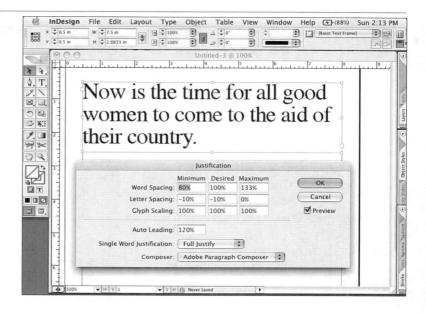

FIGURE 9.26 Paragraph spacing with less letter spacing only adjusted.

STEP 18 ▼
Managing Horizontal Space with Justification

First, don't assume your text needs to be justified for this command to apply. The term *justification* simply addresses horizontal spacing and alignment issues. You can adjust *letter spacing* separate from *word spacing* in this dialog box, and this is ideal. For all alignment options other than Justified Alignment, you use the Desired column to adjust your copy. Any number larger than 100% (which represents the spacing as is) adds space and any number less than 100% takes space out. Any number greater than 0% (which represents the spacing as is) adds space and any negative number 0% takes space out. If you are working with copy whose alignment is justified, you will work with the Minimum, Desired, and Maximum fields. This is because you must give InDesign a range to work with when you are dealing

with justified alignment because every line contains a different number of letters and words and still is forced to fit a fixed width. Therefore, you need to give InDesign a range of acceptability because every line will be treated differently.

STEP 19 ▼
In-house Digital Production

While I cannot account for the type of digital output devices, RIPs, and software you might have access to using software, it will be necessary to redistribute your pages from *reader's pairs* to simple *printer's pairs*. Printer's pairs are the pairs of pages in imposition (folding and binding) sequence. In the case of this newsletter, they are pages 8 and 1, pages 2 and 7, pages 6 and 3, and pages 4 and 5. I don't advise you to use InDesign to create printer's pairs; however, you can override master items (detach them) and turn off Allow Pages to Shuffle. Both of these options are found on the

Pages Palette menu. After turning these off, you can drag the pages into position. Again, I don't recommend this. This step is best executed by your commercial print service provider. If you still want to attempt a booklet for comping purposes, the bundled InBooklet plug-in will more than likely do the job, particularly for in-house digital production. With the layout complete, access InBooklet by going to the File pull-down menu and selecting InBooklet. Of the three tabs down the left side of the dialog box, the first tab (Layout) is where you choose your impostion style. For printer's pairs, select 2-up Saddle-stitch. This places the pages into pairs that will, when folded and stapled, read correctly. I recommend turning on the Save to Separate File option, as shown in Figure 9.27.

If no marks are necessary, select the Preview tab and navigate through your printer's pairs to ensure everything looks correct. Notice how the interior or middle spread, pages 4 and 5, remains the same. See Figure 9.28 for a reference. When you click OK, InBooklet creates a separate file for you to print from.

Another option is to export each page as an individual PDF and import the pages in printer's pairs in Acrobat. Or check out A Lowly Apprentice Production's (www.alap.com) new plug-in for Acrobat, Imposer Pro 1.0. The same developer of InBooklet for InDesign has created a similar plug-in for Acrobat. That way, no matter which application you develop your pages in, after they become PDFs, they can be imposed in Acrobat.

You will still need to be able to manage duplexing to produce this in-house, and many output devices that can fold and staple come with software that allow you to compile your pages as necessary.

FIGURE 9.27 **The InBooklet Layout tab.**

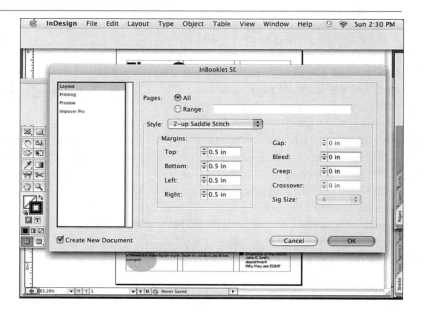

FIGURE 9.28 **The InBooklet Preview of imposed pages.**

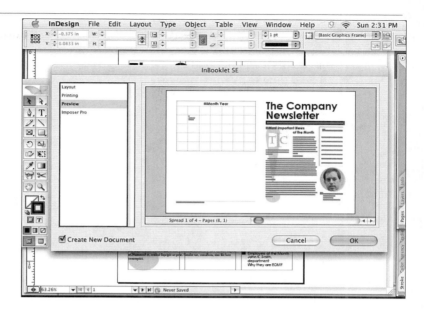

Your printer's pairs will always add up to one more than the total page count—for example, 8 + 1= 9, 2 + 7= 9, and so on.

STEP 20 ▼
Creating a PDF for Alternative Distribution

With your document open and already proofed, go to the File pull-down menu and select Export. Navigate your way to your Chapter 9 finished projects folder and name your PDF. At the bottom of the window, make sure the format is set to Adobe PDF; then click Save.

Select Preset, High Quality Print and click Export.

Final Thoughts

In this project you've executed probably the most often requested publication for production: the newsletter! This project added to your basic skill set with pagination, repeating elements, style sheets, character and nested styles, tables, and tab skills—that's a lot!

Important concepts to keep in mind include

- ▶ The method of production and delivery can be limited to internal resources and therefore a simple digital production; perhaps four pages with a basic fold will be your best option.

- ▶ If commercial offset is within your budget, allow your service provider to handle your imposition requirements so you only have to deal with layout and formatting.

▶ Consider all the elements you typically find in a newsletter. Develop basic styles for your text, and create icons you can use repeatedly that will develop meaning over time with your audience. Wrap all this into a template to save you time and increase consistency throughout your publications.

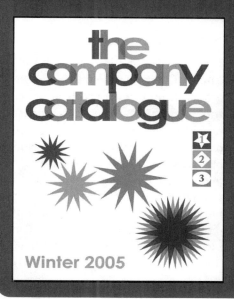

About the Project

In this chapter you will learn how to create a catalogue for your company's products or services. You will create it in such a way as to develop a template for reuse so you can deliver it in a number of ways. Along the way, you will work with spreadsheet data, engineering drawings, typographic features, master pages, and style sheets.

Prerequisites

It would be helpful if you had a basic understanding of page layout, including using the Tool palette, formatting text, and using basic page formatting skills.

@work resources

Please visit the publisher's website to access the following Chapter 10 files:

▶ **finished_projects**
▶ project files: **widget.eps, Catalogue.xls**

Planning the Project

The catalogue you will create with this project can be delivered in a variety of ways. It serves as an internal document (for anyone who must interface with a customer or distributor of your products and services) and can potentially land in front of a customer. Anyone who has had a shopping experience in which what they wanted wasn't in stock and had to be ordered has inevitably witnessed a clerk pulling out a catalogue from which to order. Everyday catalogues arrive in the mailbox for everything from clothes to seeds to hobbies...you name it, there's a catalogue for it.

What if your company doesn't produce a product, but a service? So does mine, and we have a catalogue for every type of service we perform with a brief description that sets our customers' expectations. Our catalogue is a training catalogue with all the various types of classes we offer. Catalogues are everywhere.

It will be important, once again, for you to consider your audience. With this type of publication, it is less important to consider the design or style of the piece (although it should be consistent with your image/brand) and is more important to ensure all the necessary content is available, easy to look up, and clearly described. Remember that this is a reference publication first, so pricing has to be consistent and correct. Organization is also important, so think about a table of contents or an index. Navigation icons and page numbers are also helpful.

It will also be important to release versions of your catalogue as new products or services come online or for those that are removed.

Your sales staff and distributors will come to rely on this document for accuracy. What type of information do they need access to, and how quickly does this information change?

Distribution Choices

The answer to that last question will significantly affect how many times you produce a catalogue and which production method you choose to use. If you are in an industry with high expectations of quality and color, or the product alone conveys affluence, you probably have a budget reserved for the production of your catalogue that includes a beautifully printed piece. If, on the other hand, pricing or product lines change frequently, you have probably investigated more cost-effective methods, such as PDF or HTML and distribution via the Web, FTP, or CD.

Managing Content

In any case, you have a significant amount of information to work with that is probably coming in from more than one department. Images or drawings might arrive from engineering, pricing might arrive from manufacturing, and content might arrive from marketing. You will have to manage text documents, spreadsheets, and illustrations. InDesign supports most file formats for import, but check before you begin if you suspect one of the departments submitting information might use an unsupported product. As an example, if you need to work with CAD or engineering files, you might need to investigate a filter or plug-in or open the file in a product such as Adobe Illustrator and convert it into a format that will work for you.

Production, Binding, and Finishing Considerations

Depending on the nature of the catalogue, a few things to consider include how many pages the catalogue will be. More than 64 pages will dictate something other than saddle stitching. When you get near 64 pages, the publication has a hard time remaining flat (because of the cumulative thickness of paper at the spine) and the publication's pages *creep*, meaning they don't all line up but creep backward with the inner pages protruding beyond the outer pages. If you are working on a large printed catalogue, you have to consider *perfect binding*. Talk to your print service provider about this. You will not have to do anything differently from this project, but your service provider will deal with the imposition differently.

Will this catalogue end up in a binder along with previous catalogues? If so, three-hole drilling might also factor into your layout. Make sure there is enough room in the *gutter* (binding area) of your layout to accommodate the drill. Bleed also adds to the cost because your printer must use a larger stock size to accommodate the bleed and trim. Perhaps you will produce the bulk of your catalogue in black and white and produce the cover in color. Speak with your service provider to find out whether they want you to build the cover in a separate file or will accept the cover and the remaining pages all in one file.

Finally, how will the recipients interact with the catalogue? Other than a look-up, will they use the catalogue to order from? Will the catalogue direct them to a phone number or a website for additional information or to place an order? In Chapter 11, "Making an Order Form," you will complete this project by creating an order form.

Project: Catalogue

We'll be creating a catalogue in 22 easy steps:

STEPS ▼

1. Setting up your document format
2. Creating multiple master pages
3. Creating custom columns
4. Creating tabs
5. Auto page numbering
6. Creating masters based on masters
7. Applying master pages
8. Creating the cover
9. Creating type outlines
10. Creating colors and applying blending modes
11. Transforming objects again
12. Creating Paragraph styles
13. Using the Next Style feature of paragraph styles
14. Creating anchored objects
15. Creating templates
16. Creating headers as TOC entries
17. Importing spreadsheets as tables
18. Editing tables
19. Creating a TOC
20. Preflighting your project
21. Creating a color composite proof
22. Creating a PDF for alternative distribution

These last few projects are going to get more complicated. You might want to navigate to the finished projects folder and open my version of the finished catalogue as a reference, as well as use the screen captures throughout this chapter.

STEP 1 ▼
Setting Up Your Document Format

Launch InDesign; go to the File pull-down menu; and select New, Document. Then fill out the New Document window as indicated in Figure 10.1. You will be creating a 16-page portrait layout with two columns.

FIGURE 10.1 **Fill out the window as indicated.**

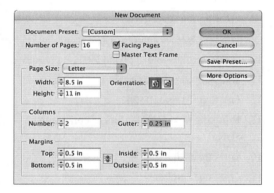

We're going to start by creating the structure by which you will lay out your template/document. First, we must consider master pages. Earlier in the chapter I talked about organizational structure. We will group three product lines into three categories and express those categories by creating three different master page sets, one for each category.

Go to the Pages palette and select Master Pages A. Go to the Palette menu and select Master Options. Leave the prefix alone, but the name should be **front/back matter**. Use the screen capture Figure 10.2 as a reference.

Click OK; you should see Master Pages A renamed in the palette. You will use this page for all pages except the body pages.

FIGURE 10.2 **The Pages palette.**

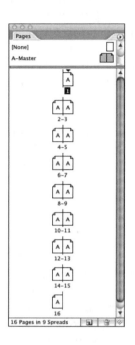

Double-click Master Pages A. We don't want columns in our *front matter* and *back matter*, so go to the Layout pull-down menu, select Margins and Columns, and change the number of columns to 1. Click OK. You should see A-front/back matter change. Double-click Page 1; it should be updated to reflect the change of no columns.

STEP 2 ▼
Creating Multiple Master Pages

Let's create *multiple master* pages. Go back to the Pages palette, select the Palette menu, and New Master. The Prefix for this master will be B, and the name will be service or product line 1 (see Figure 10.3). Click OK. Double-click Master Page B (note that the columns appear again and will continue to do so because you set this when you initially created the New Document). Once on Master Page B, we'll customize the columns.

FIGURE 10.3 **The New Master dialog box.**

STEP 3 ▼
Creating Custom Columns

Unlock the column guides by going to the View pull-down menu and selecting Grids and Guides. Deselect Lock Column Guides—now you are free to move them. Click and drag the column guide on the left page to the 2.5" marker, and click and drag the column guide on the right page to the 14.25" marker. Now lock the column guides.

STEP 4 ▼
Creating Section Tabs

Let's create tabs at the top of the pages to assist in navigating through the catalogue. Create a text box with the following coordinates and dimensions: x: −.125", y: .5", w: 2.625", h: .75". Type **Product Line 1**, format the tab, and reverse the type.

 TIP

Reverse type is a commonly used term for white type; it's "reversed out" of the black frame.

I've used Century Gothic bold, 24 points, centered horizontally and vertically, and tagged with a paper swatch. I've filled the background of the frame with black. Compare your work to Figure 10.4.

FIGURE 10.4 **The left and right masters with section tabs.**

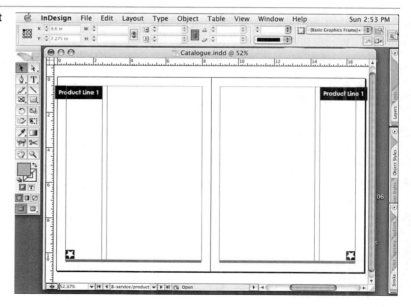

Create the same tab on the right B master using the following coordinates: x: 14.5", y: .5". (Hint: You can drag copy this element into position by pressing the Option key on the Mac or the Alt key in Windows, or you can use the Copy and Paste commands.)

STEP 5 ▼
Auto Page Numbering

Now, let's turn our attention to page numbering. Notice we didn't number the front matter and back matter masters. Only the body pages will be numbered, which is customary in most publications. We'll include the page numbering in a footer that will span the bottom of both masters.

Draw a text frame across the bottom of the left master B so it fits to the left and right margins but below the bottom margin. Set two tab stops by going to the Type pull-down menu and selecting Tabs. Set a center tab stop at the 4.25" mark and a right tab stop at the 7.5" mark. Type **Page** followed by an auto page number (insert this by going to the Type pull-down menu and selecting Insert Special Characters, Auto Page Number). You will see a *B* appear next to the word page. Press the Tab key and you should advance to the center of your text frame. Type the name

of your catalogue—I've used the company catalogue. Then tab again to the right side of the text frame and type **Winter 2005**, or whatever version you intend to publish. The text should flow to the left of the tab stop (see Figure 10.5).

FIGURE 10.5   The left master B so far.

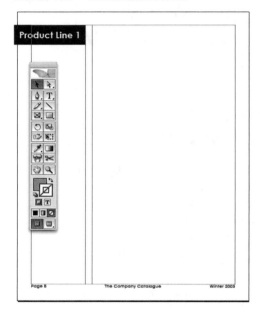

Now turn your attention to the right master. You need to mirror the footer on the right page, editing the positions of the text (from left to right, it should be Winter 2005 - The Company Catalogue - Page B), while keeping the tab stops intact.

Remember the icons we created for the brochure in Chapter 7? Open the brochure project and drag the three icons over to your new catalogue file. Change the background object to black and the foreground object to white, and then group them together. Scale them to 40% and place the star just above the page indicator on the left and right master B.

If you haven't created that project follow these steps:

Draw a square .5" in dimension and tag the fill black, no stroke. Create a star to fit inside the square and tag the fill paper, no stroke. Group the two together and place this icon above each page number.

For the next icon, create the same square (or copy the previous one) and fill it with black. Create a diamond to fit inside the square by creating a slightly smaller square and rotating it with the Rotate tool. Fill the diamond with paper; then group the two together.

For the last icon, create the same square and fill it with black. Fit an oval inside the square and tag it with paper; then group the two together.

NOTE

The star, diamond, and circle have become repeating elements in more than a couple publications in this book. If you see a pattern like that developing either by chance or deliberately, consider the use of *libraries* (as we did for the presentation project). If you have already created a library, just drag these icons into the library and label them—select File, Open, Library and find the navigation icons from the Chapter 8 finished projects folder. If you have not done that exercise, go to the File pull-down menu; select New, Library; and give the library a name, such as company library. A new palette appears. Drag each icon onto the palette and, after the icon is in the palette, double-click it and give it a name. Now you can drag and drop these icons from this independent palette/file anytime you need them. Libraries are great for repeating elements, repeating trade symbols or logos, and even that company address or mission statement you're sick of typing. Any kind of element can be dragged and stored in the library. You can even have multiple libraries, such as for each product or service line.

Next, remove all but the star icon from master page B, product/service line 1. Place two stars in opposing lower outside corners, one on each master, above the page number. Your finished master should look like Figure 10.6.

STEP 6 ▼
Creating Masters Based on Masters

The next master should be a breeze. Go to the Pages palette and select New Master, leaving the prefix at C and naming it **Service/Product line 2**. However, this time we will base this master on Master B, 2 pages. Click OK. You will see a new master appear with the name you gave it. Double-click this master. Remember that, to select a master item, you need to hold down ⌘–Shift (Mac) or Ctrl+Shift (Windows). Select the two tabs at the top of each page and edit the text to read **product line 2**. Change the icons to the diamonds at the bottom of each page.

For the last master, perform the same steps as previously mentioned, create a new master (Master D), and call it **Service/Product line 3** (base it on Master B, 2 pages). Click OK. Double-click this new master and change the tabs accordingly. In addition, change the icons to ovals—you can drag them from your library.

You should have a total of five masters now (see Figure 10.7).

FIGURE 10.6 **The finished master B pages.**

FIGURE 10.7 **The finished Pages palette.**

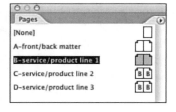

Much will depend on how you want to organize your products and services and the quantities and number of pages you have to deal with.

How do you format with a master? You can drag the master on top of the real page in the Pages palette. You can also select the page (or pages by Shift-selecting) in the Pages palette, go to the palette menu, select Apply Master, and select the appropriate master for the page or page range. See Figure 10.8 for an example.

STEP 7 ▼
Applying Master Pages

There are 16 pages in the Pages palette, all of them formatted with A. However, only the front matter and back matter should have this format. All the other pages should be formatted with the body masters. I've formatted pages 4–7 with Master B, pages 8–11 with Master C, and pages 12–14 with Master D.

Flip through your publication by double-clicking each page in the Pages palette.

The pages are now in place. Note how the off-center columns provide a structure by which the images will fall on the outside of each page, while the description and pricing will fall to the inside.

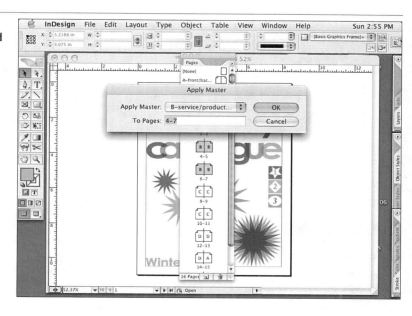

STEP 8 ▼
Creating the Cover

Let's take a break from the mechanical and have some fun. Let's talk about the *cover*. You can choose to do anything you want with the cover, but remember the production and budget considerations we spoke of at the beginning of the chapter. I've decided to make the interior of the catalogue black and white and the cover color. I'm not using images, but I'm going to build some graphics in InDesign and demonstrate some cool features at the same time. We're going to use color modes, transparency, text outlines, and the transform features of InDesign CS2.

Navigate to the cover (first page) of your publication. Let's start with the title of the catalogue. Mine is the company catalogue. Please don't worry about being exact here—and feel free to substitute and play with your own logo, company name, or branding.

I've created a text frame to fit the margins, about 4" deep, and typed my title on three separate lines. Highlight the copy and format it to the typeface you want—I've used Century Gothic bold. With the text still highlighted, tweak it a little by horizontally scaling it slightly so that it looks a little stretched. Now, make the type large enough to fill the box (see Figure 10.9 as a reference).

 TIP

I often use ⌘-Shift-> to size my text. Each time I press the < or > key, the type sizes up (or down) 2 points. This is a handy shortcut when I am unsure what type size is appropriate. However, you should not use ⌘ (Mac) or Ctrl (Windows) drag to resize the type by resizing the box the type is in. Why? If you try it, you end up with a bizarre decimal, such as 63.152 points. Do you really want your RIP to have to calculate that? And what if you have to replicate that again and again? That's not good, not efficient, and not even logical. If you must resize in this way, go back to the type size and round the point sizes off to whole numbers.

FIGURE 10.9   Your initial text frame.

STEP 9 ▼
Creating Type Outlines

With the frame selected, go to the Type pull-down menu and select Create Outlines. You are now looking at a *group* of objects. Notice also that, if you are accustomed to previous versions of InDesign, you'll notice the groups are expressed with dotted selections. It is no longer text, and no longer editable as text. Ungroup the selection and you will have three separate groups. Select just one of the lines because we want to break apart the individual letters. No grouping commands are available, so we need to release this *compound*. Go to the Object pull-down menu and select Compounds, Release. So far, so good—except if any of your letters have loops or holes, they are plugged up (see Figure 10.10).

FIGURE 10.10   Ungrouped type outlines, with compounds released and counters filled.

Select any of these letters; go to the Object pull-down menu; and select Pathfinder, Exclude Overlap. Or go to the Window pull-down menu and select Object & Layout, Pathfinder. Repeat these steps for each of your lines. In the end, every letter should be a separate, accessible object.

STEP 10 ▼
Creating Colors and Applying Blending Modes

Next, choose three colors. You can use three PANTONE colors, your company colors, three process colors—whatever you like. You should make swatches of them by selecting Swatches, New Color Swatch. We are going to color each letter with one of each color so we'll have a multicolored catalogue title. After all the letters are tagged with their colors, select all the objects and access the Transparency palette. From the Blending Mode pull-down menu, select Multiply. Now drag the letters so that they slightly overlap each other. Use Figure 10.11 as a reference. Notice how the *blending mode* of Multiply creates areas that appear as if tissue is overlapping tissue.

FIGURE 10.11   Type outlines filled with color and open loops, overlapping to create a tissue effect.

FIGURE 10.12   Headline and stars.

Some colors blend better than others, so at this point you might choose to change some colors. If you made a swatch of your color, all you have to do is remix the swatch and all the objects tagged with that color will update! Otherwise, use the eyedropper, sample the new color from your object, and squirt all the other letters with that new color. Play with this until you are satisfied.

Select each line and group them together. Next, select all three groups and, with the Alignment palette, center them and move them to the top of your cover.

Now the rest of the cover will play off the title. I've created three stars of various sizes and tagged each with one of the three colors. Use the Polygon tool to create your stars. Double-click the tool in the palette and type the number of sides (points). I've created 13-point stars. Then determine the inset (how steep the points will be in relation to the total size of the star); I've used 40%, but feel free to change the number of points and inset as you like. See Figure 10.12 as a reference.

STEP 11 ▼
Transforming Objects, Again!

Drag copy the last star to the bottom corner of your layout. Take the Rotation tool and begin to rotate the star. Then hold down the Option/Alt key and continue to rotate. If the default pivot point is not the center, click the center of the star and then rotate it slightly—about 10°–15°. Let go of your mouse before you let go of the Option key and you've made a copy! Color this new star another color. Now, let's use a new feature that I'm thrilled has been included in this new version: Transform Again. For anyone familiar with Adobe Illustrator, you already know what this can do. Go to the Object pull-down menu and select Transform Again, Transform Again. Another star is created and rotated for you—meaning the last copy and transformation you executed is actually repeated for you. Color it the third color. Select all three and choose the Multiply Blending mode again from the Transparency palette. Watch the star change, and then group all three stars together.

In the lower-left corner, I've created a text frame to indicate which version of the catalogue we are producing. I've typed Winter 2005 in Century Gothic bold, 48 points and tagged it with one of my colors.

Finally, grab those three icons from the Library palette and drag them onto the cover. Line them up with the right sides of the icon, snapping down the right margin. Make them larger—twice their original size—and apply a different color to each. Remember the order of the icons on the master pages; this should be the order down the cover. Inside each icon, type a number 1, then a 2, and then a 3 for each section of the catalogue. This will serve as a visual reminder of what they will look for inside as they navigate through the catalogue. See Figure 10.13 for the completed cover.

FIGURE 10.13   **The completed front cover.**

Now we will turn our attention to the back cover by using the elements from the front cover. Select the grouped stars and copy them. Paste them onto the back page and locate the lower-left corner of the grouped stars to the lower-left corner of the intersecting margins. Select the lower-left point of the proxy and scale the stars up to fit the right margin. Copy the icons without the numbers (or with, if you like), scale them up, and fit them across the top of the back cover. See Figure 10.14 for a reference.

FIGURE 10.14   **The completed back cover.**

On to the body of the catalogue and text! We need to create some text styles, but combining text and data can be tricky. Unfortunately, the data merge feature, new to InDesign CS2, can't create multiple data fields in documents that contain multiple pages. Depending on the size of your catalogue, you might want to invest in a catalogue plug-in designed for more sophisticated merges; however, this is outside the scope of this book.

We're going to take another approach in this book. Because this is a 16-page catalogue, with fewer than 12 pages of catalogue items, we're going to type the text and data, using paragraph styles. Fortunately, this will be a quick and easy job because InDesign enables you to string paragraph styles together. Let's go.

STEP 12 ▼
Creating Paragraph Styles

Navigate to the Paragraph Styles Options dialog. We're going to create a paragraph style for each product name, a style for the product description, a style for the column heads, and a style for the pricing.

Create a style sheet according to the following screen captures: Figures 10.15, 10.16, 10.17, 10.18, and 10.19.

FIGURE 10.15 Fill out the window as indicated for the product head. You will add the next style definition after you have completed all your styles.

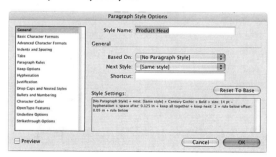

FIGURE 10.16 Fill out the window as indicated for the product description. You will add the next style definition after you have completed all your styles.

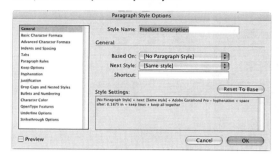

FIGURE 10.17 Fill out the window as indicated for the tab headers. You will add the next style definition after you have completed all your styles.

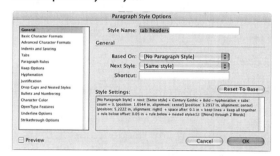

FIGURE 10.18 Fill out the window as indicated for the tab pricing. Notice that this style is based on tab headers, so you don't have to reset the tabs all over again. You will add the next style definition after you have completed all your styles.

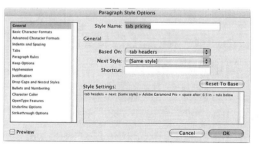

FIGURE 10.19 **Fill out the window as indicated. This style will be used for the TOC.**

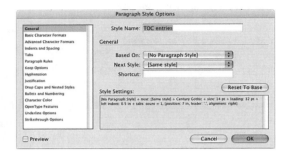

Now that we have our paragraph styles defined, let's go back to some of them and edit them. We are going to use the Next Style feature of Paragraph Styles. In preparation for this, we need to edit our new style sheets. Let's start with Product Head.

Double-click the Product Head style sheet and select Product Description near the text Next Style. Then click OK.

Double-click Product Description and for the Next Style, select Tab Headers. Click OK.

Now let's edit the paragraph style Tab Headers. Double-click this style and select the Next Style as Tab Pricing. Click OK.

Finally, edit Tab Pricing and, as the next style, select Product Head. Click OK.

STEP 13 ▼
Using the Next Style Feature of Paragraph Styles

Edit each style so the logical next style feature looks like this:

- ▸ For Product Head, the next style will be Product Description.

- ▸ For Product Description, the next style will be Tab Header.

- ▸ For Tab Header, the next style will be Tab Pricing.

- ▸ For Tab Pricing, the next style will be Product Head.

Navigate to page 4 and create a text frame to fit the right column with the following coordinates: x: 2.75", y: 1.5". With the Text tool, click in the text box. You will see a blinking text insertion point. Click the Product Head style sheet and type **Widget 1**. It formats to this new style. Press Return and you will also see a rule appear below, but when you begin typing, a new style product description is automatically applied if you set up your Product Head style sheet correctly. Type in some gibberish for a few lines and press Return again. Type **Item**, press Tab, type **Number**, press Tab, type **Qty**, press Tab, type **Price Per**, and then press Return. This takes you to yet another style. Type **Widget**, press Tab, type an item number, press Tab, type a quantity, press Tab, and then type a price. Press Return again and you are taken to the next Product Head! Check your work against Figure 10.20.

FIGURE 10.20 **The product description and pricing formatted.**

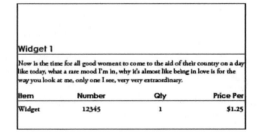

Fill this page and the next with widget entries—8 in all—by copying and pasting your initial paragraph.

Now, let's talk about associating images to the descriptions. You can always create four picture boxes in the first column and line them up with each description. This will work just fine as long as your descriptions remain relatively consistent and won't reflow. However, if you'd like to try a more robust version of inline graphics, InDesign CS2 has renamed this feature Anchored Objects with a few nifty commands under the Object pull-down menu.

STEP 14 ▼
Creating Anchored Objects

Now it's time to create some *anchored objects*. Click a text insertion point left of the W in the Widget 1 text. Go to the Object pull-down menu and select Anchored Objects, Insert. A window appears, as shown in Figure 10.21a.

Do the same for page 5. Click a text insertion point next to the W in the Widget 5 text. Go to the Object pull-down menu and select Anchored Objects, Insert. A window appears, as shown in Figure 10.21b.

Frames should appear in the left column of the left page and in the right column of your right page. If they fill with a color, tag them with a fill of None.

Repeat the previous steps and click next to each Description head to add a box attached to the description. From here, you can select each box and import your images. For the purpose of this exercise, I've provided one line drawing that you can use repeatedly as a placeholder. It is called widget.eps. Click in each box, go to the File pull-down menu, select Place, and navigate to your project files. widget.eps will actually place into the picture frame perfectly. Repeat this for all other windows.

FIGURE 10.21A Fill out the window as indicated for the left page.

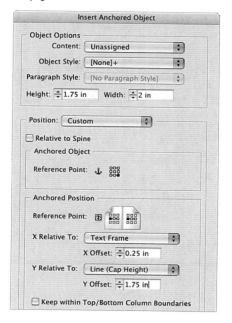

FIGURE 10.21B Fill out the window as indicated for the right page.

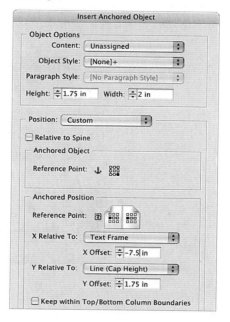

STEP 15 ▼
Creating Templates

Now you have enough ingredients to create your template. From now on, you can go to the File pull-down menu, select Save As, and select Template instead of Document.

STEP 16 ▼
Creating Headers As TOC Entries

To step through the rest of the project, you must create page headers as *TOC* entries. You do this by simply copying and pasting your initial four descriptions onto the remaining pages. To do this, execute the following: At the top of each page, I've placed a text box with the following dimensions: y: .5", w: 5.25", h:.75". The x coordinate will

change depending on whether it's the right or left page. Type a header and apply the header style sheet. Align the text vertically in the box to the bottom by either using the Control palette or going to the Object pull-down menu and selecting Text Frame Options, Vertical Justification, Bottom. Repeat this for all the body pages. See Figure 10.22 as an example.

STEP 17 ▼
Importing Spreadsheets As Tables

One page 7, I've left off or deleted the 4th description to accommodate the placement of a spreadsheet filled with pricing. Navigate to your project files and place Catalogue.xls. Turn on Show Import Options, and then fill out the import options as shown in Figure 10.23.

FIGURE 10.22 **Repeating headers formatted with the Header style sheet throughout the catalgue.**

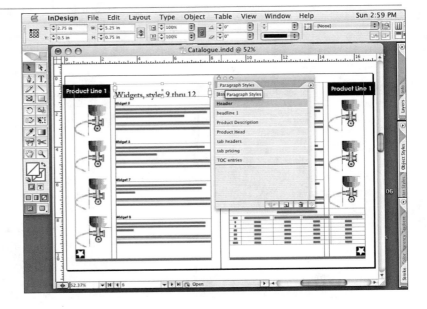

CHAPTER 10: Designing a Product Catalogue

FIGURE 10.23   The Import Options window for spread-sheets.

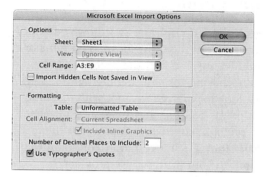

STEP 18 ▼
Editing Tables

Click and drag out a text box from the left margin to the right margin approximately 2.25 " deep. Make sure no paragraph style is applied to this table. Highlight the table with the Text tool and apply centered paragraph alignment to all the cells. Click in the upper-left cell and go to the table pull-down menu and insert, row, above the one you are currently in. Select all the cells in the new row, go to the Table pull-down menu, and select Merge Cells. Click Centered Alignment and add a table title. See Figure 10.24 for the finished table.

FIGURE 10.24   The finished table.

Quantity Pricing on Widgets					
qty	Widgets, Style 1-4	Widgets, Style 5-8	Widgets, Style 9-12		Widgets, Style 13-16
1	1.00	1.00	1.25		1.50
5	0.90	0.90	1.10		1.40
10	0.80	0.80	1.00		1.30
25	0.75	0.75	0.90		1.20
50	0.65	0.65	0.80		1.10
100	0.50	0.50	0.75		1.00

Do the same for the end of section 2 and section 3.

Now all that are left are the front matter and back matter. The front matter is covered in

this project. The back matter is covered in Chapter 11.

The front matter, pages 2 and 3, will include publication information and a table of contents. I've created a text box that fits the margins of page 2, but vertically justified to the bottom of the page. Using the product description style sheet, but with centered alignment, I've typed the catalogue production information including the title of the catalogue, the production date, who it was published by, when it was published, how it was created, and who to credit for various components. See Figure 10.25 as a guide for how the *inside cover* should look. I've also copied stars from the front cover, randomly arranged them, and filled them with black.

FIGURE 10.25   The inside cover with production credits.

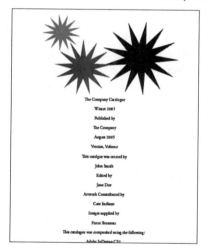

STEP 19 ▼
Creating a TOC

Now let's turn our attention to the table of contents. Move to page 3 and create a text frame that fits the margin. Leave a text insertion point in the box. Go to the Layout pull-down menu and select Table of Contents. Fill out the window according to Figure 10.26. Note you will select the style sheet header to identify all text that should be included in the TOC. You will choose the style you created, called TOC entries, to apply to the contents items to format the TOC entries. Click OK.

> ### ⊗ NOTE
>
> Like indexing, TOCs should be constructed toward the end of production when there is less chance that major items or entries will change, reflow to other pages will occur, and so on. In the event this happens, you can re-create a TOC and it will update your entries.

Add your icons across the bottom of your TOC. Scale the icons to twice their size as you did on the cover, but leave them black and white. See Figure 10.27 for the completed TOC.

Prior to printing, always save your document. If this document is based on a template, save it under a different name.

STEP 20 ▼
Preflighting Your Project

Essentially, InDesign uses a yellow caution or warning sign (the same for missing fonts or modified links) to indicate problems. When you're clicking through the Preflight dialog box, look for the yellow signs with exclamation points because they indicate a problem. The preflight command checks your file to ensure that it is in acceptable condition to submit to your print service provider. It checks for fonts, links, images, colors, inks, your print settings, and external plug-ins you might have. All this information impacts your print service provider.

Essentially, InDesign uses the color red to indicate problems. When you are clicking through the Preflight dialog box, look for red xs, which indicate a problem. You might have a problem such as a font used by the document is not turned on in your font management utility, you've moved or modified an image since you placed it in your document, or you used an RGB image. If you have errors or warnings, you need to cancel out of this dialog box, fix the problem, and run the preflight again.

FIGURE 10.26   **The Table of Contents window.**

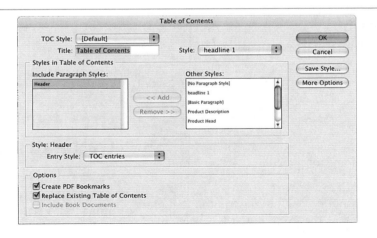

FIGURE 10.27   The finished table of contents.

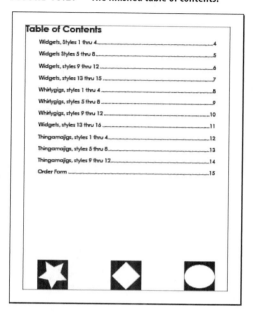

Table of Contents

STEP 21 ▼
Creating a Color Composite Proof

Let's print a content proof. Go to the File pull-down menu and select Print. Choose the appropriate settings for the printer that is available to you. On the General tab, choose one copy. On the Setup tab, select 8.5" × 11" and vertical orientation. Leave the Scale setting alone. On the Marks and Bleed tab, turn off all the options. On the Output tab, if possible, print a color composite output for your work; if not, select Grayscale. On the Graphics tab, the default settings should work. The remaining tabs can be ignored for now. Print and review your proof, make any necessary adjustments, and save your changes. Then print it again.

STEP 22 ▼
Creating a PDF for Alternative Distribution

With your document open and already proofed, go to the File pull-down menu and select Export. Navigate to your Chapter 10 folder, finished projects folder and name your PDF. At the bottom of the window, make sure the format is set to Adobe PDF. Click Save.

Select Preset, High Quality Print and click Export.

> **⊗ NOTE**
>
> If you want to add navigation to your PDF, you can do so in either InDesign or Acrobat. If you would like to create navigation using hyperlinking in InDesign, refer to Chapter 8, "Putting Together an Interactive Presentation." You might even want to use the navigation icon library you created for that project. You can drag and drop the icons on each page, and then hyperlink them.

Final Thoughts

In this project you've picked up some intermediate layout skills and worked with some new InDesign features. Most importantly, you've constructed a common and often requested type of publication, the catalogue.

Here are some important concepts to keep in mind:

▶ Make sure your organizational structure is easy to navigate.

▶ Construct designs with a template in mind—use multiple masters, styles, and swatches.

- ▶ Be mindful of how often the piece will be produced and structure the layout as cost effectively as possible.

- ▶ Keep an eye on the future when it comes to editing and revisions, and take advantage of features such as anchored objects and libraries.

- ▶ Finally, use blending modes and transparency options that can add a lot of impact without a lot of overhead.

CHAPTER 11: Making an Order Form

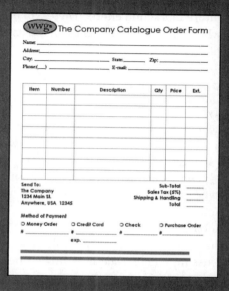

About the Project

In this chapter you will learn how to create an order form. It can be included in the back of your catalogue from the previous chapter. You can create it to be filled out in printed form, filled out as a PDF form, or have form fields added in Adobe Acrobat 7.0 Professional to be filled out on a website. This can appear as a one-page, simple project; however, that is typographically intensive.

Prerequisites

It would be helpful if you had a basic understanding of page layout, including using the Tool palette, formatting text, and performing basic page formatting skills.

@work resources

Please visit the publisher's website to access the following Chapter 11 files:

- ▶ **finished projects**
- ▶ Project file [**wwglogo.eps**]

Planning the Project

The order form you will create in this project can be delivered in a variety of ways. Working with forms is a common technical layout challenge, which is often avoided because of a limited understanding of typographical controls. In this chapter we explore a variety of ways to create the lines, grids, and text positions necessary for the precision of forms.

Forms are here to stay, and more and more marketing efforts are geared toward capturing as much information about customers as possible. We encounter forms everywhere, when joining organizations, participating with schools, providing information online, applying for credit cards, and so on. Forms play a key role in employees' interactions with their human resources department as well, and analog or paper forms are commonly converted to electronic forms that can be downloaded, filled out, and mailed back or simply filled out dynamically on a company's FTP site.

Managing Content

You will need to determine the type of data you need to capture with your form. Perhaps the form is not for commerce but for capturing demographic information about your potential customer base. Perhaps your customer is trying to request information from you by filling out a form—a form you compose and is expressly designed to capture information you need or want, such as a survey. Or perhaps you are selling something and want to passively sell by offering a form for your customers to fill out and identify what they want from your catalogue.

In addition to the information that's important to capture specific to the transaction, it's a great opportunity while you have your audience's attention to capture additional information that will be valuable to you in future marketing efforts. These will be times when you want to reach them via email, cell phone, or PDA.

Production Considerations

Typically, when we learn to type (in high school) we learn rudimentary keyboard skills. Those skills are generally geared to word processing and correspondence. This is not typesetting, which is the precise positioning of type on your page. And the precise positioning of characters is imperative with forms. All too frequently forms we create reveal spaces instead of *tabs*, tabs instead of indents, underlines instead of *leaders*, or drawn lines instead of rules or *tables*.

Will this form change frequently or remain fairly static for a significant length of time? Most printed forms are black and white, making them ideal for in-house production. Some projects, such as the previous chapter's catalogue, might need to be included in the binding.

Production considerations for forms are minimal. For print, black-and-white output (digital or offset) and whether it will be bound are about all the production considerations you will have to ponder. If the form will be distributed electronically, file size will play a factor. If you restrict the content to text characters and a vector logo, it will travel efficiently. With this type of distribution, you have the benefit of using color more liberally without the consequence of increased cost.

Distribution Considerations

Will the form need to arrive electronically? Yesterday I received an email from my daughter's high school with a PDF form attached for a plant sale they were having as a fundraiser. I printed it, filled it out, and sent it to school with my daughter. If they had taken it one step further, I could have filled it out electronically and sent it as an attachment back to them.

If your form will one day be distributed, filled out, and then mailed back to you electronically, plan for that eventuality now! Make sure you leave enough horizontal and vertical space in your form to add electronic fields.

Going one step further, you could place it on your web page and capture the data in a meaningful way into your company customer relationship management system. That system could then place this customer into a regular rotation of marketing events customized based on his buying patterns.

So, plan for the type of information you need to capture both for the immediate request and for future marketing efforts. Keep it simple and easy to understand. In other words, don't make it difficult or confusing for the customer to give you the information you want. Be sure to clearly identify tax and shipping/handling costs and whether a return policy is in place.

Project: Order Form

We'll be creating a form in eight easy steps:

STEPS ▼

1. Setting up your document format
2. Creating form fields with tab leaders
3. Inserting and formatting a table

4. Learning table behavior
5. Formatting row and column strokes and row height
6. Inserting special characters
7. Creating a color composite proof
8. Creating a PDF for alternative distribution

STEP 1 ▼
Setting Up Your Document Format

Launch InDesign, go to the File pull-down menu, and select New, Document. Fill out the New Document window as indicated in Figure 11.1. You will be creating a one-page portrait layout with one column.

FIGURE 11.1   Fill out the window as indicated.

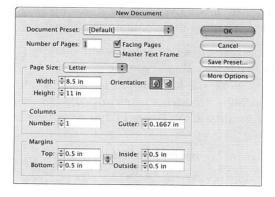

Alternatively, you can open your catalogue file created in Chapter 10, navigate to page 15, and follow the instructions from here.

Select the Type tool and draw a text frame to fit the margins of your page. Label your form. I've typed The Company Catalogue Form and formatted it with Century Gothic Regular, 24 points, right alignment, space after .2".

STEP 2 ▼
Creating Form Fields with Tab Leaders

Press Return and let's begin some typographic control. We're going to set up a traditional form with categories and line leaders. We will use the Tab palette to accomplish the setup, and each line will require different tab structures. Let's begin with the first line.

First, let's look at the text format. We've just composed the heading of the form and we don't want to continue along the same format. Change the font to Adobe Caslon Pro, 14 points, left alignment, 0 space after. Now, open the Tab palette by going to either the Type or Window pull-down menu.

If the Tab palette doesn't align with the text frame, position it and then click the magnet—it will snap into place as long as there is sufficient room above the frame.

We're going to set a single tab with a line leader. Place a single right tab stop at the 7½" mark with an underline leader. Type an underline character to avoid any gaps between the characters. Use Figure 11.2 as a reference.

FIGURE 11.2   **Fill out the Tab window as indicated.**

 NOTE

Differences in font kerning affect your underline characters forming a continuous line. Zoom in on your leaders after they are created and print them. You can have up to eight characters in the leader field of the Tab palette, but I have found typing two underline characters together seems to avoid gaps.

Type **Name:** and then press the Tab key. You should see a line appear and stop at the right side of the text box. Press Return.

The next line will have the same tab stops. Type **Address:** and then press the Tab key. Again, a line should appear and stop at the edge of the text box. Press Return. Figure 11.3 shows your progress so far.

FIGURE 11.3   **The form so far.**

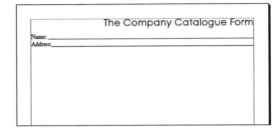

The next line will have different tab stops for the city, state, and ZIP Code. I like to think of them as *fields* and to refer to each field with curly brackets. I use a beginning bracket and an ending bracket for the field. The first bracket begins with the left indent, and the end of the first field is a right tab stop with a line leader. The next field begins at the bracket with a left tab stop and ends with a right tab stop and a leader. Finally, the ZIP Code begins with a left tab stop and ends with a right tab stop at the 7½" mark and a line leader.

Here's an example:

{City: }   {State: }   {Zip: }

The bracketed fields represent the city, state, and ZIP Code. Each field starts at a specific point and ends at a specific point, as does the next field and the next field.

Figure 11.4 shows what the tab palette will look like.

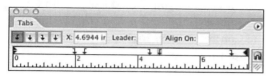

Clear the tab ruler using the palette menu. Let's create the brackets. Using Figure 11.3 as a guide, set the tab stops. Every right tab has a line leader attached. Type **City:** and press Tab. Then press Tab again and type **State:**. Press Tab twice, type **Zip:**, and press Tab one last time. Finally, press Return.

The phone and email information is the last in this section. Clear the Tab palette and set two brackets, using Figure 11.5 as a guide. Again, all right tab stops have line leaders attached to them. Type **Phone:**, press Tab twice, type **E-mail:**, and press Tab again. Finally, press Return.

Before we leave this section, highlight all four lines and open up the leading by selecting 24 points. Figure 11.5 shows your progress thus far.

FIGURE 11.5   **The top third of your form.**

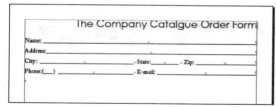

STEP 3 ▼
Inserting and Formatting a Table

Return to the end of your fields with the Type tool and clear the Tab palette. Now we are going to insert a table. Insert two returns between the top section and the table. Make sure that no paragraph styles are currently selected. Go to the Table pull-down menu and select Insert Table. Fill out the window as shown in Figure 11.6.

FIGURE 11.6   **Fill out the window as indicated.**

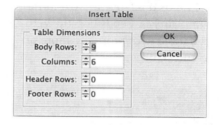

STEP 4 ▼
Learning Table Behavior

Let's first take a quick look at table behavior. With the Text tool selected, hover over the top of the first column until you see the cursor change to a down arrow. Click with the arrow in this state and notice that you can quickly select a column. Do the same for a row by hovering over the beginning of a row until you see your cursor change to a right arrow; then click to highlight the row. Hover over any of the lines dividing the tables cells and notice that your cursor changes to a double-headed arrow (see Figure 11.7 as an example).

Turn on special characters and you will see a pound sign in every cell. (You see this in every text box, symbolizing the end of the copy or story; this convention has been used in copy-writing for a long time.)

If you click and drag, you can move the lines. With either your column arrow or your row arrow, drag a selection until your entire table is selected. You will do this when you want to change all the lines, *rows, columns,* or cells. Use the Table Options commands for alternating features. Use the Cell Options commands to affect selected cells.

STEP 5 ▼
Formatting Row and Column Strokes and Row Height

Using Figure 11.8 as a reference, we'll format row and column *strokes*. Reposition the vertical lines in the table to appropriate more or less space for each category.

TIP

To avoid displacing other columns when moving a column edge within a table, hold down the Shift key.

In the top row, type **Item, Number, Description, Qty, Price, Extended**. To move to each cell in the table, press the Tab key, which advances you

to each cell. Select the entire table and make the vertical height of all the rows .45" tall. Remember that you should leave room for form fields in the future. You can do this in the Control palette, Table palette, or Table pull-down menu.

TIP

To create tab stops inside a table cell, you use the Insert Special Character command under the Type pull-down menu to select a tab character or bring up the Tab palette. Notice that it snaps to the top of a single cell and the indents form the left and right wall of the cell! You can set a tab inside a cell in this way as well.

Highlight the top row and format the text as Century Gothic, 14 points, bold, and centered alignment both horizontally and vertically.

Insert a return after the table and you should find your text insertion point on the next line directly below the table you just created.

FIGURE 11.7 **Selecting columns or rows in tables.**

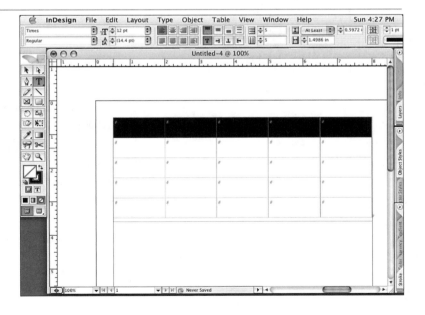

FIGURE 11.8 **Reposition vertical column edges and fill out the window as indicated.**

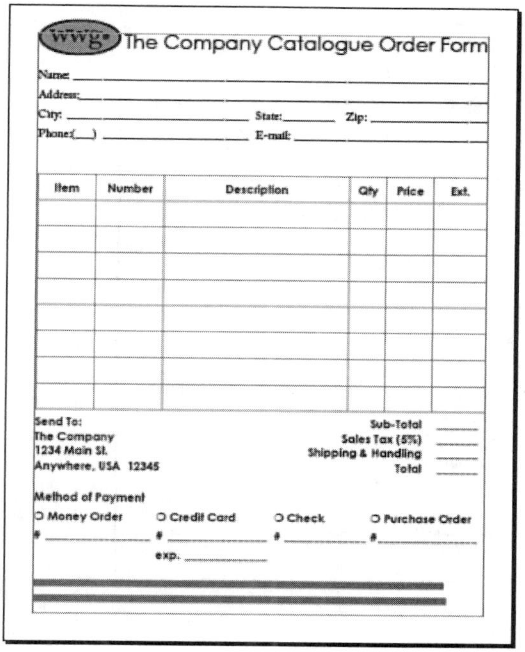

NOTE

The text insertion point will be gigantic—the full vertical height of the table—treating the table as if it were an anchored object. Press Return to advance to the next line and it will return to normal size.

Before leaving the topic of tables, feel free to experiment with the look of your table by varying the lines and fills. Try merging cells together or splitting them apart for special effects.

Now, back to the form. Click below the table to create two distinct pieces of information. One will be a return address and the other tax and shipping information. Open the Tab palette and make sure the ruler is clear. Create a right tab stop at the 6.25" mark. Create a left tab stop at the 6.5" mark and then a right tab stop at the 7.5" mark with a line leader. Use Figure 11.9 as a guide for how these two distinct, but physically side-by-side, groups of text should look.

FIGURE 11.9 **Your side-by-side paragraphs.**

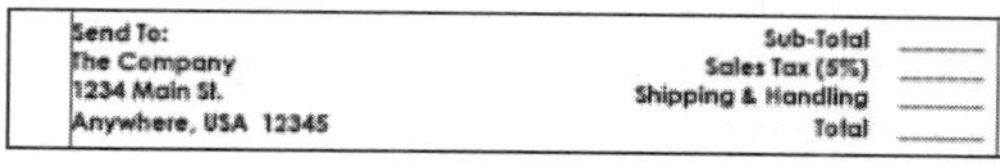

I've formatted the text in these two paragraphs with Century Gothic Bold, 14 points, 18-point leading. The last line of copy should have space after of .2". Press Return.

STEP 6 ▼ Inserting Special Characters

Next comes the section for method of payment. Type **Method of Payment** and format it as Century Gothic, 14 points. I've offered four options for payment; however, your circumstances will be unique, so you might want to change this. I've set four left tab stops across the width of the text box. Type in a dingbat of your choice, followed by a space, followed by the first method, followed by a tab. Then type a dingbat, a space, the next method, and so on. Use Figure 11.10 as a reference. Press Return at the end of the line.

FIGURE 11.10 **Your initial tab stops for the method of payment.**

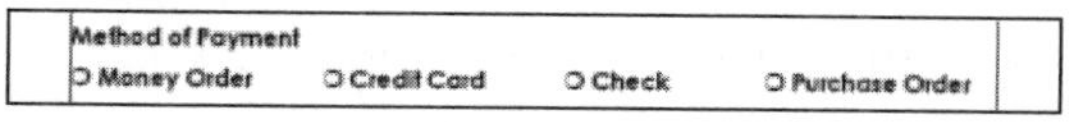

You might have additional information to capture, such as a credit card number, a check number, and so on. You should have a text insertion point at the beginning of the line just beneath the payment options. Open the Tab palette again; you should see the same tab stops as the line before. We are going to keep them and add to them. You will simply create right tab stops with line leaders to create the form fields as before. Visually position three left tab stops before all but the first pound sign and four right tab stops where you want your lines to stop.

Type a pound sign, then two tab stops, a pound sign, and two more tabs. Then type another pound sign, two more tabs, the last pound sign, and a final tab. I've formatted this section again with Century Gothic, 14 points, 24-point leading, and no space after. Use Figure 11.11 as a reference.

FIGURE 11.11 The method of payment section, complete.

Method of Payment
○ Money Order ○ Credit Card ○ Check ○ Purchase Order
________ # ________ # ________ # ________
exp. ________

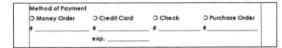

The bottom of your form might include tax information, shipping and handling qualifiers, and possibly a return policy. I've formatted this with Adobe Caslon 12 points, left alignment.

Finally, for the finishing touch, do one of two things:

- Place the file `wwglogo.eps` (found in your project files folder for this chapter) in the upper-left corner of your form with the following x,y coordinate: .5",.25".
- Use the star(s) found on the inside cover of the catalogue project in black and white and position it in the upper-left corner of your form.

Save your work. Use Figure 11.12 to tweak your layout.

FIGURE 11.12 Your form complete.

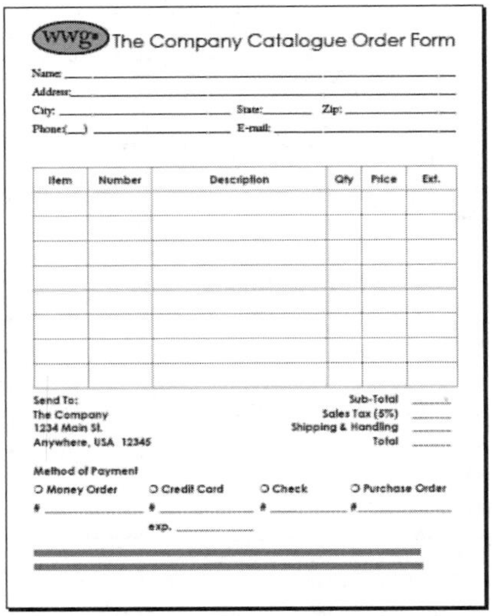
The Company Catalogue Order Form
Name:
Address:
City: State: Zip:
Phone:( ) E-mail:

Item	Number	Description	Qty	Price	Ext.

Send To:
The Company
1234 Main St.
Anywhere, USA 12345

Sub-Total
Sales Tax (5%)
Shipping & Handling
Total

Method of Payment
○ Money Order ○ Credit Card ○ Check ○ Purchase Order
________ # ________ # ________ # ________
exp. ________

STEP 7 ▼

Creating a Color Composite Proof

Let's print a content proof. Go to the File pull-down menu and select Print. Select the appropriate settings for the printer that is available to you. On the General tab, select one copy. On the Setup tab, select 8.5" x 11" and vertical orientation. Leave the Scale setting alone. On the Marks and Bleed tab, turn off all the options. On the Output tab, if possible, print a color composite output for your work; if not, select Grayscale. On the Graphics tab, the default settings should work. The remaining tabs can be ignored for now. Print and review your proof, make any necessary adjustments, and save your changes. Print it again.

STEP 8 ▼
Creating a PDF for Alternative Distribution

With your document open and already proofed, go to the File pull-down menu and select Export. Navigate to your Chapter 11, finished projects folder and name your PDF. At the bottom of the window, make sure the format is set to Adobe PDF. Click Save.

Set the Preset to high-quality print if the recipient will be printing this form and then manually filling it out. Then click Export. If, on the other hand, the recipient will be viewing this online and your goal is to create a small PDF, select Screen.

While interactive forms fall outside the scope of this book, Acrobat Professional 7 contains excellent tools to add electronic form fields to your layout so the document can be filled out electronically and sent back to you.

Final Thoughts

In this project you've picked up some intermediate typographic skills and had an opportunity to consider and capture additional important data for your marketing efforts.

Important concepts to keep in mind include

- ▶ Tabs are the only convention you should use for the accurate positioning of stops on a line.
- ▶ Tables offer another form option, and InDesign CS2 offers many great features for controlling the format of tables.
- ▶ Leaders play a key role in formatting forms. Being able to manage and control them is critical to creating forms.
- ▶ Plan for the distribution of your form, not only in print but electronically as well, by making sure you have plenty of space to add form fields later.

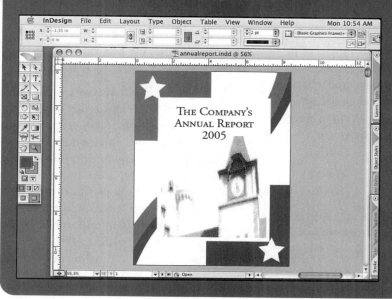

About the Project

In this chapter you will learn how to create an annual report, probably one of the most sophisticated and longest marketing and communication pieces you will ever create. It will likely be created for print and also made available for distribution to shareholders and others via the company website.

Prerequisites

It would be helpful if you had an intermediate understanding of page layout, including a reasonable command of all the tools, primary and secondary palettes, text formatting (including style sheets), and pagination skills (including page numbering) .

@work resources

Please visit the publisher's website to access the following Chapter 12 files:

▶ **finished projects**

▶ Project files [**cabinet.tif, DMLOGOgray.eps, lilly1gray.tif, logogray.eps, OverallRevenue.eps, Pete2.tif, RevenuebyProduct.eps, shareholder.eps, wwglogogray.eps**]

Planning the Project

A lot of time goes into planning an annual report. It is a communications device whose purpose is to convey essential information about a company's performance on an annual basis. That performance would include the sales accomplishments of products or services, new initiatives, stock or valuation information, key personnel changes or additions, and any other noteworthy programs (perhaps engineering achievements, new certifications achieved, HR benefits added, and so on).

 TIP

For a great reference for what is typically included in an annual report, visit Tips for Creating a Good Annual Report at http://www.zpub.com/sf/arl/arl-tips.html.

The purpose of the annual report is to review the year for stakeholders of the company. Content for this project will likely come from a variety of sources, such as internal departments, external vendors, and independent partners.

In planning the report, you will have to convey to your contributors the kind of information you will need. If the content is data, it will be particularly important that the data is valid, accurate, and in a usable format. Images and graphics should be consistent with your brand, and the report should reflect the success of your company and its accomplishments. Images as well as words should be used to convey a consistent message to your company's stakeholders.

Communicate to your contributors what kind of file formats you would like to receive. Stress that minimal formatting should be

applied to this content—you do not want to spend time stripping or undoing their formatting in an effort to apply your own. Before you begin laying out your content, the creative direction of the project should have been approved. You can create comps of some concepts for approval before content ever arrives. When the files start coming in, the layout should come together quickly.

A budget has probably been established for this project. This is generally a nice printed piece with multiple colors, formal binding, finishing features, and long document features such as credits and indexes. A four-color job on quality stock that will be mailed in a 9" × 12" envelope will contribute to the cost of the project. Special photography, language translation, and software plug-ins to handle the formatting of financial data all add to the cost and timeline of the project.

Remember that, although this project is primarily used as a device for accountability, it can also be used as a marketing tool, particularly when your company is interested in attracting investors, convincing a bank of the importance of a loan, or convincing a potential strategic partner to join forces. This is an opportunity to represent the company. For inspiration, Google "annual reports"; you will be surprised at how many sites offer libraries of annual reports you can view online or download.

Given how often throughout this book I have stressed the importance of a strong relationship with your print provider, no publication would warrant a thorough planning with your service provider more than an annual report. The run length will likely be shorter than some of your other marketing initiatives, but the planning is just as important.

Be mindful of the fact that you will convert this print publication into a PDF that can be distributed electronically. This will allow you to enrich the recipients' experience. Interactivity can be introduced into the report by using hyperlinks for navigation purposes as well as pointers to websites. Movies can be embedded such as a brief message from the CEO or chairman of the board. In addition, animation of a product demonstrating usability accomplishes a number of things, such as showing how the product works, what the product looks like, how it might be engineered, and how you are using technology to extend your message in a dynamic way.

Managing Content

This content will contain financial information, and numeric data requires some specific formatting skills. You might be dealing with multiple currency issues or need to decide how you want to abbreviate large numbers. If tabular data needs to be formatted, you might want to consider fonts with math-specific glyphs.

A decision you might want to resolve prior to content coming in is whether you will use tabs to handle your financial data or tables. Tables offer benefits such as the independence of each table cell, the ability to apply fills and strokes independently, as well as unique visual applications such as merging cells and importing images.

Consider expressing all this data in a graphical context instead of endless columns. Interpret the data for the reader using interesting graphs and charts. Adobe Illustrator is ideal for creating charts or graphs that are visually interesting and meaningful. You can add depth and dimension and impose designs onto your charts.

Your information might have to be attributed to resources or partners who will validate or certify your data, such as the company's accounting firm or stock information from the index your company's stock trades in. If this is the case, plan for footnotes in your document. If there will be a significant number of tables or charts, you can build a list that readers can use to flip to them quickly.

Additionally, a table of contents (TOC) is always useful to help readers navigate. InDesign enables you to use its TOC feature to automatically create bookmarks in your PDFs. If the annual report ends up being lengthy or contains a lot of varied information, consider using the index feature so recipients can quickly look up the information they are most interested in.

As indicated in the previous section, text will more than likely come from a variety of sources. It is important to stress to your sources that you want as little formatting as possible, so that you don't have to spend your time stripping unnecessary formatting out of the text before you can apply your own. Ask your sources to just type the text in and run a spell check. Ask them to use only one return between paragraphs. Ask them not to use spaces when they should be using tabs, and ask them not to use tabs when they should be using indents. You might choose to link your text files in InDesign as you do your image files. If the text files change or are updated over time, you can update the link in your publication to reflect the change in your layout; however, you will lose any formatting you have applied in InDesign.

Photography should be planned and shot well in advance of your deadline. It should reflect the company and its brand and should be managed at a resolution and color space consistent with your production considerations. This is one of the most formal publications you will ever produce. You might choose to work with *duotones*, *tritones*, or *quadtones* utilizing interesting combinations of spot colors such as metallics. Make sure the photographer understands how the images will be adjusted and produced. EPS and TIFF are typically used for continuous tone images.

If you are on a limited budget and can't afford to shoot your images, consider Adobe's new Stock Photo service located in Adobe Bridge under Favorites. This takes you to Adobe's new service, which is available on Bridge users. There you can search through images from different *stock photography* vendors, download comp images, and purchase high-resolution images for production. For more information, tour the Overview feature as soon as you click Adobe Stock Photos in your Favorites tab of Bridge.

If graphic elements will be used in your layout, they should also be consistent with the brand and serve a purpose, perhaps to distinguish one section of the publication from another, to distinguish one product or service from another, or used as visual navigation elements. EPS files are commonly used for illustrative graphics.

Finally, consider the pages of the publication themselves. It is unlikely you will choose a format you typically see in newsletters or magazine publishing that are three or four columns wide. Remember that this is one of the most important publications a company uses to sell stakes in the company, so it should capture the company culture and management philosophy.

Many companies prefer to express this information in a very formal format; however, if

you sell novelty party items, it would be inappropriate to create a formal annual report. In this case, you should create an annual report that expresses the fun products you manufacture. The text and data might be extremely comprehensive and complicated, so don't make it difficult to read by threading the text all over the place. Do break up text-heavy pages with large, easy-to-interpret graphics.

Production Considerations

This is typically a big budget item because companies choose to spend more on this once-a-year document designed to impress and sell the company itself. I've reviewed many splendid annual reports where no expense was spared, from varied stock (think about combining a text weight and a *vellum* for special effect), to photography shot on location for this specific event, to unique finishing options including *die cuts*, *foil stamping*, *embossing*, and *spot varnishes*.

This isn't a publication you can afford to make mistakes with—errors in either the content or in the production could be very costly. Your print provider will assist you with the color correction for your images, and it is important that your color expectations are clearly communicated and that you have confidence in the proofing options offered by your provider.

Proofing early and often is a good rule of thumb. You, of course, will have control over content and when your project leaves you, the content should not be in question. There are many types of proofs, and design/content proofing should take place throughout the layout process. The best practice suggests a two-proof cycle, meaning two pairs of eyes, not including yours, should review the project for content accuracy prior to delivery to the print service provider. For this particular type of project it is likely you will have more than two pairs of eyes proofing, and it is also recommended that financial data be independently reviewed as well.

After the content has been approved and you have preflighted your work with the *preflight* and package features of InDesign CS2, you will submit your package to your print service provider with previously agreed-to files and documentation. You need to send some type of *content proof* that production operators can refer to when checking your pages for production repairs. How you choose to do that is between you and your printer; at the very least, you should send a black-and-white laser proof. However, a color proof or a low-resolution PDF would be even better.

Why does your service provider need a reference to process your job? Pagination and text flow are two important checks in a production workflow. Your service provider needs to ensure that this job contains the number of pages, colors, fonts, and images expected. If there is a discrepancy between what the *job ticket* or the content proof states and what they find in the file, they will have to stop processing the job and contact you to resolve these issues. It would be imprudent to process the job when it doesn't match the supplied descriptions.

After a file has been given to the print service provider, the file should be preflighted again. The printer will check to ensure that they can verify they have everything they need from you to process the job and validate that the quality and integrity of the project are in line with the estimate and job ticket. It's at this point that your provider might place a call to you and let you know about missing resource files or major discrepancies between the digital file and the quote or job ticket.

If the file passes preflight, it travels on to prepress where the next step—file repair and/or preparation—takes place. Because 70% of all incoming files require work at this stage, it is highly likely that yours will as well. Although the file might pass initial preflight, work might still be necessary to ensure that the job images and prints correctly. For example, if there is insufficient bleed, prepress production operators will have to modify your page layout file to provide bleed. If there is not enough image to fill a bleed area, they will have to perform retouching to extend the image.

After the pages are corrected, the next two steps include trapping and imposition. InDesign CS2 comes with *trapping* presets that can be modified for specific production requirements and, though very capable, InDesign trapping pays off only in a RIP that utilizes Adobe In-Rip trapping. Your service provider will probably want to handle this production step themselves because they fully understand and appreciate the tolerances of their presses when combined with your stock and ink choices. Finally, imposition takes place and is, in part, determined by your binding choices and the number of pages and sheet size involved.

Your choices of review during these production steps might include page proofs (for content changes), contract proofs (for color corrections and approvals), and imposition proofs (if you would like to see how your pages will fold and trim). The technologies your service provider uses to deliver these types of proofs will vary. Digital proofing in conjunction with computer-to-plate systems is now a common combination found in many print service providers. If you are working with a printer who uses a film-based workflow, analog proofs such as Matchprints or Cromalins, might also be an option.

Digital proofs can be created with varying technologies, including laser, inkjet, ablation, dye sublimation, phase change, and a variety of thermal applications. For this project, it's important that your type proofs are crisp and clean, that your images accurately reflect your color correction requests, and that the overall proof accurately sets your expectations for your press check. A press check for a publication this formal is warranted and recommended.

Distribution Options

How will you get the annual report to the necessary recipients? You will undoubtedly use a carrier of your choosing, such as the U.S. Postal Service, or you might prefer an alternative carrier if there are timely delivery requirements. As I've stated throughout the book, the time to determine your distribution choices is at the beginning of the project. Deadlines, timelines, budget, and shipping requirements should be accounted for prior to laying out the project.

Senior management might want this project or some version of this project posted on the company website for public access. This version of the annual report will likely be downloaded as a PDF in a resolution suitable for laser or reasonable quality inkjet output. If you regularly distribute publications via your website, you should include a link to the Adobe website in the event the recipient doesn't have Acrobat Reader installed.

Remember, this is a requirement for opening a PDF, and although Acrobat Reader is free, you can't assume everyone has it installed on their desktops.

Now that we've discussed your options and considerations for planning an annual report, let's create a sample report so you can gain some experience!

Project: Annual Report

We'll be creating an annual report in 12 easy steps:

STEPS ▼

1. Setting up your document format
2. Editing a master page and basing one master on another
3. Organizing your front matter
4. Using all caps and small caps to convey formality
5. Adding bullets and numbering
6. Creating footnotes
7. Adding decorative elements to your strokes
8. Formatting financial data
9. Creating an index
10. Preflighting your project
11. Creating a color composite proof
12. Review and approval

The last few projects in this book have been challenging and this one is no exception. You might want to navigate to the finished projects folder and open the finished catalogue as a reference, as well as use the screen captures throughout this chapter.

STEP 1 ▼
Setting Up Your Document Format

Launch InDesign; go to the File pull-down menu; and select New, Document. Fill out the New Document window as indicated in Figure 12.1. You will be creating a 32-page portrait layout with one column.

FIGURE 12.1   Fill out the window as indicated.

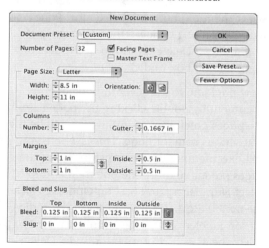

STEP 2 ▼
Editing a Master Page and Basing One Master on Another

You can proceed to edit Master Page A by adding a footer at the bottom of the left and right masters including an auto page number. Draw a text frame across the bottom, being sure to line up both sides of the text box with the margins of each page. Select Insert Special Characters from the Type pull-down menu; then select Auto Page Number and type **The Company Annual Report**. Choose an appropriate company font to format the text. I've chosen Adobe Garamond Regular, 12 points. If it is a left page, I've chosen left alignment (using the Paragraph button in the Control palette). If it's a right page, I've used right alignment. See Figure 12.2 as an example.

FIGURE 12.2 **The left master formatted with an auto page number and running footer.**

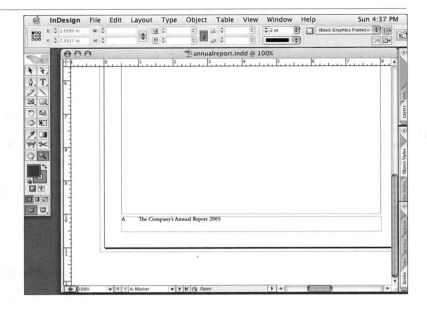

Create a new master based on Master Page A by selecting the New Master command from the Pages palette. Double-click Master Page B, go to the Layout pull-down menu, and select Margins and Columns. Create a two-column layout with a .25" gutter. You will now have two masters to work with throughout the annual report. The "A" Master has a single-column format and the "B" Master has a two-column format. See Figure 12.3 as a guide for master page formats.

STEP 3 ▼
Organizing Your Front Matter

Begin by identifying (approximately) your *front matter*—the cover, inside cover, and TOC. Let's take care of the page numbering issues right now. Navigate to the cover and remove the footer, which is a master item, at the bottom of the page. To access this item, you must press ⌘-Shift (Mac) or Ctrl+Shift (PC) to override Master items. Delete this item. Do this

for all your front matter pages. Navigate to your *back matter*, which will be pages 29, 30, 31, and 32, and remove those footers as well.

Navigate to the first page in your document (your cover) and go to the Pages palette. Go to the palette menu and select Numbering and Section. Click the box to Start Section and select the radio button labeled Start Page Numbering at 1. Choose the numbering style of i, ii, iii, iv. Delete anything in the Section Prefix dialog box and click OK.

Now navigate to the seventh page of your document by double-clicking the page icon in the pages palette (page vii), which will be the first serious content page. This is where you will execute another section start. Go to the Pages palette and use the palette menu to select Numbering and Section Options. Click the box to Start Section and select the radio button labeled Start Page Numbering at 1. Select the 1, 2, 3, 4 numbering style. Delete anything in the Section Prefix dialog box and click OK.

FIGURE 12.3   Master Page B
so far.

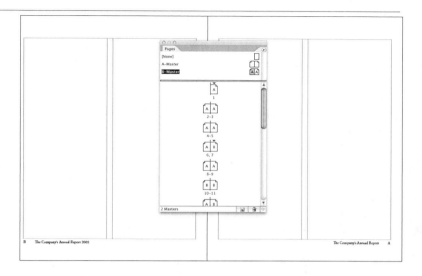

Now we can turn our attention back to the cover; feel free to experiment with the cover. I used a patriotic theme and used InDesign tools to create the graphics. I created two spot colors as swatches to use throughout the project—a patriotic blue and a red, PANTONE Reflex Blue C (for coated), and PANTONE 485 C. I've placed the company.tif image on the cover and distorted it deliberately by anamorphically scaling it (the vertical only) to stretch it to fill the negative space or empty space on the cover. For the title of the report, I've used Adobe Garamond Regular, 48-point type, 48-point leading, centered alignment. Select Text Frame Options from the Object pull-down menu. These options have been reorganized in CS2. Click the Baseline Options tab and set the first baseline offset to Cap Height and the Minimum to 1". This is one of the ways you can control where your first baseline starts in a text frame. Feel free to add your colors to the Swatches palette with the New Swatch command and experiment with your layout. Figure 12.4 shows my cover so far.

FIGURE 12.4   The annual report cover.

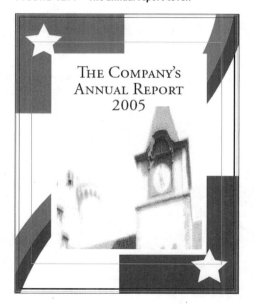

On the inside cover, draw a text frame smaller than the page and centered to the page. I decided to use a quote, which I formatted as Adobe Garamond Regular, 36 points, justified. On the third page I placed an image, pretending it's the featured company product or an image that represents the primary company service. Again, I've drawn a rectangular graphic frame smaller than the page and centered. Select the Place command from the File pull-down menu to bring in this image, `cabinet.tif`, and visually approximate its position on the page. See Figure 12.5 to compare your first spread.

> **⊠ NOTE**
>
> I've created the first credit by drawing a small, thin text frame. Rotate it on its side and type information regarding the photographer (here I've added the copyright date and name of the photographer). For all the credits in this project, I've used Century Gothic Regular, 10 points. Make a paragraph style, called credit, and tag all those elements with this style sheet. I've used the copyright symbol, which you can find by selecting Insert Special Characters from the Type pull-down menu.

STEP 4 ▼
Using All Caps and Small Caps to Convey Formality

I've chosen to add the company mission statement and core values to page 4. Again, I've created a text frame, smaller than the page. Throughout this project you'll notice I've been using All Caps and *Small Caps* as text treatments. I've deliberately chosen these styles to add formality to the project. For page 4, I've centered the copy and formatted it with Adobe Garamond, Regular, 32 points for the text Mission Statement and Core Values. For the entries under each of these headings, I've formatted the copy Adobe Garamond Italic, 24 points. I've used 36-point leading for both areas of this page.

We've covered generating TOCs in Chapter 10, "Designing a Product Catalogue." This feature is dependent on you using paragraph styles and tagging entries that you want to include in your TOC. In my project, I've typed approximate categories and subcategories. I've played with the format, which I will use as the basis for a paragraph style.

FIGURE 12.5 **Pages 2 and 3 formatted.**

"Quote: Od tet lutpatet, quat lut laore dolorti onulput nonum vulla consequat num dolortio et luptatisim quat, venit ilit nis nim nim iuscilit aut luptatet vel dolorem vel ulputpat veliquisl ut nis at vulla faccum iusto delissequis atuercidunt."
— PETE BROSSEAU, FOUNDER
THE COMPANY

Note that the main headings are in all caps, Adobe Garamond Regular, 12 points, and Red and that the subcategories are normal case, black text, 12 points, and indented. Also, a tab stop with dot leaders has been attached. We've created these in Chapter 9, "Developing a Newsletter." All the leading is 18 points. Use Figure 12.6 as a reference for the layout of this spread.

The next spread contains an image of the company's founder, the company story, and a graphical element. Begin by creating a rectangular graphic frame and placing the image Pete2.tif in the frame. I've set this image off to the left side of the page. Slightly overlapping the image, I've drawn a red vertical rectangle, which contains the text The Company Story. I've formatted the heading in small caps and tagged it with a fill of paper. Throughout the project, I've liberally used the Type menu's Fill with Placeholder Text option.

Drag the right page of the Master B set onto the seventh page in the layout. It should reflect a two-column format. Across the top of the page, draw a text frame that will contain the header information that introduces the first major element of the annual report: the letter from the CEO. I've formatted the first line with all caps, Adobe Garamond Regular, 24 points. The second line introduces the person, with the same typeface and small caps followed by a comma; then I've reduced an all cap version to 14 points to describe the position. These paragraph styles will be repeated throughout this publication. At this time, it would be wise to save these formats as paragraph styles so they can be reused throughout the layout.

The first few lines of the letter are 24-point type on 36-point leading. Then two linked text frames are added below using the column guides. The text is linked from the first frame to the second and then the third. Draw a large text frame to fit the margins of page 8 and link the third frame from page 7 to this frame on page 8. On page 7 you can fill the empty frames with placeholder text. I've formatted the text in frames 2, 3, and 4 with Century Gothic 12 points, left alignment and have added room for a signature. See Figure 12.7 to compare your spread to mine.

FIGURE 12.6   Pages 4 and 5 formatted.

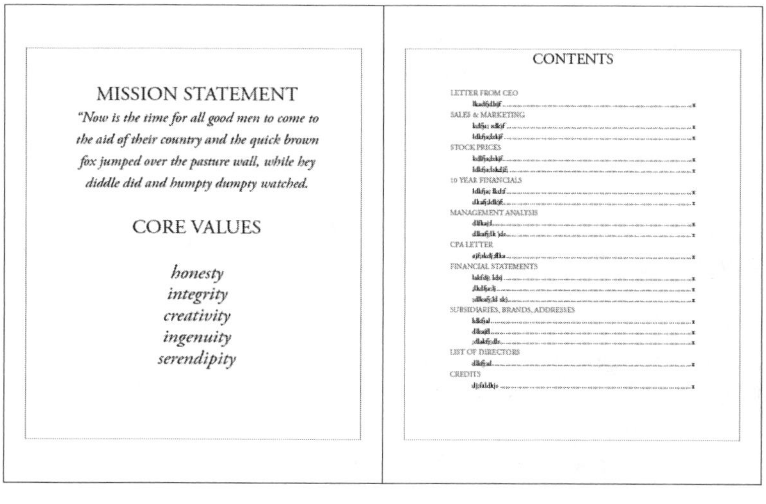

MISSION STATEMENT

"Now is the time for all good men to come to the aid of their country and the quick brown fox jumped over the pasture wall, while hey diddle did and humpty dumpty watched.

CORE VALUES

honesty
integrity
creativity
ingenuity
serendipity

CONTENTS

LETTER FROM CEO
SALES & MARKETING
STOCK PRICES
10 YEAR FINANCIALS
MANAGEMENT ANALYSIS
CPA LETTER
FINANCIAL STATEMENTS
SUBSIDIARIES, BRANDS, ADDRESSES
LIST OF DIRECTORS
CREDITS

FIGURE 12.7   Pages 6 and 7
of the Pages palette formatted.
The seventh page will contain
the number 1 as a result of the
auto page numbering placed on
the masters and the section
starts you created.

STEP 5 ▼
Adding Bullets and Numbering

You've already begun page 8. It is filled with
placeholder text with room left in the middle
of the page for a bulleted list and at the
bottom for a signature.

If there are certain key points, elements, or
initiatives the CEO would like to call the
reader's attention to, you can easily do so.
I've simply typed Item One, pressed Return,
typed Item Two, pressed Return, and so forth.
Highlight the items and with the Paragraph
button selected in the Control palette, pull
down the triangle in the upper-right corner
of the palette and select Bullets and
Numbering. Fill out the dialog box
according to Figure 12.8.

Create a rectangle graphic frame to fit the
margin guides for page 9 and place the
image called lilly1gray.tif. You will have to
anamorphically scale this image. Take the
lock off the scale fields in the Control palette.
With the Direct Selection tool, click the image
itself and only vertically scale the image to
175%. Tag this image with the red swatch.

FIGURE 12.8   The bullets and numbering dialog box.

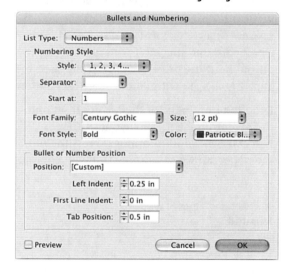

Add a text frame on top of this image; type
Sales and Marketing; and format it with
Adobe Garamond Bold, 36 points, right
aligned. Position this frame at 8.5" for the y
coordinate. Note that another image credit
has been added on the lower-left corner of the
image. Review your work (see Figure 12.9).

FIGURE 12.9   Pages 8 and 9
of the Pages palette formatted,
and the auto numbering will
reflect pages 2 and 3 on the
pages themselves.

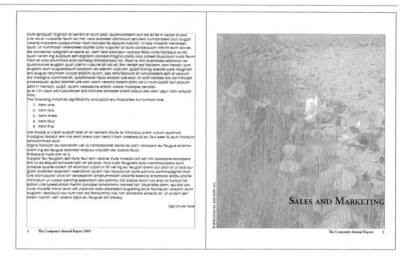

Apply Master Pages B to the next two pages—
10 and 11. Draw a rectangular graphic frame
at the top of both pages with the following
coordinates: x: .5", y: .5", w: 7.5", h: 4".
Place the image OverallRevenue.eps on page
10 and RevenuebyProduct.eps on page 11. Add
credits to both of these charts directly underneath each graphic frame. I've placed them
on the lower-right side of each frame. Then
create four text frames (one in each column
of the spread) under the graphs; link them all
together; fill them with placeholder text; and
format them with Century Gothic, regular, 12
points.

STEP 6 ▼
Creating Footnotes

Now we have a new feature to cover: creating
footnotes. It is not unusual to have to attribute information or quotes to published work,
and the new footnote feature is ideal for this
requirement. Highlight the text or click a text
insertion point somewhere in the body of the
paragraph you need to credit to a

publication. Go to the Type pull-down menu
and select Insert Footnote. A small, super-
scripted number 1 will appear next to the text
you highlighted, and a new number 1 will
appear at the bottom of the page with a
short, horizontal line above it separating the
footnote from the copy. The text insertion
point is next to this number 1, waiting for
you to enter the publication name and date.

NOTE

For more information on formal document features
and usage of these features, refer to the *Chicago
Manual of Style*—the de facto standard in reference
for publishing. For more information, see Appendix B,
"Resources."

Execute the same steps somewhere on page
11 and note that it will execute a second footnote with the number 2. You can set the
option for sequential numbering by selecting
Document Footnote Options from the Type
pull-down menu. See Figure 12.10 to compare
your finished spread.

FIGURE 12.10 **Pages 10 and 11 of the Pages palette formatted and the auto numbering will reflect pages 4 and 5 on the pages themselves.**

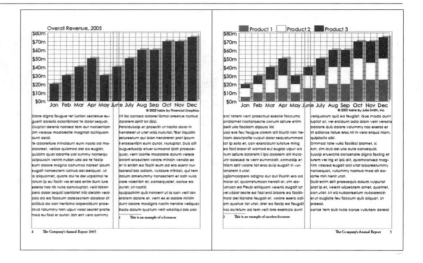

For the next spread, on page 12 I've added headers called `Shareholder Information` set in Adobe Garamond Regular, 24 points, centered alignment, small caps. Then on page 13, I've added a header called `Summaries of Financial Figures, 10 Years`, with the same formatting as page 12, except the alignment for this header is left aligned.

Create a rectangular graphic frame with the following coordinates: x: .5", y: 1.825", w: 5.25", h:5.7". Place the image `Shareholder.eps` in this frame and manually position it with the Direct Selection tool. To the right of this frame, create a text frame and type the label **Earnings and Dividends Per Share**. I've broken up the lines with soft returns and formatted the text with Century Gothic Regular, 18 points, 30-point leading, centered alignment. Add a credit below the chart. At the bottom of this page, I have added another text frame to fit the left, right, and bottom margins and have added placeholder text that will describe the chart above it. This text is formatted with Adobe Garamond, 12 points, left aligned.

STEP 7 ▼
Adding Decorative Elements to Your Strokes

On page 13 we will draw a swoosh with the Pen tool and apply a red 50-point stroke. See Figure 12.11 as an example. Now we'll add an arrowhead to the new vector. This graphic represents an upward trend in numbers and will act as a timeline as well. Now add lines along the timeline with solid circle starts or ends, and add a text frame to each describing each year's performance. I've formatted each text entry with Adobe Garamond Regular, 18 points. See Figure 12.12 for guidance in drawing your figure.

Drag the right Master Page B to page 13 so you have a two-column format. Below the graphic I've created two linked text frames and filled them with placeholder text formatted with Century Gothic, 12 points, left aligned. Our spread is now complete; see Figure 12.13 for the results.

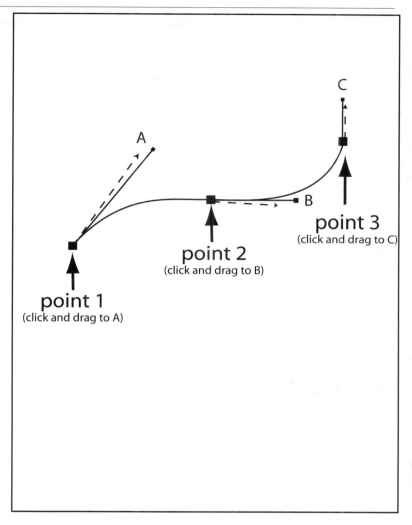

Pages 14 and 15 are formatted using the same elements and formats you used for pages 7 and 8. The only additional element I added was a sprinkling of five-sided stars that I tucked behind the text by using the Object menu's Arrange, Send to Back command. Compare your layout to mine using Figure 12.14.

Next we'll break up the layout by adding another image. On page 16, draw a rectangular graphic frame and place the image lilly1gray.tif again. Anamorphically scale the image with the Direct Selection tool—select and vertically scale it only by 175%. Tag this image with the patriotic blue swatch and then add a credit to the image. Format page 17 as you have formatted pages 7 and 8 with a text frame spread across the top. Drag Master Page B to page 17; then draw two text frames to fit the column, link them together, and fill them with placeholder text. Format them according to previous pages. Check your work against Figure 12.15.

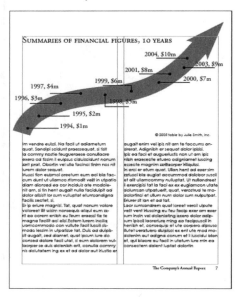

STEP 8 ▼
Formatting Financial Data

For the purpose of this part of the exercise, you will use both `Financialstatements.doc` and `Financialstatements1.doc`, both of which are tabbed text documents. I've created header text frames on pages 18 and 19 in the upper corners. Type the header **Financial Statements** formatted with Adobe Garamond Regular, 24 points, small caps. Left align it on page 18 and right align it on page 19. Below these headers draw large text frames to fit the margins; then import `FinancialStatements.doc` onto page 18 and `FinancialStatements1.doc` on page 19.

Option #1

Depending on who is submitting this information and how, you might choose to convert this information (perhaps from a spreadsheet) into a table or import it as tab-delimited text. You will likely have to set tabs off to the right. The first line of each page, which states `Year Ended 31 December`, should be set to a centered tab at about the 6" mark.

The next line highlighted should have centered tabs set to 5", 6", and 7". The remainder of the financial information should be highlighted and formatted with decimal tab stops at the 5", 6", and 7" marks.

FIGURE 12.13   **Pages 12 and 13 of the Pages palette formatted; the auto numbering will reflect pages 6 and 7 on the pages themselves.**

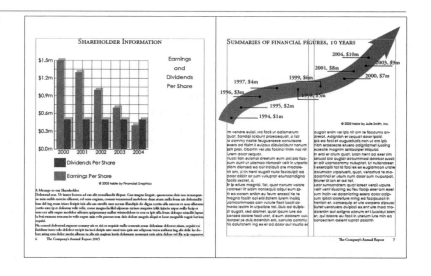

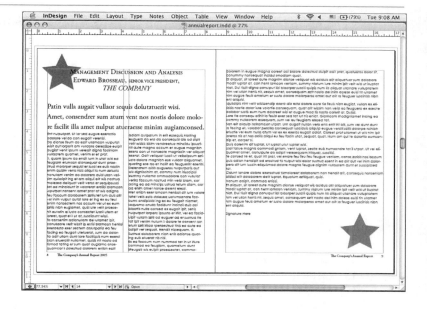

Notice how I've used the Rule Below option for a couple of lines with 1-point weight and an offset of .05". Note: Paragraph Rules are found in the Paragraph palette menu. All this text is set to Adobe Garamond Regular, 12-point type, 18-point leading, with some carriage returns between key lines of information.

For page 19 and the next set of financials, all the previous tab stop information holds true—the only difference is the treatment of certain subtotal lines, where I've used both Rule Above (offset of .175") and Rule Below. Also note that I've added paragraph spacing around these lines. While the text formatting has changed, I've reduced the leading on this page to 16 points to fit all the information on the same page. This is very important: Trying to read tabbed information that is spread over two pages means you have to repeat headers for readability. At that point, you would be better off using a table with repeat header rows.

Option #2

Place these text files on each page, respectively. With the text highlighted, go to the Table pull-down menu and select Convert Text to Table. Leave the defaults alone and click OK. Highlight your columns with the Type tool to change alignments. If you need to add tab stops within cells, highlight a column, open the Tab palette, and set a tab (probably decimal) for that column. Experiment with table options versus cell options. Don't forget color—this is where a product like Woodwing's Smart Styles can come in handy. After you develop a format for your tables, you can save that format as a table style using Woodwing's plug-in and apply table styles to all your financial data so it all has the same look and feel.

Note I've chosen not to use commas but to designate all numbers expressed in millions. Limiting the number of punctuation marks with numeric data is helpful, and I needed to keep the decimal marks because of the earnings per share entry, which is expressed in cents. Use Figure 12.16 to compare your work.

The next spread identifies the directors and officers of the company. If you have pictures of them, you should use them. Here I've just centered the list, with the headers formatted in small caps, the names in italic, 24 points for the headings, and 18 points for the names.

For page 21, draw a graphic frame to fit the margins. Use the Place command to import `lilly1gray.tif` again and scale it vertically by 175%. Tag the image with the Red swatch and add a text frame at y: 8.5". Type **Subsidiaries, Brands and Addresses** and format it

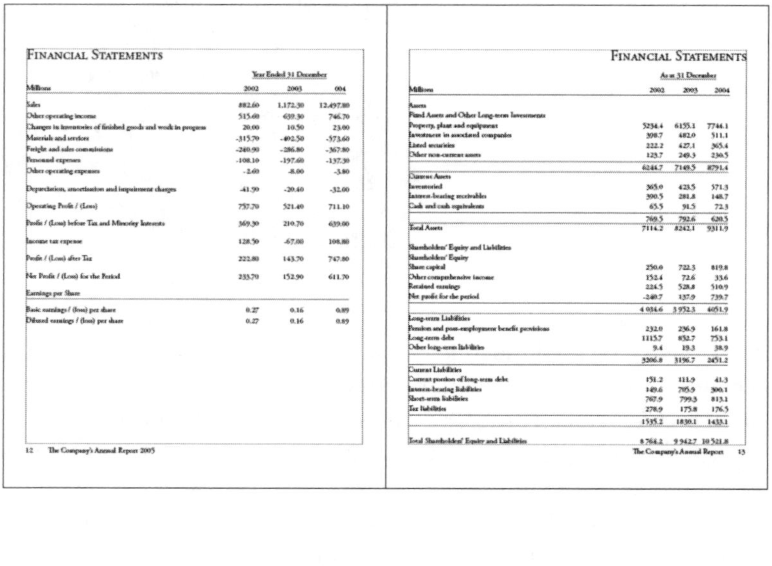

FIGURE 12.16   Pages 18 and 19 of the Pages palette with financial data formatting. You will see auto page numbers 12 and 13 on the pages themselves.

CHAPTER 12: Producing an Annual Report

with small caps, Adobe Garamond Bold. Don't forget to add your credit for the image. Review your work as shown in Figure 12.17.

Page 20 contains logos and descriptions of all the companies or subsidiaries your company owns. I've used three logos that, if you've created the previous projects, you'll recognize. I've scaled each logo I've imported proportionally to fit my box. Of course, I can do this with these graphics because they are vectors and I shouldn't have to deal with any quality issues as a result of my scaling. Next to each logo I've created text frames that contain brief information about each company, where they are located, when they were acquired, how they complement the company, and any other pertinent contact information. I've formatted the text with Century Gothic Regular, 12-point type, left aligned.

For page 23, I've used the same formatting features as for pages 7 and 8. This page, though, contains information from human resources and new initiatives that have been taken to enhance employee benefits while controlling costs. See Figure 12.18 to review this spread.

Continue the HR article to page 24, in a single column, by linking the last text frame on page 23 to this large one on page 24. Fill it with placeholder text.

On page 25, we'll place another rectangular graphic frame, place lilly1gray.tif, and tag it with the patriotic blue swatch. Credit the image and create a text frame at the following coordinate: y: 8.5". This should contain the text Advanced Product Concepts, formatted with Adobe Garamond Bold, 36 points, right aligned. Position it to the right of the layout (use Figure 12.19 as a reference).

Repeat pages 7 and 8 here; this section is used for advanced manufacturing (see Figure 12.20) .

Like the pages for directors and officers, page 28 contains a list of credits for the production of the annual report. Finally, select the Table of Contents command from the Layout menu.

FIGURE 12.17 Pages 20 and 21 of the Pages palette formatted; the auto numbering will reflect pages 14 and 15 on the pages themselves.

FIGURE 12.18 Pages 22 and 23 of the Pages palette formatted; the auto numbering will reflect pages 16 and 17 on the pages themselves.

FIGURE 12.19 Pages 24 and 25 of the Pages palette formatted; the auto numbering will reflect pages 18 and 19 on the pages themselves.

Make sure More Options is clicked. Select the Credit Paragraph style and add it to the list to include, just as you would for making a TOC. We are simply using this feature to create a list with page numbers. Select the TOC Body Text for Entry Style and After Entry for Page Number. Between Entry and Number, enter ", **page**". Click OK and the text icon should load up with a collection of all the credits tagged with the Credit Paragraph style. Click your icon and watch your list generate.

Your entries should look like this:

Table by Julie Smith, Inc., page 5

Both the publication personnel and the illustration and photography credits should be centered. Format the postions with small caps, Adobe Garamond Regular, 18 points, and format the names with the italic version of this face. The credits should be formatted Adobe Garamond Regular, 12 points, 18-point leading. Use Figure 12.21 to review page 28.

CHAPTER 12: **Producing an Annual Report**

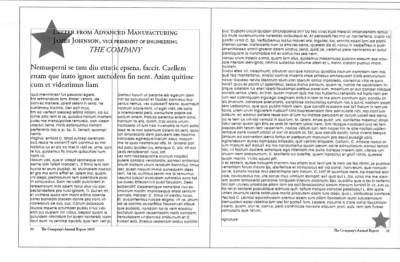

STEP 9 ▼
Creating an Index

I've chosen to treat page 29 as an *index*, with any carryover to page 30. Page 31 is the inside back cover, which is typically left blank, and page 32 is the back cover. Apply the right Master Page B to page 28 in preparation for the index.

To create an index, you have to create index entries. Go to the Window pull-down menu and select Type and Tables, Index. A floating palette opens. You will move through your document, highlighting words or phrases you want to add to the index. These words or phrases should be relevant and terms recipients will likely search for.

Navigate to a page and highlight a word you want to add to the index. Use the drop-down palette menu to select New Page Reference, or click the button directly next to the trash icon at the bottom of the palette.

A dialog box opens with your word already entered into the top level. For the purpose of

FIGURE 12.21 **Page 28 of the Pages palette formatted; the auto numbering will reflect page 22 on the page itself.**

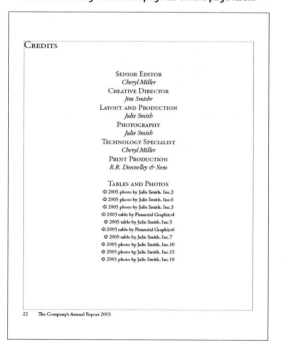

this index, leave the defaults alone (see Figure 12.22 for a sample of the Index dialog box).

Click the Add All button and every instance of this word is recorded in your index. Click Done and move to the next word you would like to add—repeat as necessary. Note that you can add index entries throughout the layout timeline.

After you generate an index, if you feel you've left out entries, you can either update the existing index or delete it and generate a new one.

After you have all the entries added, navigate to page 29. You are now ready to generate the index, either with the palette menu or by clicking the middle button at the bottom of the Index palette.

A dialog box opens, and you can click the More Options button. Type a title for your index, and notice that it creates and applies a style called Index Title, which you can edit later to reflect your own paragraph styles. Note: "Index Title" is applied only to the title of the index, not the entire index. InDesign generates styles on the fly for all index entries if you don't create and specify styles on your own. Make sure Include Index Section Headings is turned on. Leave everything else alone. Click OK.

A text icon appears; click and drag it into the first column. An overflow symbol will appear, indicating there is more to the index. Click the outport, the small square in the lower-right corner of the text frame, in this case, containing a red plus or overflow symbol. Or click the overflow symbol in the out port in the large square in the lower-right corner of the text frame. Then you can Shift-click (auto flow) the remaining text into the area you want to fill. You will see alphabetic entries with index section heads.

 TIP

InDesign allows for the automatic threading or flowing of text with a feature called auto flow. When your text icon loads up—say, from the generation of an index—hold down the Shift key. Note the icon no longer looks like a small paragraph but a serpentine arrow. This is the autoflow symbol. If you Shift-click with this symbol, InDesign autoflows the text into the columns for you.

Open the Paragraph Styles palette and click an index section head. If you want to change the style, double-click the style in the Paragraph palette and change the

FIGURE 12.22   The Index palette and entry dialog box.

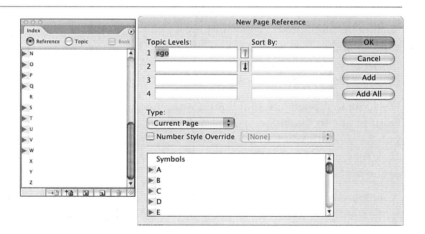

formatting. The section heads' styles will all update when you are finished. You can do the same for the index entries themselves (see Figure 12.23 for an example of what your index might look like). If there is still overflow in the second column, move to page 30, apply the left Master Page B, and continue to thread your index into these columns. Again, page 31, the inside back cover, is left blank.

FIGURE 12.23   Your index page(s).

Page 32, the back cover, should reflect the front cover. You can either repeat the front or select specific elements to copy to the back cover. I will leave the back cover up to you.

STEP 10 ▼
Preflighting Your Project

Make sure you have saved your work. Go to the File pull-down menu and select Preflight.

The preflight command checks your file to make sure it is in acceptable condition to submit to your print service provider. It checks for fonts, links, images, colors, inks, print, and external plug-ins. All of this information impacts your print service provider.

InDesign uses a yellow caution triangle to indicate problems. When you are clicking through the Preflight dialog box, look for these warnings indicating a problem. You might have a problem such as a font used by the document is not turned on in your font management utility, you've moved or modified an image since you placed it in your document, or you placed an RGB image. If you see errors or warnings, you need to exit this dialog box, fix the problem, and run the preflight again.

STEP 11 ▼
Creating a Color Composite Proof

Let's print a content proof. Go to the File pull-down menu and select Print. Choose the appropriate settings for the printer available to you. On the General tab, choose one copy. On the Setup tab select 8.5" ×11" and vertical orientation. Leave the scale alone. On the Marks and Bleed, turn off all the options. On the Output tab, if possible, print a color composite output for your work; if not, select Grayscale. On the Graphics tab, the default settings should work. The remaining tabs can be ignored for now. Print and review your proof, make any necessary adjustments, and save your changes. Print it again.

Absolute page numbering has been used in this project. The preference setting you choose also impacts printing. Absolute page numbering uses only the physical sequence of pages. If you want to print page 1, your cover will print. If you want to print the page with the number 1 in the lower-right corner, you must print page 7. The same holds true for the Export feature: If you want to export this file as a PDF, the same rule applies. Export All Pages does just that, but if you want to export only a portion of your pages, it uses the absolute numbering and ignores the auto page numbering in use by the document. Folios (visible page numbers on the actual pages themselves) reflect numbering as a result of section starts, not the "absolute" page numbering.

STEP 12 ▼
Review and Approval

This type of publication will probably go through at least two proofing cycles for content and perhaps another for color approval. (Be careful with this one because everyone perceives color differently. So, limit the number of contributors at this step and trust your print service provider.) Adobe Acrobat 7 Professional is an ideal tool for this application. You can create a PDF and, with the email review feature, designate who you want to participate in the review by entering their email addresses. Emails are automatically distributed and recipients are invited to create comments (annotations) regarding the PDF. After those comments are recorded, they are sent back to the originator of the review. From there, you can take those comments, correct the layout, create a new PDF, and start the cycle again until all the content is approved. The best part of all is that the recipients do not have to own Acrobat themselves—only Acrobat Reader 7, which is a free download from Adobe. The initiator of the review can simply customize the review options and enable Reader commenting. This feature can expedite the review and approval process.

Final Thoughts

In this project you've picked up some intermediate layout skills. You've worked with some new InDesign features as well. Most importantly, you've constructed a publication that requires a lot of planning. It requires attention to formatting and formal navigation and crediting features you wouldn't ordinarily see in most marketing material.

Important concepts to keep in mind include

- Get all the contributors to the project on board with assignments, clear instructions, and deadlines. Manage them and keep in touch with reminders and feedback about submissions.

- Plan the project with your print service provider in advance of the actual construction, and work out all the details from substrates and ink through special binding and finishing requirements.

- Decide how you want to handle the financial data you will receive—specifically, tabbed text or tables. The formatting for these choices will be different depending on which feature you go with.

- Translate some of the data into graphically rich visuals that are clearly labeled and easy to read.

- Finally, proof early and often. Have your review cycle planned so the people participating in the reviews know what their roles and deadlines are.

PART III: Appendixes

anamorphic   Differing scale effects along perpendicular (x,y) axis applied to an image. It's the opposite of proportional scaling (equal effects on both axes).

anchored objects   Formerly known as *inline graphics*, these are objects attached to text that reflow with text as it is edited and reflowed.

aqueous coating   A water-based coating typically used all over a printed piece, as in a flood coated document. Because of its viscosity, it's difficult to limit it to specific areas.

back matter   The last pages in a long document that include appendixes, indexes, and any blank pages left at the back.

bleed   The area used to align objects needed to extend beyond the trimline of your printed document.

blending mode   Found in the Transparency palette, it allows you to mix objects together and have colors combine rather than replace each other in different ways.

calibrated   A device functioning up to its vendor's standards.

center spread   The center two pages of a publication.

characterized   Refers to the creation of a device profile, which is a description of the device's unique color rendering capabilities.

clipping path A vector outline of a raster image that has the effect of creating a smooth edge while knocking out the background behind the outlined foreground.

CMYK Process color that is the basic ink set for commercial printers. It stands for cyan, magenta, yellow, black. (*K*, instead of *B*, is used for black because *B* could mistakenly be thought to stand for blue.) CMYK is a subtractive color model that uses pigments to absorb colors from the visual spectrum. The remaining reflected colors of light determine how the human eye perceives the color in the printed piece. You can mix CMYK to form approximately 5,000 colors.

collapsible palette bays The dock on the right side of the InDesign interface that allows floating palettes to be stored and slide out as needed.

collateral A term used for printed materials used to present information about your business and its capabilities, products, or services.

color management The process of controlling the rendition of color when multiple devices are involved.

Color palette Contains a defined color list from which you can work for all your content.

color separations The process of converting color art or continuous tone color photos into four process colors (cyan, magenta, yellow, and black) for printing.

columns Information placed vertically in a table.

compound Created using Pathfinder operations or by selecting Object, Compound Paths, Make. Two or more selected objects are united and moved to the same plane. The appearance of the resulting object is determined by the options chosen.

constraining Applying a constraint to shape or motion by holding down the Shift key.

content proof A proof that represents a reasonable facsimile of the layout. It's used to approve content only and not for color correction.

cover It's typically a separate or different substrate from the body of the publication, unless you're using a self-cover, meaning it's comprised of the same material as the body pages.

creep The effect of pages not meeting equally at the face trim of a publication; it's seen most frequently in saddle-stitched binding.

data source A file that contains your mailing data. It typically includes contact information such as the company name, contact information, address, and so on.

demographics Characteristics of populations that identify consumer markets.

die cuts A finishing technique that cuts stock in unusual shapes or edges by striking the stock with a metal die; it's popular in the commercial greeting card industry.

digital A printing method that directly delivers pigment to the substrate using electrostatically charged toner, toner-slurry, or sprayed ink.

digital proofs   Proofs made from a digital output device. Unlike analog proofs, which require film, digital proofs are made directly from the digital file to a digital output device.

dingbat   A special type character that is graphical in nature.

drag copy   A keyboard shortcut for all Adobe products that allows the user to hold down either the Option or Alt key while an object is in motion, which will automatically create a duplicate or copy of the object.

drop cap   Not to be confused with an initial cap, a drop cap is a large character that drops down into the body of the paragraph. The lines in the paragraph wrap around it.

drop shadow   The simulation of a shadow offset in two directions.

duotones   A picture composed of two colors, typically black plus a spot color. These two colors are printed at different angles with black always printed on a 45° angle.

duplexed   A page printed on both sides via an output device (many copiers and network printers have this feature).

em space   The size of the letter *m* in the type-face and point size currently selected. So, an em space would equal 10 points if you were using 10-point type.

embossing   A finishing technique that lowers the surface of stock in a specific shape by striking the stock with a metal stamp.

EPS   Stands for Encapsulated PostScript: PostScript language artwork, which is a common file format for vector artwork.

feathering   Creating a faded, blurry effect around the edge of an image.

file link   Managed by the InDesign Links palette, this feature allows you to maintain a list of all the resources you've placed in your publication. Unless images are embedded (and this is not a recommended practice for application files), images are linked to the publication and only a low-resolution thumbnail preview is used within the InDesign file. This allows for efficient management of layout files.

fill   Solid color within an object.

flexographic   A printing method by which content is imaged onto a rubber plate that stretches to accommodate three-dimensional objects. It's well suited for packaging and labels but is not recommended for high-resolution printing or printing that requires substantial type.

foil stamping   A finishing technique that adds metallic foil to a specific area by stamping it into position. It's commonly seen on diplo-mas, religious materials, and even business cards.

fold lines   Marks used by commercial printers to tell the binder workers where to fold.

font   A digital version of a type family and its faces.

footnote   A note placed at the bottom of a page that cites a reference for something mentioned in the text.

front matter   The first pages in a long docu-ment that include publishing credits, a table of contents, an introduction, or a foreword.

fulfillment   The act of stocking or reserving preprinted material or inventory for use over a period of time.

full bleed   Printing beyond all the edges of a page to compensate for misregistration on press so that, when trimmed, color has printed all the way to the edge of the page.

gamut   A range or available palette of color.

gate fold   Generally symmetrical, with two or more panels folding into the center from opposing sides.

GIF   The Graphic Interchange Format, which is a web raster file format and one of the oldest web file formats.

group   A relationship of selected items that, when selected, all select and transform together. Grouped objects can be ungrouped, or individual elements can be accessed without ungrouping using the Direct Selection tool. In InDesign CS2, when grouped objects are selected, they are represented by a dotted outline.

gutter   A printing term that represents additional space required for perfect and case binding.

hard return   A line break that creates a new paragraph. It's created by pressing Enter.

hidden characters   Nonprinting characters that manage the position of text, including carriage returns, soft returns, tabs, spaces, and so on.

hyperlink   A link or reference from some point in one document to another document, another place in the same document, or a URL.

ICC profiles   The International Color Consortium is the governing body for color standards, and its profiles are the adopted methodology for characterizing devices and their color gamuts.

indentation   A paragraph command that moves all lines in a paragraph in from the left and right or the first line in from the left. A left indent moves all the lines of a paragraph in from the left. A right indent moves all the lines of a paragraphic in from the right. A first line indent moves the first line of a paragraph in from the left of the left indent.

index   A navigational device for long documents that assists the reader in finding a specific topic mentioned in the document.

inside cover   The text printed on the back (inside) page of the front cover.

interactive   An element that enables the user to interact with the file, not just read it.

intranet   An internal company website that is not available to the public.

job ticket   Documentation used by a print service provider to define the parameters of the production of a job. The job ticket typically includes the job number, client name, deadlines for all phases of production, finished size, number of pages, number of colors, binding and imposition requirements, color correction instructions, and so on.

JPEG   The Joint Photographic Experts Group. A compressed raster file format, it utilizes a lossy compression scheme that removes data to achieve compression.

justification   The adjustment of horizontal space throughout an entire paragraph. It handles letter and word spacing separately.

justified   Text that is horizontally or vertically aligned.

kerning   The horizontal adjustment of space between a pair of characters.

knockout/reverse   An object or text revealed by removing color (ink) from a background to reveal the paper color beneath. You may also see the term knockout defined as a silhouette.

l*a*b   The international color standard that measures lightness (the *l*), the green-red axis (the *a*), and the blue-yellow axis (the *b*).

lamination   A thin layer of a clear, protective material bonded to the surface of the substrate by applying both heat and pressure.

landscape   The horizontal, or wide, orientation of a printed piece.

layers   An organization tool that allows you to group elements into stacks and identify them, such as the content layer.

leaders   Characters that fill between the end of text and a tab stop. Typically, leaders are used in forms, tables of contents, and indexes. Leaders commonly appear as dots (for TOCs and indexes) or lines (for forms).

letter spacing   The adjustment of space between letters only, leaving word spacing alone.

libraries   The InDesign equivalent of a repository in the form of a separate file that, when opened, becomes a palette that holds frequently used objects such as text, graphics, and unassigned (neither text nor graphic, which is useful for basic object shapes).

master page   An underlying master layout that contains repeating elements on each normal page of your file, such as repeating column and ruler guides, headers and footers, and page numbers.

masthead   The title of the publication, which remains the same every time the publication is produced (for example, the masthead of every issue of *Rolling Stone* is "Rolling Stone").

merged document   The result of a data merge or the combination of the data source and target document. This is a completely separate document and does not affect the original layout.

metafile   A digital file format capable of containing both raster and vector graphics.

object styles   These are saved styles for graphical elements that include all sorts of attributes. They're found in the Object Styles palette menu or the Control palette.

offset   Method of printing that involves cylinders, a blanket, oily inks, and water. The image on the printing plate is first offset to a rubber blanket, and then the blanket transfers the image to the paper—hence the term offset.

offset lithography   The most popular commercial printing process involving plates, blankets, cylinders, water, and ink.

OpenType   A new cross-platform font file format.

paper grain   The direction of cellulose fibers created in paper during the paper-making process.

paragraph rules   Lines that are attached to paragraphs and flow and resize as text moves through a text block(s).

paragraph styles   Predefined formats for paragraph text. Style can carry attributes including font, size, spacing, and hyphenation. They are useful for creating a consistent look within a publication or across several publications.

PDF The Portable Document Format was innovated by Adobe systems for the purpose of easily distributing content. Its characteristics include self-contained resources and cross-platform compatibility.

PDF/x A subset of the file format. PDF is designed for reliable prepress processing. It ensures the PDF contains correct content for this type of print workflow.

perfect binding A binding method that requires extra space at the gutter to accommodate the bend or fold of the paper. The gutter edge is ground and glued. Examples include magazines and paperback books.

placeholder text Dummy text used to create a template. It's useful when copy for a publication isn't readily available because it allows for the continued development of the publication pertaining to formatting text.

planning Meeting with your print production vendor and any additional vendors in the production process about things such as binding, finishing, and mailing that will be involved in the job to preview the job and offer guidance for how to create the job so that it has optimum manufacturing success.

portrait The vertical or tall orientation of a printed piece.

preflight The act of verifying that all resource files are included with a digital project and validating that the files and layout are of sufficient quality so they can move forward into the print production workflow.

preset Stored settings for later reuse.

printer's pairs A publication's layout in imposition order so that when it is folded, cut, and bound, it reads correctly.

process colors Colors made up of screen tints of cyan, magenta, yellow, and black printing inks.

proofs Reasonable facsimiles or simulations of the expected printed outcome, such as content proofs, contract proofs, page proofs, and imposition proofs.

proxy A mechanism on either the Control palette or Transformation palette that establishes the point of origin.

PSD The Photoshop native file format, which can contain multiple layers and transparency.

quadtones A picture composed of four colors, typically black plus three spot colors. These colors are printed at different angles with black always printed on a 45° angle.

raster An image composed of an array of pixels arranged in rows and columns.

reader's pairs A publication's layout in reading order.

RGB It is projected color—the basic light set for viewing instruments including monitors, televisions, projectors, and handheld devices. It stands for red, green, and blue. These are the colors the human eye identifies, or perceives. RGB is an additive color model that uses light to mix from the visual spectrum. You can mix these colors to form approximately 16 million colors.

rows Information placed horizontally in a table.

scoring The process of mechanically creasing the paper to facilitate folding while guarding against cracking of paper and board. This is essential when heavy (thick) papers are folded.

self-mailer   A marketing piece that is mailed without an envelope. It includes a return address, an addressee, and some form of postage. Examples of this are postcards, newsletters, catalogues, and so on.

serigraphic   This printing method, also called *screen*, transfers an image to a screen (synthetic or natural fiber) that has been stretched over a frame. The image is etched in a chemical emulsion, blocks ink in certain areas, and lets ink through in others. The screen itself acts as the carrier for the ink, which is pushed through the mesh with a squeegee onto the substrate underneath. It's recommended for a variety of substrates (signage), cloth, and specialty items.

small caps   A style of typeface in which the first character is a true, standard height capital and the remaining letters are capital in smaller scale. In InDesign small caps are set to 70% of actual size. This percentage can be adjusted in the Advanced Type Preferences.

soft return   A line break that doesn't create a new paragraph. It's created by pressing Shift+Enter.

spot color   A special ink, other than cyan, yellow, magenta, and black (which are process colors), given its own unit on the printing press. These inks are developed and manufactured by companies such as PANTONE and Toyo. They are designed to expand the color gamut of process inks beyond the 5,000+ colors that can be mixed with process colors. Colors that are difficult to create from process inks, such as oranges, navy blues, metallics, and pastels, can be achieved with these special inks.

spot varnishes   Clear coating in specific areas to give the image greater emphasis.

stock photography   Noncopyrighted images made available for purchase.

stroke   A line or frame containing both color and weight properties, which straddles the vector or outline of an object. Strokes are applied to a table to visually divide the data.

subscript   The opposite of superscript, it sets a character below and to the side of another character—for example, H_2O.

substrate   A broader term than *stock*, it refers to the substance upon which you print— paper, cloth, glass, and so on.

superscript   To set a character above and to the side of another character and at a reduced size—for example, X^2.

SVG   The Scalable Vector Graphics file format, which creates a vector graphic file format intended for web graphics.

swatches   Saved color definitions.

SWF   Shockwave Flash, a Macromedia file format that creates scalable and compact web graphics and is well suited for interactive, animated web graphics.

table   Another formatting device used to line up information in both a horizontal and vertical manner. Tables allow for the organization of data or information in an easy-to-read format.

tabs   Physical stops placed on a ruler. Each stop is characterized by its own alignment properties. When the Tab key is pressed to move to a stop, those alignment properties cause the text to move in a specific direction and create alignment or columns.

tagging to apply a characteristic to an element as used throughout this book as in to tag an object with a colored fill or to tag some text with a paragraph style. Interchangeable with the word "apply."

target document The layout created to receive the data.

template A standard document preset with layout, graphics, and text.

text wrap A floating palette that enables you to control the flow of text around another element as opposed to text flowing on top of or underneath an element. This feature creates interesting visual effects with type by creating a boundary around an object that repels text away.

thread When you thread text, you take blocks of text and link them together for the purpose of flowing text on a page or throughout the pages of a file.

TIFF The Tagged Image File Format is a raster file format primarily found in print workflows.

TOC stands for table of contents, which generally expresses broad categories of a publication's organization.

tracking The horizontal adjustment of space across highlighted text.

transformation A function that changes the position or direction of the axes of an element.

transparency The degree of opacity found in an element.

trapping The compensation for press misregistration by expanding or retracting abutting colors in a layout.

tritones A picture composed of three colors, typically black plus two spot colors. These colors are printed at different angles with black always printed on a 45° angle.

type family A group of typefaces within the same design pattern, such as Palatino Roman, Palatino Bold, and Palatino Italic.

typeface Variations within a type family.

UV 1) Ultraviolet ink used for outdoor signage because it resists the elements, particularly fading. 2) An ultraviolet coating used to protect a printed piece from light damage.

varnish A common coating typically used to highlight specific areas of a printed piece, commonly used on coated stock.

vector Object-oriented graphics represented as separate shapes using outlines of lines, arcs, and curves.

Vellum A type of stock or paper made up of fibers that make the paper translucent.

wide format An industry term referring to roll-fed, wide inkjet plotters used for large or oversize pieces, typically posters, banners, and signage.

word spacing The adjustment of space between words only, leaving letter spacing alone.

XML The Extensible Markup Language is used to repurpose content particularly for the Web, but it can be used to tag any document structure.

Using the Publisher's Website for All InDesign @work Project Files

All the projects in this book use resource files located on the publisher's website. They are organized by chapter, and each chapter contains both project files as well as finished projects so you can compare your layouts with mine.

To download the book's project/resource files, go to http://www.samspublishing.com. Enter this book's ISBN (without the hyphens) in the Search box and click Search. When the book's title is displayed, click the title to go to a page where you can download the project Zip files.

> 🚫 **CAUTION**
>
> Be sure you extract all the files from each Zip file with the Use Folder Names option (for PC users) selected so you can get the same folders on your computer as included in each Zip file. Mac users can simply double-click the downloaded Zip file and the folder structure should appear intact, as named.

The Adobe Website and Transparency

The transparency feature in InDesign is a powerful, creative option that many publishers are using in their layouts. How to use it effectively and ensure it produces properly is the question. Because InDesign can apply transparency to both vector and raster elements, when combining those elements together, flattening decisions are required to determine how these elements combine when they're output. Features that invoke transparency include

- ▶ The Transparency palette (found on the Window pull-down menu)
- ▶ Drop Shadow (found on the Object pull-down menu)
- ▶ Feather (found on the Object pull-down menu)

When any of these features are used, transparency is invoked. You can confirm this by looking at the Pages palette. Pages that contain transparency have a checkerboard appearance. This is an Adobe convention used throughout the Creative Suite to indicate transparency.

Assuming you intend to print the publication or export it in a PDF version lower than 6.0, you will need to flatten it. You can flatten at the page level using the Flattener Preview palette or the Pages palette or at the document level while printing or exporting.

For more information on flattening, visit Adobe's website for an excellent guide on the topic. You can download it as a PDF and keep it as a desktop reference. Use the following URL:

http://www.adobe.com/products/creativesuite/pdfs/dgt.pdf

Popular Plug-ins

I can't speak for all the plug-ins available on the market, but there are a few that I either have used or have clients using. These come highly recommended:

- ▶ **Woodwing Software**—Provides some valuable plug-ins for InDesign. Its Smart Series of plug-ins is handy, and you can download free 30-day trial versions of its products. Smart Styles, as an example, allows you to store table styles (much like paragraph, character, and object styles) so that, once you develop some tables that work well with your company brand, you can simply define them as styles and tag all your tables in the same way. This is an enormous time-saver, not to mention great for content consistency. Check out Woodwing's website at www.woodwing.com.

- ▶ Given the trend in advertising toward personalization rather than mass marketing, it's noteworthy to include variable data publishing. Several developers in this market space are creating plug-ins for InDesign so that marketing and communication professionals can take customer data and merge this with InDesign layouts to create personal marketing pieces. This goes beyond the simple DataMerge feature found in InDesign CS2. One of the notable applications is XMPie's product UDirect. For more information on this plug-in and other developers, go to Adobe's Variable Data Publishing Resource Center at http://www.adobe.com/products/vdp/main.html.

- ▶ **Cacidi Systems**—This company has a plug-in that batch processes multiple Quark and PageMaker files into InDesign fairly quickly and efficiently. Cacidi also offers several plug-ins for catalog publishers. Go to www.cacidi.com.

> ## ⊗ NOTE
>
> All the plug-ins previously mentioned range in price from $65 to $2,500. As with all plug-ins, it is important that you verify with the developer that the plug-in you are interested in is compatible with the new version of InDesign. If a trial download is available, you should try the product to determine whether you might experience technical difficulties.

- ▶ **Adobe**—You can visit Adobe's website (www.adobe.com) for a listing of plug-ins for InDesign at http://www.adobe.com/products/plugins/indesign/main.html. The Adobe User Group website (http://www.indesignusergroup.com/thirdparty/plug_ins/_plug_ins.php) has a nice listing as well.

Local Resources

You should look into the following local resources for assistance with your new acquisition or upgrade. Networking with other users can provide invaluable feedback. In addition, training is always a great way to kick start the learning process. Look for an Adobe Certified Instructor in your area. Finally, I've collected many references over the years that I have found to be useful; I gladly pass some of those recommendations on to you here.

User Groups and Associations

Many people don't realize that they have local resources, such as an InDesign Users Group, available to them. Being able to connect with other professionals using this product, possibly for the first time, is a wonderful networking opportunity and a local resource at the same time. Use the following website to locate a user group near you: http://www.indesignusergroup.com/.

Don't have one? Consider starting one in your area. You will note that the user group website has additional resources and useful links for all kinds of information.

In addition to a specific user group, try locating a chapter of the American Institute of Graphic Arts (AIGA) at www.aiga.org. You will meet many professionals working with InDesign. Do you find yourself in a corporate environment? Try the International Association of Business Communicators (IABC) at www.iabc.com. These two organiza-

tions are broader in scope, but they often have technology user groups that might prove useful to you.

Training

No doubt, training is a subject near and dear to my heart. Nothing can replace instructor-led training, and to locate an Adobe Certified Instructor, visit the Adobe website at http://partners.adobe.com/public/partnerfinder/tp/show_find.do.

Your local community college might offer options, and don't forget your local art centers. We have a wonderful resource here in Indianapolis, called the Indianapolis Art Center, and they have a computer lab that offers design classes on popular software.

If local instruction is not available to you or your budget won't allow for it, explore the many options Adobe provides at http://www.adobe.com/support/training.html.

Publications: Print and Web

As always, turn to the developer as a first choice for information.

- ▶ A wealth of information, support, downloads, papers, best practices, and referrals to a variety of ASN participants can be found at http://partners.adobe.com/public/main.html.

- ▶ Sign up for available resources found at http://www.adobe.com/support/main.html. There you will discover all kinds of resources, from the Adobe Studio chock full of ideas, tips, and techniques, to Adobe's new quarterly online magazine called *Proxy* (http://www.sadobeproxy.com/).

- Yet another new magazine new on the market is *InDesign Magazine*, published in association with Creativepro.com (www.creativepro.com). You can find it at http://www.indesignmag.com/idm/index.html. Creativepro.com is a great resource website for all your communication needs. You will find familiar names contributing to their editorial content and reviews.

- To learn more about the world of digital printing, turn to www.printondemand.com.

- Because, throughout the book, we frequently mention the making of PDFs as a reliable method for distributing content, I recommend Adobe's website for more information about this file format. You should also check out the huge PDF resource site http://www.planetpdf.com, as well as PDFzone (http://www.pdfzone.com/).

Finally, I recommend the following books:

- I am particularly fond of the reference book series *Visual QuickStart Guides* and recommend them to all my trainees as tried-and-true desk references. Aside from my book for your on-the-job projects, I also recommend *InDesign CS for Mac and Windows* by Sandee Cohen (Peachpit Press, ISBN 0321322010). It is well written and well organized—truly a complete desk reference.

- Every publisher of content should have the *Chicago Manual of Style*, the style standard for best practices in publishing (University of Chicago Press Staff, ISBN 0226104036).

Appendix C: Printing Processes

The following printing processes are covered, including common commercial printing workflows: offset, gravure, screen, flexo, and digital.

Offset

The most common form of commercial printing, offset is a printing process in which a printing plate is made; then it is mounted onto a cylinder, rolled in a mixture of ink and water, and then offset onto a blanket, which in turn rolls over paper.

This method of printing is by far the most common and the option you will choose repeatedly to address the majority of your printing requirements. Build references or resources of stock samples as well as ink catalogues, and include chip books or fans, which will assist you with your production choices. It is also helpful to have a good understanding of bindery and finishing options. The following is an overview of the offset method.

Sheetfed Versus Web

There are two categories of offset: sheetfed and web. *Sheetfed* sends cut sheets of paper through a printing press, whereas a *web* press sends paper through a press from giant rolls of paper, which are later cut.

The applications for offset are numerous. Almost all examples in this book could be accomplished with offset, sheetfed printing. Publications that are typically printed on web presses include newspapers, books, and magazines, which are typically printed in large quantities. This is a more economical method of printing because the run lengths are long, thereby decreasing the cost per piece. Because the paper is not precut, the cost for this resource is lower. The more impressions you can get from a plate, the less expensive each impression is. Web presses can print on both sides of paper at the same time as the web (rolled paper) runs through the web press—again an economization.

Chemistry

Offset printing involves the creation of print-ing plates that have *oleophilic*, or oil-attracting, areas (the image) and *hydrophilic*, or water-attracting, areas (the nonimageable area). The printing press uses a combination of water and ink, and the chemicals then migrate to the appropriate areas on the plate. There is already some moisture in the paper itself, which actually assists in the printing process; however, too much moisture in the paper will ultimately cause problems as the paper eventually cures or dries and shrinks.

A lot of skill is involved in getting the chem-istry or balance between water and ink just right. So, unlike any other printing process, achieving optimum color requires several passes before the press operator pulls a press sheet he is satisfied with. The goal—aside from managing a schedule, mounting plates, mixing and managing chemistry, loading paper, and maintaining the press—is to come as close as possible to matching the proof you signed.

Proofing

Sometimes the proof you signed is made from the same films that made the printing plate the press operator is using. The benefit of this method of proofing is that the plate and the proof are made from a common source, which should result in the printed piece more

closely matching the proof. The downsides to this type of proofing are cost and time. Now that more than half of all commercial print-ing plants in this country are direct-to-plate (a method in which the printer can send your file directly to plate, without having to image film), a proof made from film is not an avail-able choice because no film has been made.

Digital proofing has emerged hand in hand with direct-to-plate. The same file that gener-ates the plate generates the proof. This is a great economy of time and money. The trick is to get the digital proofing device to image or create color to match the printing plate production. When consistent color can be achieved to match digital proof to plate, everyone wins. The printer achieves economy of the manufacturing process and therefore the customer wins, as well.

As we've discussed previously in this book, printers can employ a variety of proofing technologies, and there are pros and cons to each. Just remember that pleasing color can be achieved at lower resolutions (twice your linescreen), whereas most of us would like to see crisp, clean type, which is achieved at higher resolutions. You will ultimately get this from your printing plate, but it might be difficult to achieve depending on which digital proof option you choose.

Print Workflow

As I've said repeatedly, you can't communi-cate too much with your commercial print service provider. While commercial printers have been developing many mechanisms for making the submission, preflighting, proof-ing, and tracking of your print projects as easy as possible, it is still important that every aspect of the manufacturing process is well planned and that you understand everything that will happen to your job.

The workflow might look like this (and yes, I'm sketching out the ideal, both process as well as quality control) in the following sections.

Estimating

You contact your sales representative at your primary provider to discuss an upcoming job you are about to begin. You sit down with the sales rep to sketch out the job specifications, to the best of your ability, including the run length, the number of colors, the number of pages, the stock choices, the binding styles, and any finishing requirements. Your rep returns an estimate to you based on the parameters you submitted.

Planning

At this point, you should have solidified the project, resources, staff, and format of the project. You'll call your rep and notify her of any changes that would affect the estimate, along with a schedule. At this point in time, you should participate in a planning meeting with your print service provider if a) the job is important; b) the job is complex; or c) you don't have much experience with this printer or in working with any printer. Often a planning meeting will point out issues on the creative side that might not translate too well in print production, and guidance can be offered to structure a piece in a way that will satisfy the creative request—which is very valuable. On the manufacturing side, planners within your service provider will plan the manufacturing process; line up the necessary resources; and map out the workflow including which press, sheet size, and bindery

equipment will be necessary to process the job.

Submission and Preflighting

After you have completed your project—including proofing and approval—and your own preflight, it's time to turn the project over to your service provider. Depending on your service provider's requirements, you might burn your files to CD or DVD or submit your files via FTP. Your service provider might have web-based preflighting so that, when you submit your work to their workflow via their website, you can receive a preflight report (usually via email) to notify you of the status of your job.

 NOTE

Your goal is to submit as complete a project as possible. The less intervention the prepress operator needs to make with your files, the faster the job will move through the system and the less charges you will incur.

The role of preflight is to verify that all resources are present and validate that the quality of those resources is sufficient enough to move through the workflow with little intervention. If intervention in the form of correcting problems such as fonts, color, and image resolution is necessary, you will probably be presented with the choice of either correcting the problems yourself or having your provider correct the problems.

Prepress

Once preflighted, your job will move into prepress where additional work will be performed. If corrections to your file need to be made regarding fonts, color, or images, this will take place next.

If changes or corrections are unnecessary, meaning you've followed my advice and created a bullet-proof PDFx job that requires no intervention by prepress, you might be working with a commercial printer with an automated PDF workflow such as Creo's Prinergy or Artwork System's Nexus. These systems will take your PDF and, using predefined scripts, process your jobs through the next few steps automatically, instead of operators executing these steps individually or manually.

If, on the other hand, certain changes to your project need to take place to prepare it for production, your original application file will be edited. These changes can include adding bleeds, adding marks, preparing images that crossover bind, trapping, and imposing your project.

> **NOTE**
>
> To *trap* a file means to slightly overlap abutting colored areas so that, when paper wiggles on press (and it will), abutting colors still appear to touch rather than pull apart to reveal the paper. Why does paper wiggle on press? Paper is usually held in place along one edge, the gripper edge. The edge of the paper away from the gripper edge could span as much as 40". The farther away from the gripper edge you travel, the less steady the paper is; it can therefore move slightly, but enough to affect how elements on the paper, particularly abutting colored elements, print closely to each other. Therefore, the technique of trapping is employed. Special software examines touching objects in your file and their color values and determines the adjustments that are required. Trapping is just one of many skills a prepress operator must have to process your files correctly.

At this point in the process, you might have asked for some type of proof so you see the finished product prior to trap and imposition. This is a digital proof, such as a content proof used to approve the content of the page(s) but not the color. Or, if you've asked your service provider to perform color correction on your images, you can request a contract proof for the purpose of approval of your images. A contract proof is usually generated on a high-quality color proofing device designed to print images, specifically color, very well.

> **NOTE**
>
> To *impose* a file means to take the pages you will lay out in reading order and reorder those pages to accommodate the binding style you have chosen. Even if you are not binding your project—such as in the case of a postcard—imposition still takes place (that is, multiple up). Imposition has two purposes: to make the most of a sheet of paper and to position pages on that paper so that, when the sheet is folded, cut, and bound, the pages are back in reading order again. Imposition accounts for *creep*, the byproduct of folding many pages together. Pages creep backward, with the innermost pages appearing longer than the outer pages. Imposition calculates the amount of space needed to add back into the layout to compensate for creep.

After your job is trapped and imposed, if you are printing a multipage job, you might have another type of proof generated. This is a page proof, generated from a wide format device that can image the large imposed sheets that are then folded and trimmed down to show you a mock-up of the finished project.

Plating

Finally, your job is ready to plate and print. The prepress operator will release your job to plate, and the digital file will be sent to a machine that will rip your file to machine pixels and laser the image to a special plate mounted on a cylinder. Plates typically go through some type of processing to wash and bake them. Baking hardens them so that they can hold up under constant impressions. Plates are typically inspected and proofed to ensure they match the imposition proof. The plates are then released to the pressroom.

Press

The press operator(s) will manage the chemistry and mount the plates and paper. Depending on the number of colors in your job, each unit on the press will contain a color (CMYK) and a plate for that color. The press operator will execute several passes or runs of paper, adjusting the chemistry to get the press proofs to match the contract proof. When he feels he has accomplished this, a press check, if requested, will take place. The best effort (press sheet) will be taken to a light booth or a customer lounge with a light booth and viewed under optimum conditions and compared to the contract proof. If approval is given, the job will run. If additional tweaking needs to occur, then it's back to adjusting the press until a proof is pulled that is satisfactory. After the job has run and is moved to the bindery, the press operator(s) will be responsible for breaking down the press, removing the plates, cleaning them, and so on.

Bindery

From the press, the sheets are moved into the bindery where folding, binding, and cutting occur. From the bindery, the job is checked (this check is usually called *quality control [QC]*) and then sent to shipping or fulfillment.

Shipping will send the job wherever it's requested. Fulfillment is a value-added service your print provider might offer, in which they warehouse your finished goods for you and take care of drawing down the inventory and sending it wherever you need, thereby becoming by extension your own distribution center.

Shipping

Once shipped, you are invoiced for the work. Depending on how well the job was produced and how many problems were experienced along the way, you might be asked to participate or you might instigate a review of the project in an attempt to identify areas for improvement.

For a great, firsthand look at the technological advances of this form of printing, go to a trade show such as Print, which is hosted by GASC.org and typically held at McCormick Place in Chicago each September. There, you can walk the floors and see all manner of printing presses and technologies that are innovating this industry.

This is the cycle for offset commercial printing. What follows are descriptions of other types of commercial printing processes and recommendations for applications for each of those processes. The workflow for each varies slightly to accommodate any differences in press preparation, but generally file preparation is handled the same regardless of the printing process.

Gravure

Gravure is a process in which large, heavy, metal cylinders are engraved with the image to be printed for each color or page. The cylinders roll in ink and the excess is wiped off, leaving only the ink in the etching. As the cylinder rolls over the paper, the ink is deposited directly to paper.

Gravure printing is a cousin to long-run web offset. However, in this printing process, the image is not offset onto some type of receiver. These cylinders are extremely durable and last longer than offset plates. Gravure is used frequently for long printing runs for publications that have large circulations, such as magazines. Other long-run items might include wallpaper and some flexible packaging.

Some important aspects of gravure worth noting are that no chemistry is involved with gravure printing and no mixing of ink and water occurs (only ink is used, which means consistent color can be achieved quickly). As you can imagine, etching the page image into hard metal creates a very fine, quality reproduction and is occasionally used for fine art reproduction. However, creating these etched cylinders is expensive, which makes them practical for only long run lengths. These hard cylinders are ideal for long runs also because, once a plate gives out, there are no more impressions left to be made. Make another plate with new chemistry and you risk inconsistency throughout the run. These metal cylinders run for millions of impressions. Money is printed with this process.

Screen Printing

Everyone thinks of T-shirts when they hear *screen printing* (also known as *serigraphic printing*), but I've worked with a few screen printers and, believe me, the only t-shirts around were on the backs of the employees. The

opportunity for creativity in large form is astounding. I've witnessed everything from billboards to vehicle signage, to outdoor signs to 3D in-store retail displays that would really knock your socks off.

This method of printing is appropriate for signage; printing on fabric; novelty items; and unique surfaces like glass, circuit boards, wall coverings, and even linoleum. This method of printing uses process as well as spot color inks; however, they are formulated thicker and dry more quickly. Signage requires that these inks be able to stand up to all sorts of environmental issues. Substrates are much more varied than offset and, beyond paper, choices include plastic, nylon, and all sorts of synthetics in between.

Screen printing is a printing process in which positive films are used to expose photosensitive stencil and the wet stencil is applied to the fabric screen (the equivalent of a plate). As the stencil dries, it adheres to the fabric plate. The plate is mounted on a press that looks like a series of tables. The substrate feeds its way through each press unit. At the first unit, the screen is lowered to the substrate, ink floods the screen, and is then squeegee'd through the screen to the substrate below. Then the substrate moves on to the next unit until all color is applied. After the piece moves off press, it enters a finishing area where options including mounting, sewing, grommets, and vents are applied.

Innovations in screen printing include direct-to-screen technology, which eliminates the use of film—much like computer-to-plate technology for offset printing. A computerized mechanical head sprays wax onto the screen or plate in the negative areas, leaving areas of mesh for ink to pass through. It is extremely fast and accurate.

Additionally, because there is so much expertise in large format signage with commercial screen printing, many of these commercial printers have added wide-format digital output devices as well. Run lengths and the types of ink/substrate combinations dictate whether a job will run conventional or digital.

Substrates and inks in screen printing are different from offset, and creatives therefore need to think differently when they design for this process. The substrates typically found in screen printing range from paper to fabric to plastic and all types of synthetic materials selected for their ability to endure all kinds of environments. Because of these substrate choices, inks for screen printing tend to be thick. However, drying time can be boosted with heat sources and, like the synthetic substrates, these inks can withstand a variety of environmental considerations. Signage tends to image a lot of solid color, so trapping is intense in this line of printing (as it is in packaging) and these jobs must be carefully planned. Colored substrate is not uncommon in this application, and there are many methods for employing white inks under other inks to achieve your color choices.

This is definitely a printing method that warrants consultation prior to the creative process getting started so that you fully understand how to construct for the screen process and the limitations of the process when it comes to attempting something such as matching a screened sign to an offset produced piece. Different methodologies, delivery mechanisms, substrates, and inks make that a challenging request; however, it can be done. As one of my clients told me with a wink, "The magic is in the ink."

 TIP

For more information about this printing method and for a firsthand look at technologies innovating this industry, check out SGIA.org. Their annual trade show is typically held in the fall in New Orleans. Here you will see all manner of large format specialty graphics.

Flexography

The flexographic printing process is known as a *relief* printing process because the flexible rubber plate is made by carving or removing the negative or nonprinting area of the rubber—kind of like a giant rubber stamp. The image area that receives the ink is raised above the nonimage area. The raised surface of the plate comes into direct contact with the substrate by applying pressure.

Like most printing processes, flexography can be produced with analog or digital plates. Computer-to-plate technology is in the mainstream of flexo workflows as well, and laser platemakers remove (or *ablate*) the nonprinting areas of the plate.

Because the type of ink used in flexographic printing does not require absorption into the substrate to facilitate drying, flexo is used in conjunction with nonporous substrates required for various types of food packaging as well as many plastics. It is also well suited for printing large areas of solid color. Flexographic inks are very fluid, dry rapidly, and are most often water-based—again, important in food packaging.

Flexography's fast-drying inks and high-speed presses make this method ideal for printing long runs of continuous patterns (for example, gift wrap and wallpaper). There is no chemistry involved, so printers can come up to consistent color very quickly at the beginning of their press runs. It is the most common form of relief printing on the market.

As with most forms of packaging, trapping is a key step in this process, with solid inks the norm. Multiple up imposition or gang impositions are also common to package printing. Consult with your flexographic printer when preparing your design to make the most of this printing process.

Organizations to visit online include www.fta-ffta.org/ and flexoexchange.com.

Digital

Digital printing for short-run production has been around for a while in the black-and-white category. Typical examples are technical documentation and in-plant short-run production of black-only communications, but in-roads to color laser and inkjet technology and applications allowing for customization of digital output have led to an explosion in this printing technology.

Applications for this technology include in-plant short-run production, variable data publishing, direct mail, and just-in-time publishing including books on demand.

The equipment used for digital printing includes variable imaging digital presses (computer-to-paper), digital desktop printers, digital copiers, and direct imaging presses (computer-to-plate-on-press). For the purpose of this discussion, I am going to leave out copiers, desktop printers, and direct-to-press imaging and concentrate on laser and inkjet technology in the digital press category. These are the two most common forms of digital printing found on the commercial market and in-plant production today.

Computer-to-paper devices abound on the market as copier manufacturers have taken their imaging technology and applied it to the graphic arts market. Many commercial printers have added digital devices to service short-run requests. Technologies that characterize digital output include the use of electrophotography for imaging as well as *duplex* printing, or printers that can print on both sides of the paper in one pass.

Here's how it works: From the computer, the digital file or layout is sent to the RIP (the computer attached to the output device), which takes your PostScript data, interprets the math, and creates an image mapped out in machine pixels on a grid. From the RIP, the image is sent to the marking engine and then onto the drum, where toner is attracted to the laser-imaged areas of the drum, which is then deposited onto your paper. It is extremely important to follow the manufacturer's guidelines when it comes to using stock specifically designed for digital output because extreme heat is involved to bond the color to the substrate. The toners that create the color can be a dry mixture or liquid. Dry toner images are fixed onto the substrate with heat, whereas liquid toner images dry shortly after the liquid toner makes contact with the substrate. The paper passes through each set of drums and comes into contact with the toner; then it makes its final pass through a heating set of rollers and then a cooling set of rollers before the paper emerges.

✗ NOTE

Digital devices can be sheetfed or web; rolls of paper can be attached to the front end with finishing options attached to the back end of these presses to cut, fold, and bind multipage documents.

Considerations when designing for digital include not only a working understanding of the process, but also differences in your manufacturing supplies. For example, the same machine that will produce your job will also proof your job—a distinct advantage because your proof will match your production. But toner is not the same thing as ink and there is no spot color option with these devices. So, you must design for process color. I advise a good swatch reference specific to your device.

If you will be combining both offset and digital in a large campaign, understand that getting your digital pieces to match your offset pieces will be problematic. If the entire job can stay digital, you are better off using that option. As indicated earlier, paper for digital production is specific and you should have adequate references for stock choices for this type of production as well. For example, toner will not stick well to a coarse surface such as you would find on linen or recycled stock.

Spreading color over large areas is not advisable because it is difficult for toner to bond evenly over great distance. Take advantage of what these color devices do very well, and use photographic images instead and you will be very pleased.

Inkjet technology is another form of digital printing for production and, as mentioned earlier, it has found a home in wide-format devices. The two basic technologies in this category are *continuous flow* and *drop on demand*. Continuous flow uses a static charge to deliver the ink (made of dye, not pigment) to the substrate and uncharged droplets are collected and recycled. Drop on demand squeezes out drops as needed so inks have faster dry times.

Everything from posters to signs, from point-of-purchase merchandising to fine art can be produced from these devices. Because these devices use highly concentrated dyes, color reproduction is very good. Inks are also available in UV, which will resist fading. A variety of substrate choices are available, including bond and coated papers, proofing, backlit, self-adhesive (for mounting on rigid surfaces such as foam core), and synthetic banner material.

 NOTE

For more information on digital printing, visit dpia.org, printondemand.com, and the Digital Printing Council at www.gain.net.

Appendix D: Workflow

Your digital workflows should support the creative/marketing function, whose primary goal is to sell the product or service of a given company. As these images suggest, the message, brand, or content can be repurposed and distributed in a number of ways. The means you use to further marketing strategies are examined in this appendix.

I use the term *workflows* because there are several that take place concurrently and are discussed throughout this appendix:

- ▶ **Creative**—This workflow involves the assembly of your resources, the layout of your content, and the production of your content based on delivery or distribution strategies.

- ▶ **Asset**—This workflow includes the organization, management, retrieval, and archiving of all your digital assets.

- ▶ **Repurposing content**—This workflow includes taking content in one form and changing it to become compatible for another method of distribution.

- ▶ **Review and approval**—This workflow is the communication between all approving investors in the production of your content.

- ▶ **Job management and tracking**—This workflow includes assigning tasks, tracking those tasks, and managing them through to conclusion.

- ▶ **Quality control**—This workflow involves the hand-offs throughout the previously listed workflows and how they affect delivery of content.

Throughout each of these workflows there should be quality control measures built in to ensure that all the workflows are performing to best practices and standard operating procedures.

If you're reading this book, you are probably responsible for the creation and delivery of content in some form or another. So, let me illustrate the concept of content distribution in the context of workflow with the following example.

Example of Content Distribution

Your marketing department develops a strategy to drive consumers to a specific page on your company's website because, statistically, they know that if they can get a consumer to this page, their close rate goes up by 40%. So, the challenge is how to get consumers to log on. The answer might be a combination of strategies: direct mail, telemarketing, emails, and broadcast orchestrated around a theme or message that ties the campaign together. Resources for each of these distribution points are very different:

▶ Direct mail requires page layout and print graphics.

▶ Telemarketing requires valid, qualified data.

▶ Emails require both valid, qualified data as well as brief, well-formulated content.

▶ Broadcast might require video or animation targeted to specific demographics on specific outlets at specific times of the day.

You might be required to supply a good portion of this content and therefore should have a firm understanding of the requirements each of these distribution points will demand. You'll also need a well-organized set of tools, assets, and skills to be able to call on an efficient workflow to meet these demands.

Assessing Your Current Workflows

So, why not take a snapshot of where you are today within your job function or department to evaluate your current situation and plan for the growth or evolution of that function?

Technology that supports your digital workflows includes desktop hardware and software, network infrastructure, repositories for your assets (such as servers and drives), output devices, and your staff's technical skill set.

When planning strategically, one of the first steps is to inventory what you already possess. That includes your physical technology, your assets, and your staff's skill sets. Take a look at the following list to inventory your technologies, methodologies, and skills:

▶ Review tools, including hardware and software

▶ Repositories and librarian utilities

▶ Methods for repurposing and distributing content

▶ Methods for reviewing and approving your content

▶ Methods for tracking and managing jobs

▶ Experience and skill levels for all methods of creation/production for distribution

Let's take each workflow individually and examine the technology required and the options that exist in the present market for each. Let's start with the creative workflow.

Creative Workflow

The creative workflow is the process of gathering resources, talents, and skills for the purpose of publishing content. The creative workflow involves planning the creation, composition, production, and distribution of the content. This section discusses the major components of the creative workflow and describes typical strategies and best practices.

Hardware Found in the Creative Workflow

What differentiates a marketing/graphic arts workstation or network from general office productivity?

The demands of the creative workflow are extremely different from those of the average technology user in a business setting. Time and again, DesktopMedia is called in to work with an IT staff that cannot support the marketing/graphic art function within its organization because the equipment, storage requirements, bandwidth, platform, and file sizes require a different IT skill set than the majority of the customers they are required to support.

A graphic arts workstation must have an extremely fast processor, with a large and fast hard drive, a large amount of memory, a fast video card, a large and accurate monitor, input devices (including tablets and scanners), and an operating system designed to support the graphic arts function.

Cross-platform

I'm not going to get into a discussion of dueling platforms. I am an unabashed Mac user and have been for the last 16 years. It is ideal for this industry segment, not only for OS X's easy and efficient interface, but because software developers for this industry typically develop with the Mac in mind. However, large, corporate environments typically have all flavors of PCs running some version of Windows. Adobe has made great strides in developing for the Windows platform, and all its applications are identical regardless of platform. In addition, OpenType has awesome cross-platform capabilities.

Your network infrastructure is composed of wiring, switches, and servers and will likely be structured as a client/server configuration. A *client/server* network means everyone has access to a centralized repository of data, which is easily backed up and secured. Growth of the department is thus easier to manage. The network created to support the client/server structure is efficient and looks like a hub with spokes connecting the desktops (see Figure D.1 for an example of a client/server network in a graphics art department). Any client computer could be physically down without disturbing the other participants on the network. Special attention must be paid to the uptime of this server, though. If the server must be consistently functioning 8 hours a day, 5 days a week, special attention to the configuration of the server to build in redundancy and reduce the risk of failure is very important. Redundant array of inexpensive disks (RAID) technology utilizes multiple redundant drives to ensure against disk failure.

The speed of your network and its bandwidth is critical. Moving large files around quickly and efficiently and accessing the outside world and your external customers with these large files requires an infrastructure to support your functions. Gigabit speed and T1 access are commonly found supporting the graphic arts function. Switches designed to manage your network traffic at speeds appropriate for your activity are also equally important to match with your infrastructure. In other words, it makes no sense to have a very fast computer but a very slow network. To have P4 or G5 technology on an old, slow network is like putting a Ferrari on a dirt road. See Figure D.1 for an example of an infrastructure layout.

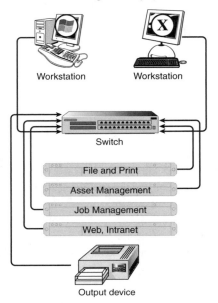

Everyone is experiencing exponential growth of their resource files. The following questions should be answered during your inventory exercise. Where should we put them? How can we quickly access them? Do they need to be online, near-line, or offline? How secure are they? If you lost all your files in a fire, what would the consequences be and how quickly could you reconstruct these files?

Software Tools for the Creative Workflow

Platform aside, an inventory of your current software tools is a worthwhile exercise. You will be able to determine which tools you currently possess, whether they are legitimate licenses, whether you have current versions, and whether there are gaps in the inventory that you need to fill.

The Adobe Creative Suite

You need a strong tool set "and you need the right tool for the right job." Thus, I recommend an all-Adobe workflow. You should have a tool for every job requirement designed to integrate efficiently together. While there is overlap in some functional areas, no one would advocate using InDesign for illustration or illustration for image editing. The three core products of InDesign, Illustrator, and Photoshop (as shown in Figure D.2) are must-haves in anyone's toolbox.

Repositories should be examined for their capacity, speed, and accessibility and then configured and sized accordingly. Many of my clients choose to segment their repositories by workflow. For example, they might have a server for file and print, a server for digital asset management, a server for creating PDFs, a server for job management, and so on. Capacities for digital assets or file and print are far more significant than job management, for example.

FIGURE D.2   The Adobe Creative Suite, Standard Edition.

InDesign

Illustrator

Photoshop

Acrobat

I view Acrobat as the "finishing" option for a significant amount of your composited content. You can finish a layout using Acrobat for the shear purpose of making it a universally accepted file format. You can finish your layout by ensuring it has the proper security. You can finish your layout by adding interactivity, form fields, or a signature. And you can finish your layout by turning it into a slide presentation.

Suitcase

Another tool I strongly recommend is a good font management utility as well as some strict standards for font technology. It is detrimental to the efficiency of your system to have your fonts loaded in your system folder, "turned on" all the time, hogging your memory. This is acceptable only if you had a few fonts you work with on a regular basis, but if you have many fonts you like to choose from, font management is necessary. I recommend the combination of Extensis Suitcase and Adobe's OpenType font technology. Suitcase allows you to manage your font library by giving you the ability to turn you fonts on and off when you need them. Adobe's OpenType technology, as previously discussed in this book, allows cross-platform compatibility, single file structure, and extended character sets. All Adobe products are designed to take advantage of this font technology.

Microsoft Office

I also recommend Microsoft's set of office productivity applications, which give you the tools you need for editing documents, working with financial data, and creating templates for slide presentations. Branding control extends to correspondence and slide presentations as well as advertising. So, don't forget about the content generated every day by different people in the organization. Make sure there are clear guidelines for company correspondence, specifying usage of fonts, logos, and so on. Additionally, slide presentations should be consistent from any department and should begin with a set of templates accessible by everyone.

InCopy

Depending on how your workgroup is structured, you might consider InCopy, an add-on application for publishing environments. If you have copywriting job functions within your department, InCopy will work in conjunction with InDesign, adding assignment and annotation functionality to your InDesign workflow. Copywriters can work with InCopy to develop written content and be able to preview its placement in a layout without ever having to leave their desks.

FTP Utilities

The File Transport Protocol (FTP) enables you to transfer files using the Internet instead of email. Email is not an acceptable method of moving graphic art files because most email products encrypt and compress attachments, which can have disastrous effects on your files—particularly the fonts. Additionally, most email programs impose a file size limit for attachments. None of this is the case for FTP, which is a straight transfer of data with no interference placed on the files being transported. The only limitation here is the size of your bandwidth to the Internet, which can affect the speed of your transfer. Consider using an FTP utility that enables you to perform this function easily. Products to consider include Fetch, Transmit, CuteFTP, and WSFTP.

Output Devices

Inventory your current output devices and reassess your needs. As always, define and redefine your requirements for output: black-and-white output versus color, content proofing, color proofing, contract proofing, short-run digital in-plant production, variable data, finishing options, and wide format. There are many needs in graphic arts and marketing for output, and many devices on the market cater to those various needs. Define your requirements, both immediate and for the next 3 years, and review only those devices that meet those requirements.

Inkjets

For example, perhaps a small footprint desktop printer is all you require. In this category of printer, the technology options are inkjet or laser. Weigh your decision carefully when considering a small footprint inkjet. The entry price points are attractive. However, when you factor in the price of consumables over the course of a year or the lifetime of the device (never more than 3 years), it might make more sense to purchase a color laser. Additionally, modestly priced inkjets do not support the PostScript language and you might not be happy with the quality of your graphics upon output.

Desktop Lasers

Decide whether you need the device to be networkable, meaning it's accessible by others on the network. The page languages the device supports are also important; in graphic arts you should always purchase the Adobe PostScript language, level 3. Consider the duty cycle of the device. How many pages per minute will you need to produce? And remember that color output will be slower than black and white.

Which type of stock will you need to run through these devices and in what quantities? It's imperative to factor in the manufacturer's recommended stock and the ink, dye, and toner into your purchasing decisions. Will you need to print on wide format? Will you need UV inks to prevent fading or to stand up to strong lights? Will you have additional finishing requirements? Is it more cost-effective to generate this output in-house digitally or with an outside vendor offset? Quantity is generally the trigger—the longer the run, the more cost-effective offset printing is.

In general, the key factors in deciding a laser purchase include color, the cost of toner, the duty cycle, and the size and weight of the substrates you want to use.

Networked Digital Copiers and Laser Printers

This industry has exploded as commercial printers have entered the short-run digital markets and many companies are bringing these devices into their own in-plant production areas. They offer high-speed, just-in-time production of all kinds of materials, including technical documentation, manuals, marketing material, newsletters, catalogues, and even books.

These devices are often shared by workgroups, and many brands on the market today can cater to the graphic arts market. See Appendix C, "Printing Processes," where digital production printing is covered in more depth. Also see the section "Variable Data Publishing" for information on which of these devices are well suited for your purposes.

Many manufacturers provide onsite analysis of your output requirements to match the best model for your production demands.

Wide Format Inkjet

Wide format inkjets have become more affordable, and many are appearing in-plant and have many uses. Oversize pieces that cannot be produced on the devices previously mentioned have a home in the wide format market. Many industries use these devices, including retail, sports and entertainment, and even manufacturing.

These devices are essentially large inkjets. The technology of these devices is covered in Appendix C, but I thought it best to include these devices here as well as because they can be an important part of the creative workflow. Quantity and timing will dictate this purchase. If you need to quickly turn around small quantities of banners, posters, signage, CAD drawings, and so on, a device like this is a logical purchase.

Key features that will factor into your decision-making include the quality of color, the speed, the size (the width of the paper), and a variety of substrates. If you need this device to function as a color proofer, special attention needs to be paid to the RIP and the rendering of images. See Figure D.3 for an example of each of the devices I've just described.

After you have narrowed down the list, it's important to test output. Spend a little time selecting representative jobs you would use this device for. If it's a PostScript device, make sure the device has a valid, current printer description (PPD) for the platform you work

on. Send these test files to the device, and then evaluate that output for speed, color, and finishing options. Determine whether the footprint for the device will fit in the area you intend. Does this device require much maintenance or special ventilation? Will you have to calibrate the device on a regular basis? Are service contracts available, and local personnel to service the device?

Be careful about long-term financing on these devices. A 5-year financial commitment for a device you outgrow in 3 years will leave you locked in, at the very least, to this vendor or manufacturer with your only recourse to upgrade with this organization and/or brand.

Variable Data Publishing

Digital output devices capable of producing high-speed color output can have many uses. If this is a current requirement or a 3-year strategic marketing goal, you should consider variable data and short-run digital production. As mentioned previously, personalized marketing is a maturing software segment with many applications on the market that allow you to marry your data with your page layout. You've long been mail merging in MS Word, haven't you? You can take it a step further with "if/then" expressions commonly found in programming. For example, you could say, "If my customer likes chocolate ice cream then insert a picture of ice cream in this graphic frame." You can create custom marketing pieces that look like they were designed specifically for their recipients.

FIGURE D.3 **Common output devices found in the creative workflow.**

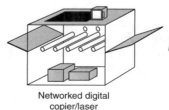

Desktop inkjet

Networked laser

Networked digital copier/laser

Wide format inkjet

As previously indicated, visit Adobe's website at http://www.adobe.com/products/vdp/ for more information on variable data publishing.

Organizing, Managing, Retrieving, and Archiving— The Asset Workflow

Now let's discuss software applications for your various repositories. Let's start with the organization, management, retrieval, and archiving of your assets. We'll then discuss the assets themselves, the hardware they sit on, and the software you might use to manage them.

Digital Assets

What is a digital asset? A *digital asset* is an electronic resource, such as a scanned picture, a video or audio clip, a web page, a text document, and so on. These assets represent a significant financial investment, which is why they are termed a digital *asset* and not a liability. Losing them would impose significant hardship on your company. So, when grappling with this asset, let's look to time-savers by examining digital asset management options. See Figure D.4 for file examples.

FIGURE D.4   **All sorts of file formats can be digital assets.**

Text   Image   Sound   Movie

All sorts of assets can be managed, including text documents (memos, press releases, and copy), slides (PowerPoint, Keynote, or Acrobat), printed marketing (such as the examples in this book), eDocs (PDFs), email, graphic files (illustrations, images, or a combination of the two), video files, animation, audio clips, and so on.

Let's look at the quantity and nature of these assets. Do you keep multiple versions of a project? Indefinitely? Is this a problem? Do you keep multiple versions of image files? Perhaps in different color spaces or resolutions? Do you edit images for a specific publication thereby creating a different version of the image? The question becomes whether you have to store all this. And, how you can make sure you're using the right one.

I like to qualify assets into two categories: current production and some type of library or archive set. *Current production* is what it implies: all assets that are currently in production. These assets are checked out or copied from your asset archive. Within current production, you need to have a designation for assets that are being used for that production. Those assets, once produced, will be thrown away unless they're modified from the original in some way and merit archiving. See Figure D.5 for a graphical example of current production versus a library or archive.

Let's drill down, specifically to images and talk about color space. All workflows, with the exception of print, are RGB. You acquire images (via a scanner or digital camera) in RGB and display images on projectors, televisions, and websites in RGB. Heck, even your eyeballs are RGB receptors. This color space describes a gamut of approximately 16 million colors. The only workflow that requires a CMYK color space is print. This color space is approximately 5,000 colors with spot color inks extending that gamut somewhat further.

Some of my clients prefer to store their image assets in the largest color space possible, at the highest resolution possible, knowing that

they can convert to other spaces and resample the resolution down in a controllable fashion. After those images are produced, they are thrown away. They always have the original image in the broadest gamut with the most information stored in their library. There is a great deal to be said for the efficiency of this organizational structure.

One concern is where the color conversion takes place. Does it occur at the local desktop(s)? Do you leave that to your print vendor instead? What if you have more than one? Or what if you use different printing technologies—sometimes offset and sometimes digital? The answers to these questions might prohibit an all-RGB workflow. Generally, the tighter control you have over your output (using a single vendor for all output, as an example), the greater the consistency in your color output. If this isn't achievable, you might have to deal with duplicate assets, such as an original RGB version and a converted CMYK version. As long as the resolution is high enough to

FIGURE D.5 **The difference between current production and archive.**

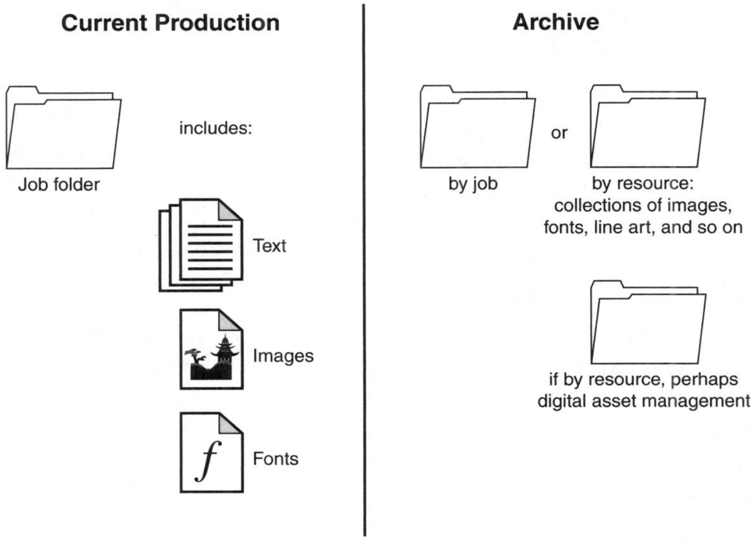

Current Production

Job folder

includes:

Text

Images

Fonts

Archive

by job

or

by resource: collections of images, fonts, line art, and so on

if by resource, perhaps digital asset management

account for your highest-quality print jobs and largest production sizes (do you frequently produce posters?), you can always downsample for any distribution requirement.

Asset Management Hardware

Assuming everyone in your workgroup shares a common repository, and even if you are a one-person Swiss army knife, there is still some logic to separating your digital assets from your local drive. Your local drive houses your applications and current production. CDs, DVDs, or an external storage device can warehouse assets you do not use on a daily basis, thereby keeping your internal drive as efficient as possible. The tool(s) you are currently using to organize this data should be examined.

The capacity of your repository and the nature of that repository fall into three categories: online storage (which is on the internal hard drives of the server itself), near-line storage (which is stored on an external device attached to your server, such as an external RAID or DVD jukebox), or offline storage (CDs or DVDs burned and organized in a rack).

Each choice brings consequences both positive and negative. Your first two choices are automated, in which retrieving assets can be done directly from your desktop. Online storage is the fastest solution and the easiest to secure with a backup. However, your ability to grow your storage will likely be limited and expensive. Near-line storage is a tad slower because there is an external device attached to your server resulting in a slight lag time in retrieving assets. However, your storage capacity is limitless. Finally, offline storage represents the least-expensive option

with limitless storage capacity, but it's the slowest approach. The process is a manual one, so when you look up an image in a catalogue, you must get up and physically locate and mount the disk to retrieve the image.

Asset Management Software

How do you currently look up assets? If the answer to this inventory question is a simple folder structure and the operating system's "Find" command, you are most likely experiencing frustration. As your assets grow, the time it takes to locate something lengthens. Everyone contributing to this repository might have their own way of naming and organizing projects, which can increase your search time. Versions of assets might be starting to take over, and costly mistakes might be leading to incorrect content being distributed.

With the Creative Suite comes some built-in assistance: Adobe's Version Cue and Bridge, which provides navigational control and functions like a creative hub. These products are designed to create a common workspace for you to organize your projects with your Adobe assets. Version Cue manages different versions of a file and notifies users, like a librarian, whether the asset is checked out by someone. Bridge, as the name implies, is the bridge between all applications. It's a common area where your projects can be viewed, much like Photoshop's previous feature File Browser— except it's accessible by all of Adobe's Creative Suite applications.

Looking beyond these built-in solutions, we can turn our attention to a software product class or category known as *digital asset management* (or just *asset management*).

These products use metadata to make cataloging, searching, retrieving, and archiving much easier. *Metadata* is information about the content, quality, condition, and other characteristics of data—in this case your accumulated resource files used for content distribution. Certain metadata, such as the date the file was created, is appended to a file upon creation. This simple metadata is something you've been working with all along. But what if you wanted to be able to search by a description or keywords, brand, SKU, or barcode?

Digital asset management (DAM) software allows you to create your own search criteria, add metadata specific to your requirements for searching, store this information in the form of catalogues, retrieve your asset, and deliver it right to your desktop. Think beyond images—your PDFs, layouts, and Word documents can all be catalogued and retrieved. See Figure D.6 for a catalogue example.

How do you select the appropriate application? You first define your requirements for the solution. You must ensure that whatever you select will accommodate your file formats, the quantity of assets you currently possess, and (projecting out approximately 3 years) how many more you think you'll create. The solution must support the color spaces you typically store and allow for customization of search criteria. You might want to give access to your image catalogues to others, either inside or outside your organization. You also might want to control how others access those catalogues—for example, whether you want to give them high-resolution images or low-resolution PDFs. Controlling distribution might not be an immediate need, but in a few years, you might regret not choosing an application that enables you to control access and distribution.

If your assets exceed your local drive or you find yourself spending a lot of unnecessary time searching through CDs, it's probably time to step up to some type of DAM

FIGURE D.6 **Your catalogue with thumbnail and metadata that is linked to the resource file, anywhere you would like it to reside.**

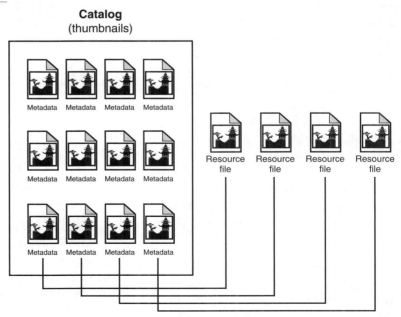

application. The simplest configuration is a local workstation with catalogues containing thumbnails and attached metadata by which you can search and locate images. After the image you want is located, your DAM application knows where to find the actual file and the name and location of the disk it resides on. From this simple configuration, a solution can grow to a client/server relationship. Software clients can access catalogues on the server, which can return the requested image. Those images can be warehoused online, near-line, or offline. Examples of products to look at include Extensis Portfolio and Canto Cumulus.

Another capacity consideration is the quantity of files. Depending on the quantity of assets, you might need a database to drive the DAM interface. If you already have a database standard, such as SQL, this can factor into your decision. Of course, this will also increase the cost of the solution.

The benefits of a strong, easy-to-use DAM solution are many. You can quickly access your library and find the correct image—no more costly exercises in searching through drives and CDs looking for a file, not knowing its name or whether it's the correct asset. You can make better use of your assets if you can get to them. You can give access to others so more people can benefit from this resource, which should cut down on duplications of assets throughout the company. Greater control can be exercised over these assets as well. You can use this solution to organize and quantify your assets. This is a valuable exercise for both company valuation and insurance purposes.

From a simple search and placement for the graphic arts function (think images), to easy access of common documents within the organization (think HR forms or contracts), to

company marketing pieces (think access to the repository for your remote sales force), the possibilities are endless with a strong DAM solution.

Repurposing of Content Workflow

In my experience with content generation, most companies I work with have content and data scattered all over the company in various forms and repositories. Often these companies have separate departments for print and web. They might outsource their email marketing and likely use outside service providers for their broadcast advertising. See Figure D.7 for potential locations where your data and content might be located.

FIGURE D.7 **Your content data and skills could be scattered all over the company.**

Advertising: content, skills

Accounting: data

Marketing: strategy, data

Content is everywhere.
Content is shared.
Content is repurposed.
Why not bring it all together?

Sales: data, presentations

Web/IT: content, infrastructure

Engineering: line art, data

Consider this example: Various departments request logos and images to be repurposed from print to web to email. They are saved in various formats, color spaces, and resolutions all over the company. They are sometimes used in accordance with branding standards, but often are not. Content including product or services information, pricing, and specifications might be warehoused in engineering or manufacturing. Customer information, including various methods of contacting them, buying history, and customer service history, resides somewhere in sales or accounting.

The convergence of all this content will allow for the leveraging of that content efficiently and quickly. When marketing creates a campaign that relies on the timely release of content at specific times that leverage the results, how can you respond when all your resources are scattered all over the place in noncompliant forms? See Figure D.8 for my interpretation.

FIGURE D.8 **The recycle symbol can apply to assets as well.**

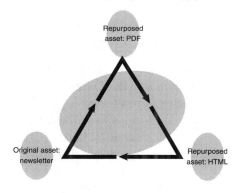

The concept of repurposing of content is nothing new to the creative. An image for the Web will need to be RGB or indexed and low-resolution, whereas the same image that needs to be printed will need to be CMYK and at a resolution of twice the intended line-screen. This is a simple example of repurposing this content for different uses. Can you not apply the same logic to data, to product descriptions and specifications, and to pricing?

To step beyond the concept of repurposing a single file or image, let's look at the role of Acrobat as one of the first utilities that allowed for the repurposing of content. You can take a layout and initially send it around the company in a small, compact, low-resolution form to act as a content proof. Then you can take the same layout and create a PDF to be posted on the website. Finally, you can take the same layout and create a PDF destined for a printing press. Thus, you've repurposed this content three ways for three different and distinct reasons.

PDF Workflows

In recent years, an explosion of PDF generation has occurred. You can use PDFs for the distribution of memos, for low-resolution proofs circulated via email for approval, and for slide presentations. PDFs can be distributed instead of printed catalogues on CDs with hyperlinks and bookmarks for easy navigation of product information and price lists. In addition, you can use PDFs for placing ads in publications and electronic billboards and for print production.

That's a lot of uses for PDFs and just as many opportunities for making them incorrectly. Yes, it's possible to make a bad PDF. If this file format has become a cornerstone in your workflow, are you optimizing its production? Do you have standards or procedures in place to ensure PDFs are created correctly and consistently? How about efficiently?

InDesign, as do all Adobe products, has the ability to create PDFs via the Export command. The Export command's tabs in InDesign look similar to the setting options you see in Distiller. These options are adequate for the bulk of PDFs you will need to generate. Distiller is still an option, and you will find more specific options available via Distiller for generating a PDF. Many print vendors would still prefer you generate a PDF with Distiller and will even distribute custom settings specific for your printer's workflow.

Another option you should consider is the concept of "certified" PDFs. A *certified* PDF is validated for a specific workflow. A common certified PDF discussed in this book is the PDF/X standard. Many products can create or validate for this standard. Enfocus has a series of products designed to expedite this process and can add this feature to virtually any application. InDesign and Distiller can create a PDF/X. Flightcheck can check to verify a PDF/X, whereas Acrobat can preflight to check a standard and validate the standard. Because many print production workflows can move this type of file quickly through their processes with little or no intervention by prepress, they can quickly produce these jobs. This is a "win-win" for both the service provider and the client. See Figure D.9 for the PDF endorsement.

FIGURE D.9 **The green checkmark, indicating certification.**

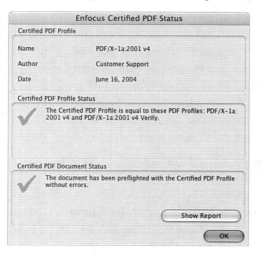

Distiller supports watched folders, a feature that attaches job settings to specific folders. Files that are dropped into these folders are automatically distilled to those specifications. The product Distiller Server allows you to set up watched folders on a server so that a workgroup can take advantage of this feature. Imagine everyone producing PDFs for specific types of output consistently. These actions can be scripted to further automate the process.

Another option for PDF generation is an online service provided by Adobe at http://createpdf.adobe.com/. This is a handy resource provided by the company that invented and defined the standards by which this versatile file format succeeds not only in graphic arts but in the general population of business and consumer creators alike.

Repurposing Content with Creative Suite, Variable Data, and XML

Let's look beyond page layout and Acrobat and turn our attention to the Creative Suite as a whole. You can start a layout in InDesign (with contributions from Illustrator and Photoshop) and Package for GoLive. You can then repurpose the content of this print layout for a web layout. Or you can take a series of images in Photoshop and create a web gallery of images. Plus, you can take the correspondence you create in MS Word and make it a form. Or you can repurpose content using the Creative Suite.

Variable Data Publishing is not limited to print, but can be used for web and email as well. It enables you to get even more from your content by creating custom, personalized pieces of marketing by using not only text and images, but customer data as well.

Imagine being able to use a customer's buying history to entice another sale. For example, say a customer receives an email indicating that a special website designed just for him is waiting at a specific website. The website contains a picture of a product or service the customer has recently purchased with a message outlining his recent purchases. Based on that history, the website states that the customer might be interested in another product, which is waiting for him. All he has to do is simply click to create an order!

Finally, the most sophisticated and strategic methodology for repurposing of content is the use of Extensible Markup Language (XML) tags for all your content. XML is a language by which you create definitions for tags that you apply to all content. These tags can then be attached to objects or frames in a layout to expedite the construction of a message. Chapter 2, "Planning for Production," reviewed the process briefly. For more information, a good starting reference book is *The Visual QuickStart Guide to XML* by Peachpit Press. You should also look up http://www.w3.org/XML/ for more information.

Review and Approval Workflows

As with all workflows, you must inventory your current solution(s). If a change needs to be made, define your requirements for your review and approval workflow. Then, look for solutions that fit those requirements. What are the common components of review and approval, and what are some of the common solutions found on the market today?

Best practices for review and approval of content typically require two proofing cycles—one by staff and another by the content creator. Often a final approval is done by someone such as a manager responsible for quality or brand control. This person checks for usage (is the logo sized per standards), correctness of content (did they use the correct image based on version and copy), production requirements, elements style, and typographic errors.

Too many reviewers and approvers can cause a complete breakdown in the system and make it difficult for the content generator to get her job done in a timely manner. But you would be surprised by the number of workflows I've seen crippled by too many contributors with no restraint or respect for the proofing cycle, calling in corrections as late as press time. Can you imagine what such a routine costs the company?

How are these proofing cycles accomplished? One option is accomplished via hard-copy proofs, perhaps first in black and white and maybe only for correct assets, placement, and text-related checks or by using PDF as a soft proof option. Then perhaps the next round of proofing centers on color, for content and tagging. Final approval and production checks might be reserved for management. An internal device might be used to accomplish this. These proofs can be distributed internally by hand-carrying them or externally via a carrier service.

Once released—and only if this job is headed for a printing press—your service provider might send you proofs, previously agreed to, in the form of page proofs, contract proofs, remote hard proofs, remote soft proofs, or onsite press checks.

PDFs can be employed in the review and approval cycle because they are easily created and distributed. If members of the cycle own Acrobat, they can mark up or annotate the

PDF with their comments. Those comments can be informally collected, and the original layout can be modified accordingly.

With the advent of Acrobat 7 Professional, the content creator can sponsor email review and approval without the recipients owning Acrobat. The creator simply generates a PDF and, using the new feature in version 7 called "Allow Reader Commenting," turns the PDF into an "intelligent document" and the PDF gives the recipient commenting tools. The only software the recipient needs is Adobe Reader 7, which is a free download from Adobe. The creator, from within Acrobat, submits the PDF for an email review. Then, after the comments are placed by the recipient, he clicks Send Comments and the creator receives the reviewer's notes. See Figure D.10 for an example.

FIGURE D.10   PDF comments.

If an email approach to review and approval entails too much traffic, you could sponsor web approval, also available in Acrobat with a WebDAV-enabled server. You could also get

a third-party web solution such as Rosebud PLM (http://www.rosebudplm.com). This method invites the reviewers to a specific URL, where they will preview the PDF and add their comments that in turn will be sent back to the creator.

To move beyond these features, you can step up to collaboration applications or online services that create common workspaces for invitees to join in, collaborate, and annotate. These begin to fall into the category of project management. Microsoft SharePoint technologies is a platform designed specifically for collaborative applications. These types of solutions should be considered when collaboration or approval, either wholly or in part, takes place outside your domain or network.

Online Proofing

Great strides have taken place in the world of remote proofing with Kodak leading the charge with RealTime Proofing technologies. This application can push pixels over the Internet to a certified monitor for contract proofing with tools that allow the reviewer to measure color, density, and ink limit!

Job Management or Tracking Workflow

When does a job become a job in your organization? When the client accepts the proposal? When someone hands you an assignment? Do you have any mechanisms to facilitate the transaction, such as a job ticket or work order? Depending on the size of your organization, maybe all this occurs verbally, on paper, or via email. But if you are part of a larger organization with a well-defined staff and budget, you might benefit from a job

---

management application. The many items you might have to track include

- Resources, such as staff, art, and photography
- Timelines and deadlines
- Budgets
- Digital assets
- Vendors

Perhaps jobs or projects are assigned within the context of a team of supporting cast, a blended group of internal staff and external vendors. Monitoring the progress of the project and knowing whether you are on time and on budget could mean spending a lot time tracking down answers to questions, or it could simply involve the click of a few keystrokes to manage and monitor your projects straight from your desktop, or anywhere. Where is the project physically? Who is working on it? What stage is it in? How much time and money do you have left?

Consider software in the following categories: job tracking, job management, project management, and time billing. There is some overlap in these categories, so I've chosen to mention them all. Several good products are on the market designed specifically for the graphic arts/marketing/communications industry.

Time billing applications can offer the simple tracking of time and resources by an individual. Project management can manage a project with multiple contributors over time, whereas job tracking can capture time and resources attributed to any or many jobs in progress at any time. Job management can monitor the progress of a project and let you know, at any given time, what stage it is in and who is working on it.

Once again, assess where you are currently with respect to job management. Is your current system effective? Can you get answers to questions quickly, or do you spend a lot of time tracking job-related information? Can you know, at any given moment, if your jobs are on time and on budget? Would there be value in increasing the efficiency of your department with job management?

This class of applications inserts a dimension of accountability that you might not currently have within your job function or workgroup. For the individual, tracking your time and resources associated with a job will help you bill consistently and more accurately estimate future projects. For the workgroup or team, job tracking and project management forces groups to clearly define their roles and responsibilities as well as their deadlines. Job management allows a workgroup to be easily monitored, in many cases from anywhere.

So, whether you are looking for a standalone application for an individual job function, a client/server application for a workgroup, or remote access for management monitoring from anywhere, there are plenty of features to choose from, including

- Job tracking
- Job cost
- Accounting
- Remote or web access
- Estimating/Planning
- Order entry
- Invoicing
- Asset management
- Customer history
- Job history
- PO management

- Scheduling
- Shipping
- Inventory
- Finished goods inventory

This category of workflow offers accountability for staff, resources, projects, timelines, and budgets. With a well-chosen product and a solid implementation, it can quickly pay for itself. How? It can pay for itself in lost time found, a more efficient use of resources and staff, and quicker and better decision-making with accurate information delivered in a timely manner.

Quality Control Throughout Your Workflows

Finally, after assessing all your workflows, take a closer look within the workflows at hand-offs and quality control (QC) check points. Anytime a project stops to be examined or moves from one phase or person to the next, opportunities exist, for better or worse, that affect the efficiency of the workflow.

Communications

One common problem area is communications, either with staff or providers (see Chapter 2 for checklists). AVO is a common acronym, and it stands for avoid verbal orders. Communication delivered only verbally is at risk for interpretation, and after time it might be remembered differently or, worse, be forgotten. Written communication is best both for communicating instructions and annotating progress. Job history is very important; recording the events as they

unfold and detailing unique hurdles or problems solved related to the project will only help future efforts become more efficient and avoid costly mistakes.

If this information is shared via a common vehicle such as job management, everyone has access to the same information. Reviewing the project after it's delivered will give all the participants the same information about the project, not just their own individual experience. Communicating clearly with external partners and vendors is extremely important, and redundancy (meaning verbal communication and following up with the same written instructions) in communication is also helpful. Remember that you can never give your vendor too much information.

Image Suppliers

Suppliers, such as photographers, have to be given clearly defined expectations regarding the job as well as any additional services you might want from them. For example, do you want your photographer to color correct the images she shoots for you? Or perhaps you would prefer your print vendor to handle all color correction and therefore do not want to pay for that service from your photographer. Maybe there is not enough money in the budget to hire a photographer, so you will opt for a stock photography service. Don't overlook Adobe's new service, which can be accessed via Bridge from any CS2 product. Digital photography is finding its way into many marketing, communication, and graphic arts departments as more are opting for this economical, easily accessed, and fast turnaround option for shots that don't necessarily require high quality. Make sure someone on staff understands how to operate the camera and how to download images either directly from the camera or via a memory stick. After they're downloaded, images should be properly named, tagged, and catalogued.

If analog images are being shot, scanning and color correction will likely take place. From an efficient workflow perspective, having your print service provider offer scanning services is a common choice to make because they can scan your images and optimize them in anticipation of their own printing presses. These are profiles, and when you open these images in Photoshop—for instance, to add a clipping path—or you place these images in InDesign, you might get a warning about an attached profile. This attached information describes the gamut adjustment between the scanner and the awaiting printing press. These profiles should be preserved and not eliminated during your portion of the workflow.

When hiring a graphic artist, clearly communicate the various distribution methods so the artist can supply you with the appropriate art in the appropriate resolution and color space. I've been in the middle of many a transaction that didn't supply usable art for a project.

Video and animation might be part of the requirement for some aspect of a marketing campaign. After these elements are developed, you might need to transfer them to tape or to the Web. The size of the frame and speed of transmission will affect the project and could represent a bottleneck.

Content Sources

If copywriters do not have a vehicle or application that can integrate into your workflow, they will likely use an application such as Word to accomplish their job function. Communicate clearly how you want those

files to be submitted. In many cases that can mean no formatting, simple carriage returns, and a spellcheck are all that's required. On the other hand, in a publishing environment, you might want to develop a hand-off where your Word documents use style tags with the same names as InDesign paragraph style sheets so that when the text arrives and is placed in the layout in the designated frames, the format definitions match up and the text flows into the layout correctly formatted.

Financial information is a common resource you have to work with. Whether it's pricing from sales, specifications from engineering, or the company balance sheet, you will have to become accustomed to how this data behaves as well as develop standards by which it's formatted, reviewed, and approved. How it's expressed and whether it needs to be translated into other currencies or measurements can have an impact on workflow. How much time is spent on struggling with these issues should motivate you to remove any time drainers from these exercises.

When searching the Web for content, keep your expectations low. Finding logos on the Internet might not always yield quality results because web graphics are typically low resolution and use a limited color space, such as indexed color (a palette of 256 colors only). In addition, there's the question of your legal rights to use those logos. Use the content at your own risk. Check to determine when the website was last updated. You can't always tell how accurate someone else's information is.

Clipping services are a common feature in marketing workflows. Staying on top of industry information and competitors' products or services is crucial to a marketing department's strategies. Clipping services monitor specific industries in publications found all over the world. They bring that information into a common repository that is searchable and can be used for research as well as strategy. All these external resources need to be communicated with regularly and accurately. But don't forget that you can build internal resources that will assist you as well.

The following are some supplies that will help your workflow and are great resources for choosing stock, ink, finishing options, fonts, and good reference material:

- I've already mentioned a great resource from AIGA, but many paper companies will gladly give you sample catalogues or fans. And don't forget stocks designed for digital as well as offset.

- Ink companies such as PANTONE and Toyo make fans of swatches for you to choose color from, which is always the best method for choosing or mixing color. A process simulator is also imperative. You should also look for swatches of digital color production. I saw a fabulous exercise by a Parsons Graduate student who created a swatch book of all the different blacks a digital output device (a Xerox iGen3) could image.

- Finishing options and samples might also prove useful. For example, when a metallic finish is desired, is it best to go with a metallic ink or a foil stamp? The answer will depend on the stock you choose and the area receiving the metallic effect.

- Develop a nice font catalogue or, better yet, use Suitcase's nifty font preview feature and have Suitcase print a font catalogue of your fonts for you. If you're budgeting, consider acquiring Adobe's OpenType Font Library, which has more than 2,200 typefaces on CD-ROM!

- Reference options, other than this book, would include *Visual QuickStart Guides*

for your major applications; *The PC Is Not a Typewriter*, by Robin Williams, Peachpit Press, ISBN 0938151495; and the *Chicago Manual of Style*. Refer to Appendix B, "Resources," for more information on procuring these references.

Final Thoughts

You can never give the printer too much information! No other industry has undergone such a massive technological manufacturing transformation in the last 20 years as the print service industry. With more and more capital investment in equipment, modern workflows, commodity pricing, and extreme turnaround times, not to mention new challenges as geography purchasing becomes far less important, your print provider needs you, their partner, to provide as much information as possible so that your job succeeds in their workflow.

As digital becomes more prevalent, higher in quality, and less expensive, you will be faced with the question of offset versus digital. Understanding the strengths and limitations of each means you will make more effective decisions. Refer to Appendix C for a discussion of printing methodologies.

When your hand-off is to a web developer, be sure you know what they need. Do they need RGB or indexed color? What file formats would they prefer? Understanding the differences between platform system palettes and understanding the various browser support, graphic file formats, and distinctions regarding transparency are imperative when giving hand-offs to with this service provider.

The design of forms goes hand in hand with the capturing of data. You need to work closely with the job function responsible for capturing the data. Collaborating with this job function will help you develop a form that will capture the correct data that can be reused in many a campaign.

A Final Example of the Possibilities of Convergence of Workflow and Content

Consider this example: A retail firm needs to sell an overstock of a specific consumer item. It's late in the day and the product needs to be moved, quickly. Marketing decides to deploy a sales strategy targeted at consumers on their way home from work. It will incorporate a sale price that expires by the end of the evening. How will they get consumers to stop by the store to make a purchase? Perhaps they can use a combination of radio broadcast, opt-in emails, opt-in cell text messaging, and digital billboards found in office buildings. Resources for each of these distribution points are very different:

- ▶ Radio broadcasts require copy, an announcer, and perhaps music or sound effects.
- ▶ Emails require valid, qualified data; brief, well-formulated content; and format options for wireless devices.
- ▶ Cell messaging must quickly and briefly convey sale price and expiration.
- ▶ Digital billboards usually support a PDF format but can push content quickly and repeatedly for a specific period of time.

Index

How can we make this index more useful? Email us at indexes@samspublishing.com

How can we make this index more useful? Email us at indexes@samspublishing.com

How can we make this index more useful? Email us at indexes@samspublishing.com

How can we make this index more useful? Email us at indexes@samspublishing.com

content

295

D

How can we make this index more useful? Email us at indexes@samspublishing.com

How can we make this index more useful? Email us at indexes@samspublishing.com

H – I

How can we make this index more useful? Email us at indexes@samspublishing.com

J – K – L

How can we make this index more useful? Email us at indexes@samspublishing.com

lpi

303

M

How can we make this index more useful? Email us at indexes@samspublishing.com

O

Object menu

Fit Content Proportionally command, 173

Fit Proportionally command, 58

Transform Again feature, 197

object styles, creating in newsletter projects, 171-172

Object Styles palette, 9, 17

New Object Style window, 171

newsletter projects, creating object styles in, 171-172

objects (anchored), creating, 201

Office (MS), creative workflows, 269

offset lithography, 50

offset printing

printing plates, 256

proofing, 256

sheetfed printing, 255

versus digital production, 134

web printing, 255

online proofing, RealTime Proofing technologies (Kodak), 280

Opacity (color mode feature), 91

OpenType Font standard

InDesign support for, 10

product sheet projects, 126

order form projects

composite proofs, creating, 214

document layout, orienting, 209

form fields with tab leaders, creating, 210-211

method of payment sections, creating, 213-214

PDF files creating as, 215

planning

content management, 208

distribution choices, 209

production choices, 208

prerequisites, 207

return address sections, creating, 213

tables, inserting/formatting, 211-212

tax and shipping information sections, creating, 213

orientation choices (business collateral projects), 48

outlines (type)

color fills, 196

color, blending, 196-197

creating, 196

oversized characters in newsletter projects, 177

P

packaging

magazine advertisement projects, 94

poster projects, 105-106

page creep, 189

page numbering

annual report projects, 223-224, 240

product catalogue projects, 192

How can we make this index more useful? Email us at indexes@samspublishing.com

How can we make this index more useful? Email us at indexes@samspublishing.com

How can we make this index more useful? Email us at indexes@samspublishing.com

How can we make this index more useful? Email us at indexes@samspublishing.com

Q - R

How can we make this index more useful? Email us at indexes@samspublishing.com

Tab palette, 15

tab stops, creating in cells, 212

Table palette, 14

tables

behavior of, 211

cells

creating tab stops, 212

moving, 212

editing, product catalogue projects, 203

formatting, 211-212

newsletter projects, creating in, 174

order form projects, inserting/formatting in, 211-212

spreadsheets, importing as (product catalogue projects), 202

text, inserting, 213

uses of, 10

tabs

newsletter projects, creating in, 167

product catalogue projects, creating in, 191-192

target documents, data merging, 145

tax and shipping information sections, creating in order form projects, 213

technology (production planning)

EPS metafiles, 32

GIF files, 33

JPEG files, 32-33

PSD files, 32

raster files, 31-33

software, 31

SVG files, 34

SWF files, 34

TIFF files, 32

vector files, 31-34

templates

business card creation projects, saving as, 60

elements of, 178

product catalogue projects, creating in, 202

production planning, 36

text

address boxes, envelope creation projects, 63

aligning

paragraph alignment, changing (magazine advertisement projects), 92

poster projects, 99

All Caps, conveying formality, 226

auto flowing, 238

auto leading, envelope creation projects, 64

bulleted text, 228

interactive presentation projects, 156

poster projects, 100

color, adding to (product sheet projects), 113

columns versus text blocks, 116

creating

business card creation projects, 58

envelope creation projects, 62

letterhead creation projects, 53

product sheet projects, 112

drop caps, product sheet projects, 125

drop shadows (magazine advertisement projects), 90

em spaces, 54

formatting

business card creation projects, 58

letterhead creation projects, 53

magazine advertisement projects, 90

postcards, 68-71

product sheet projects, 113

How can we make this index more useful? Email us at indexes@samspublishing.com

How can we make this index more useful? Email us at indexes@samspublishing.com

X – Y – Z